THE DECIBEL DIARIES

THE DECIBEL DIARIES

A JOURNEY THROUGH ROCK IN 50 CONCERTS

CARTER ALAN

ForeEdge

ForeEdge

An imprint of University Press of New England

www.upne.com

© 2017 Carter Alan

All rights reserved

Manufactured in the United States of America

Designed by April Leidig

Typeset in Ehrhardt by Copperline Book Services

For permission to reproduce any of the material
in this book, contact Permissions, University Press
of New England, One Court Street, Suite 250,
Lebanon NH 03766; or visit www.upne.com

Library of Congress Cataloging-in-Publication Data

Names: Alan, Carter.

Title: The decibel diaries: a journey through rock
in 50 concerts / Carter Alan.

Description: Lebanon NH: ForeEdge, [2017] |
Includes bibliographical references.

Identifiers: LCCN 2016038513 (print) | LCCN 2016038769 (ebook) |
ISBN 9781611687927 (pbk.) | ISBN 9781512600476 (epub, mobi & pdf)

Subjects: LCSH: Rock concerts. | Alan, Carter.

Classification: LCC ML3534 .A425 2017 (print) | LCC ML3534 (ebook) |
DDC 781.66078—dc23

LC record available at https://lccn.loc.gov/2016038513

5 4 3 2 1

*For Carrie,
and also Melon,
the purring
proofreader
who sat with me
every morning
as I wrote this.*

CONTENTS

FOREWORD

Playing classic rock masterpieces on the radio isn't enough for Carter Alan, one of America's top rock jocks. Carter wants to get into it, go deeper, and write the stories behind — as well as in front of and around — the music. His new book, *The Decibel Diaries*, is the latest in a series of acutely observed volumes that take his readers into the secret spaces of rock music, those guarded backstage areas where only the professionals are allowed access.

For anyone who writes about this world, access is everything. Carter has enjoyed major access, as I can enviously confirm. When I was a music editor at *Rolling Stone*, and later as a rock biographer, I was always jealous of the FM radio DJs I encountered backstage at big venues like Madison Square Garden, Boston Garden, and the Forum in Los Angeles. They had better access to the musicians than we scribes, and for good reason. For the rock stars, the DJs were gatekeepers to their audience. Radio was the portal to acceptance (and plutonian riches) by the fans who bought the records and filled the seats. Top jocks like Carter were garlanded with laminated credentials promising "ACCESS ALL AREAS;" they were plied with Peruvian powders and fragrant herbs by hovering promo guys (some of whom became music legends themselves); they were meeted and greeted, wined and dined, photo op-ed for *Billboard*, glad-handed, even bribed (not Carter, of course), while we pathetic critics were shunted off to dreary "hospitality suites" (actually the arena's visiting team locker room) where the rock stars never deigned to appear.

The rock jocks generally had much hotter girlfriends as well.

This access — and his curiosity about what really goes on — has propelled Carter into the exalted ranks of authors who write about rock and somehow get their books published. Example: In 1981 a teenage

Irish band called U2 came to Boston and played at a small club called the Paradise. Carter was a DJ at the city's top rock station, WBCN. He befriended U2 and was ahead of the radio curve by being one of the first jocks to play their records. This relationship turned into Carter's first book, *Outside Is America: U2 in the U.S.* Next was an insightful book about the legendary English Ur-roadie, *Life on the Road: The Incredible Rock 'n' Roll Adventures of Dinky Dawson.* After that, Carter published the best book anyone has yet written about FM rock: *Radio Free Boston: The Rise and Fall of WBCN.*

This new book is as close to a memoir as we're going to get from a major figure in classic rock media. Like a good reporter, Carter kept notes on his favorite rock concerts over the last forty years, and he uses his fifty best (and in the case of Aerosmith, those bad boys from Boston, the single worst) concerts to plot a course through four decades of the I-was-there experiences of a conscious music professional.

And he nails it. Like Carter, I live in the Boston area, and like him I've been to a lot of shows. I was present (and usually also taking notes) at six of the concerts he writes about, such as Fleetwood Mac in 1975, the Police in '78, Prince in '81, Guns N' Roses in '87, Pearl Jam in '94, Robert Plant in 2008. Then there was Joe Perry's private birthday party where the band was Cheap Trick. Carter's memories of these memorable shows completely jibe with my own, which makes me grudgingly admit that—damn it—I wish I'd written this book.

Stephen Davis

INTRODUCTION

My sister always got home before me. She was three grades ahead, and rode an earlier school bus. By the time I crawled in the front door of our rural farmhouse in eastern Pennsylvania, I would always hear her stereo blasting upstairs. Sometimes Mom yelled at her to turn it down, but she never did, just closing her door instead. You could feel the rhythm of that Ringo Starr backbeat thumping through the walls. Like every other teenager in America in 1964, she was a hopeless Beatles fanatic. The arrival of the Fab Four in New York City in February for their coronation on the Ed Sullivan Show came one week after "I Want to Hold Your Hand" went to number 1 and spent seven weeks on the top of the singles chart. The group would achieve a total dominance of American culture like no band before or since; the term Beatlemania was justified by six number-1 singles and six hit albums *in 1964 alone.* Patty would never permit her younger runt brother to even approach her sacred collection of Liverpudlian vinyl, but I didn't need to since one of those half-dozen discs was always chewing up mileage at 33⅓ on her little Sears record player. Next door in my bedroom, I learned every note whether I wanted to or not.

In short order, I realized I really wanted to. I commandeered a brown plastic radio from a closet and soon its transistors and tiny speaker groaned under the effort of keeping up with a volume knob usually pinned at "max." What it lacked in power, the little AM set made up for in reach, pulling in the local Allentown Top 40 outlet as well as the big ones in New York and Philadelphia. I loved those pop-music stations: WAEB, WABC and WFIL. The heavily echoed rants from the disc jockeys introduced each selection, identified the station, read the weather, gave the time, and perhaps even plugged a local racetrack or furniture store all during the brief instrumental introductions to the songs. It was a hysterical approach for sure, but they kept those singles pumping! Things calmed down as the Beatles changed the game again with *Sgt. Pepper's Lonely Hearts Club Band*; suddenly people started buying "long-players" and the DJs talked slower, hipper, and much less often. A scene that was squeaky clean, starched, and innocent in 1964 had now grown shoulder-length hair, wore paisley, donned love beads, and regarded its recording stars as beacons, pointing the way down the road rather than merely leaving signposts on the Top 40 hit parade. They were no longer considered "acts," but artists who created music the way Picasso or Warhol would paint his visions. Instead of the rigid conventions of the music business dictating the creation of their art, they followed the muse. By 1970, rock and roll had come a long way down Route 66, getting its kicks and leaving the city limits behind; there was an open road up ahead and a full tank of gas destined to fuel decades of dreams.

The nearly fifty-year highway that popular music covered after that point is taken up in these pages. As rock and roll traveled its course and eagerly picked up generations of hitchhikers, it changed and mutated, sometimes progressing or even devolving to its original stripped-down essence in order to remain fresh and relevant. No cruise control was set in this little red Corvette; there were always so many people from so many places reaching out to grab the wheel and work the pedals. And even though rock and roll careened madly down an erratic route filled with potholes, detours, and even collisions, this hot rod was still bound for glory. The journey of the music is filled by the stories of thousands from Elvis Presley to Guns N' Roses, singing and playing their way into the hearts of millions standing starstruck along the way. The recorded music they produced—singles and albums—charted each star's course, but the concerts and shows they performed during the ride revealed their progress (or retreat.)

This book takes place inside the "houses of the holy," visiting fifty stages for nearly a half century of hallowed-ground glimpses where greats with names like McCartney, "Slowhand," Jagger, Townshend, "Lucille," and Vaughan gambled their mojo. These stories plot rock's path like pushpins on a map, showing where we've been, but like May-belline gallopin' over the hill, not necessarily predicting what burger joint we're going to end up at. The observations from the field are meticulously documented by a fellow fan, laughably adolescent in the earliest concerts and growing into a music-business professional long before the last. Somehow, career advancement in an industry tasked with spinning art into gold never fossilized my love for the music. It simply *had* to be the healing effects of rock and roll, pushing back the relentless creep of growing cynicism that challenges all of us as we age. Don't harden your hearts! Drink down that magical panacea originally brewed on the plantations of the Delta and the streets of Memphis, then bottled in Chicago and St. Louis and shipped from America to the world! That youthful elixir, battling the attrition of time, will keep girls in those pink pedal pushers and the guys in their blue suede shoes (or at least nose rings and tats) for a long time to come.

THE DECIBEL DIARIES

CHAPTER 1

JAMES GANG

FIRST RIDE

Muhlenberg College Memorial Hall, Allentown, Pennsylvania, December 28, 1970

Listen to: "Funk 49," "The Bomber," "Lost Woman"

Look up the word "geek" in any dictionary. If there's a picture next to the definition, then it's a photo of me in 1970. As a ninth-grader wrapped in tortoiseshell glasses under short, (very) straight hair, living out in the boonies of Pennsylvania farm country, and going to school ten miles away in town, my chances at dating any of the female population at Emmaus High were nil. But, with all that downtime hanging around, whether I wanted it or not, I had plenty of time to concentrate on hobbies. A lot of the boys went for sports, but my circle of friends just gobbled up music, sharing our discoveries like those other kids traded baseball cards. As a group, we migrated from listening to the local Top 40 radio station with its screaming DJs and three-minute singles to obsessing over the new and hip "underground" radio station in Philadelphia that featured album cuts. I racked up hundreds of miles on my mom's uncool (but essential) Ford Maverick in 1970, driving past those countless rows of corn stalks on important missions to the local record store to purchase some of the best albums ever created: *Abraxas, Cosmo's Factory, Led Zeppelin III, Live at Leeds, Déjà Vu,* and *Let It Be.*

During an endless summer still gloriously free of too much responsibility, my friends and I would surrender precious poolside time to venture into Allentown and Speedy's Record Shop. In the back there was a booth featuring the names of all the latest 45s with their current chart numbers labeled on the wall and copies to purchase stocked below. After so many visits choosing singles in that rear space, we ignored it to browse through the new-album bins up front, locating the cool long-players we heard the hippie radio announcers play. Sometimes an article or advertisement in a music magazine like *Rolling Stone* or *Circus* could add some details or put a face to a scrap of musical brilliance gleaned off the airwaves, but for the most part this was virgin territory; we leaned into the racks and bought on instinct. I grabbed my buddy's arm and pointed, "Look!" There, prominently arrayed near the cash register sat a few copies of a plain white album cover dominated by the words *James Gang Rides Again* in plain black letters. I'd heard this band on the radio — a brand new cut named "Funk 49" featuring some smart-ass loud and brash guitar playing with a heavy-duty rhythm section tearing up the background. I didn't know a shred about the group, but I loved that song!

The James Gang played a brand of music swiftly gaining favor in the wake of the psychedelic explosion three years earlier, when rock first matured from its neat and tidy Edwardian-suit era of rote pop songs into an open season of no-holds-barred expression. Rock had flown off in a dozen directions, and one of those involved the act of amplification and extension: louder bands and longer solos! Growing swiftly into a charging behemoth on the backs of Jimi Hendrix, Jeff Beck, Cream, and the Who, hard rock advanced into a full-blown, high-decibel crusade, regarded with disdain by many of the folk-rockers and musicians who considered themselves artfully above its class. Despite the highbrow resistance, the advancing wall of guitars and Marshall amps could not be slowed, leading to even more glorious cacophony like heavy metal, punk rock, and death metal, still alive and crackling in high-voltage intensity forty years later. The James Gang, with its soon-to-be ax star Joe Walsh, stepped into the spotlight, representing Cleveland and attracting the attention of no less than Pete Townshend, so impressed that he insisted the group warm up for the Who on a tour of Europe, then lavished endless praise on Walsh's guitar work to anybody who'd listen. The trio went on to fame and glory for three studio albums, selling out prestigious venues like Carnegie Hall, and was bound for inevitable arena status before it all came crashing down when Walsh jettisoned the others to embark on a solo career. The James Gang's survivors would infuse fresh blood on guitar and make a go of it for several more albums, but they'd never recapture the arc of that exploding success in 1970 and '71.

I grabbed the shrink-wrapped *James Gang Rides Again* and flipped it over. A black-and-white photo of the trio straddling motorcycles on the back cover rumbled with coolness, plus the record had a $4.99 sale sticker on it. Convinced of the album's potential, my buddy and I both walked out with a copy. That vinyl provided hours of enjoyment and turned us on to the towering talent of Walsh, who not only played those guitars, but sang lead vocals and wrote most of the songs. The album vied successfully with the monsters in my collection: Led Zeppelin, Cream, and the Who, for precious turntable time. I memorized every note and word on *James Gang Rides Again* with its rocking side one and gentler acoustic-based flip which actually added some string arrangements and lots of keyboards (which Walsh also played). Weeks later, blasting like a thunderbolt out of the radio, I heard an ad for an upcoming James Gang performance at Muhlenberg College. Although I'd never been to a rock show before, as far as I was concerned, my destiny led straight through that concert hall. Even as a teenage rock 'n' roller in 1970 with rebellion in my heart, I still respected my parents 1950s *Leave it to Beaver* outlook, so I politely asked if I could go to the show and also reserve the car keys. Wonder of wonders, my folks said yes—as long as I honored the terms of my Pennsylvania "Cinderella license" which didn't permit me to drive after midnight.

The show was advertised to start at 8:00—when would people start lining up? We didn't know, so, insanely, we arrived at Muhlenberg's

Memorial Hall by noon. In retrospect, it's clear to me that a line might have already formed if it had been a Stones, Zeppelin, or Dead concert, but for the James Gang, we had the entranceway to the sports facility all to ourselves. With the temperature hovering a few degrees below freezing in the early afternoon, we stomped our feet and walked around to resist the chill. After a couple of hours of this monotony, one of the glass doors in front of us swung open suddenly like the peephole at the entrance to the Emerald City in Oz. A man in blue custodial work clothes peered out in disbelief. "Are you guys here for the concert? It's pretty early, yunno."

"We want good seats," I replied, my breath fogging the air around me.

"Well, you're gonna get them, I'm sure," he laughed, before disappearing inside and pulling the door closed. Our stamping and shuffling resumed for a few minutes before it rattled open again. This time the janitor was accompanied by an older college-aged kid with long hair, who said, "Look, you guys are going to freeze out there. If you promise to stay in the lobby, you can wait in here." I couldn't believe our luck: was it our honest faces? No, we probably just looked pathetic out there and these guys didn't want to fill out the police paperwork for "two deaths by frostbite" on school grounds.

The custodian instructed us to sit on the floor between a couple of large glass cases containing numerous Muhlenberg sports trophies, then we rubbed the feeling back into our extremities and remained as inconspicuous as possible. Gradually over the slow hours the sky outside turned dark, then suddenly we heard loud blasts of guitar and a steady whacking on various drums echoing rudely through the hall. The tentative reports soon coalesced into a song and I shouted at one of the workers walking by, "What's going on in there?"

"They're doing sound check," he tossed back, obviously on some important mission. I'd never heard of sound check. "What's that?" I asked. He looked back blankly, "They're just getting the sound levels adjusted for the show," then disappeared. We should have gotten up to take a look, but fear of being booted from our warm oasis kept us pinned firmly against the wall.

The brief, unexpected rendition of a couple of songs helped pass the time as I noticed a ragged line of people beginning to assemble in front of the outside doors. By now, we were such a part of the scenery that even the new figures that showed up, including several policemen, barely gave us a glance. When the janitor began unlocking the front entrance, we stole away from the wall and pushed through the inner doors into the empty basketball arena. An unobtrusive walk accelerated into a sprint as we rushed across the open court and right up to the stage at the far end. In seconds, it seemed, the whole floor had filled up behind us with people sitting cross-legged and chattering excitedly while staking out some personal space. Despite the No Smoking signs, a bluish haze quickly blurred the air, while a pungent earthy odor assaulted our noses. "Is that . . . ?" I'd certainly heard all about pot, but never saw it or smoked it; now I sure knew what it smelled like: horse manure. Maybe it was homegrown—we had a lot of horses around eastern Pennsylvania. The stage stood only a couple feet high, up to my knees, and we were positioned right in front of the center microphone when a local band called Fiasco came out to warm up, blasting off with some jazzy funk rock with horns and guitars blaring. As a first-time concertgoer, I found the high volume astonishing, but couldn't deny the exhilaration of hearing and seeing the performance happening right in front of me.

After Fiasco's set, it took hours, it seemed, before the James Gang got onstage. Unknown to us, a disturbance had ensued outside the hall when several hundred fans arrived to discover that the show had completely sold out. Angered at the prospect of returning home or back to the dorm without seeing the band, they'd gone on a noisy rant that left minimal damage, but required a police detail to disperse. There were also rumors floating about of a bomb scare, but no one asked the audience to exit the building. I had no idea how long bands delayed going onstage, but eventually I'd discover that some, like the Rolling Stones and Guns N' Roses, could make their audiences sit in boredom for two hours before pulling the trigger. Finally, Joe Walsh, bassist Dale Peters, and drummer Jim Fox walked out and took charge. Standing at attention to greet them, my head looked dead on with Walsh's guitar, which he swiped once to explode a massive chord through the building that made Fiasco's set sound like an acoustic show. Off they went, the volume punishing my ear canals, but revealing awesome delights from the new album and several cuts from the band's obscure first record that we'd never been able to find. "Funk 49" came early and got everybody in the house on board; I thought the sheer heaviness of "The Bomber" would collapse the roof, while a long jam on a cover song called "Lost Woman" allowed each member the chance to solo—for a satisfyingly long time.

During it all, I must have annoyed Walsh to no end, since I persistently waved my *James Gang Rides Again* album cover in his face whenever he looked up. He never reached down to sign it, which you'd think would have solved everything. At one point he moved over to the other side of the stage for a while and I'm convinced that was my fault. But, if my inexperience regarding what a sound check was or what pot smelled like implied my lowly status as a concert tenderfoot, that I'd neglected to even bring along a pen or a magic marker only confirmed it. Joe Walsh couldn't have signed my record even if he wanted to! As it turned out, though, I'd have several more encounters with the young guitarist, who'd soon be elevated to the lofty heights of rock stardom as a solo artist and then become even more famous as a member of the Eagles in future years. His personal success and eventual battles with excess would typify many stars of the era and even rock itself, which accelerated down history's drag strip in a burst of fantastic creativity, only to realize that the damn race car had no brakes. Joe Walsh would be one of the lucky ones to survive beyond the long skid marks he left behind, but many around him would never be as fortunate.

CHAPTER 2

NEIL YOUNG & THE STRAY GATORS

DON'T BE DENIED

Orlando Sports Stadium, February 1, 1973

Listen to: "Down by the River," "The Needle and the Damage Done," "Tonight's the Night"

What could go wrong? All I had to do was stick my thumb out for a 250-mile jaunt up Florida's east coast, then bang a left into Orlando. For millions of people, that destination meant one thing: shaking mitts with Mickey Mouse at the recently opened Disney World. I had a different goal, if not exactly a way to get there: nothing less than a concert from one of rock music's great eccentrics, Neil Young. In 1973 he was riding high on the hippy cred of Buffalo Springfield, and as the fourth wheel in the monumental, mega-selling Crosby, Stills, Nash & Young, before setting off on his own with a quartet of idiosyncratic, important solo albums that had given the world such classics as "Cowgirl in the Sand," "Cinnamon Girl," "Southern Man" and "Down By the River." Artist, enigma, country hippy, and L.A. scenester, Young had already proven himself by acting on instinct and faithfully following his muse. So, in that regard, maybe he was like Walt Disney's famous character: you wondered who the real person was wandering around inside the mouse outfit.

A year earlier, Neil Young's latest album, *Harvest*, had transported the singer-songwriter to the top of the charts behind its mainstream hit "Heart of Gold." It was an uncomfortable place to be, as the artist admitted while looking back in his scrawled liner notes to the 1977 compilation *Decade*—"This song put me in the middle of the road. Travelling there soon became a bore so I headed for the ditch." Young's sudden jump in fame meant that he'd be touring the big places this time around: boxy 20,000-seat sports arenas with disastrous music-killing acoustics and cold concrete or parquet floors. But, hey, it was Neil Young! Plus, Linda Ronstadt, the prettiest singer in L.A., would be warming up the show. Of course, how could we have known that the massive sixty-five-date run, one that would later be referred to as the Time Fades Away Tour, had become Neil's nadir, a dark place so repugnant to the singer, that a live album culled from those dates remained his only record unreleased on compact disc forty years later.

The seeds of this discontent would have been easy to see, but in the early seventies no E Network, TMZ, or Internet existed to instantly spread the word of Young's cascading debacle. The fastest one could count on fresh information about a favorite rock star might be every couple of weeks in *Rolling Stone* or monthly in other mags. People didn't realize that the man who had made "Heart of Gold," who should have been celebrating his number-1 hit, was actually experiencing a consuming depression following the recent death of his friend and collaborator, guitarist Danny Whitten. This name has become a mere footnote in rock history, but Whitten's presence on guitar along with his band Crazy Horse had given Young the sturdy catalyst he needed to reach beyond a crippling indecisiveness and triumphantly finish his second album *Everybody Knows This Is Nowhere* in 1970. The success of this release renewed the star's confidence and got his solo career on track after a disappointing debut. But his collaborator couldn't beat the heroin, inspiring Young to write "The Needle and the Damage Done," lamenting a supreme talent crippled by utter dependency. When Whitten got the call to join Young's touring band for the upcoming mega-tour, he was unable to break free from his debilitating drug haze. The guitarist was sent packing back to L.A. with a stipend, but promptly overdosed and died that very same night. The specter of Whitten's demise continually haunted Young and settled thickly over the entire three-month tour.

The mood seemed to descend over our hitchhiking trip as well. About 140 miles up the coast highway in Vero Beach, as night came on, two local thugs approached my buddy Phil and me, drew fishing knives, and relieved us of some pocket cash and my watch. Then the inevitable: "Give us your wallets!" Despite our lack of weapons we refused, and after a brief standoff, the pair took off (without gutting us like groupers, thankfully). With our moods soured and barely ten bucks between us, we nonetheless pressed on and arrived at a friend's doorstep at Rollins College late that night. This was still the era of general-admission concerts, so no sleeping in; we arose early and spent most of the day in line at the Orlando Sports Stadium, where a nearby dirt road threw great clouds of choking dust into the air and all over the early birds whenever a vehicle passed. It was worth it. When the doors opened and after a thorough pat-down by local police (they didn't mess around in Florida in '73: you definitely went to jail if they found a joint) we hurtled inside, racing through the arena in front of a human wave. Phil and I ran all the way up to the barrier in front of the stage, collapsing against it to stake our claim. Front row! If we spelled each other through our infrequent visits to the bathroom, we'd be able to defend our small bit of prime real estate and stare right into the red of Neil Young's eyes.

As the hours passed, the arena filled up noisily. The smell of marijuana drifted lightly about despite the penalties if caught, and small bottles of liquor that had been smuggled in close to the body were everywhere. Finally the houselights dimmed, and pandemonium rose as young country-rock sex kitten Linda Ronstadt got onstage and worked through her set. With her many solo hits still a couple of years away, most people didn't know who the talented singer was (though they'd probably heard her feathery backup vocals on Neil's "Heart of Gold" without realizing it) and spent more time talking to their friends than listening. Clearly, the inattention of the crowd, plus the frequent catcalls and shouts for Neil Young, got to Ronstadt, who tried in vain to screen out the bedlam and concentrate on performing. The second that her contracted set time was up, she murmured a fleeting goodbye and beat it quickly off the stage. As the house lights came back up, the warm-up singer already forgotten (she would have her revenge as a headlining star after 1974's *Heart Like a Wheel* went platinum), the audience turned toward their more pressing matters—like going to the bathroom or getting a burger.

Up front during intermission, the area tightened and our personal space vanished as determined interlopers angled closer. Drunken confrontations flared up all around, but with our backs to the wall we successfully warded off all invaders. "It's getting harder to move," I croaked. "Move?" Phil replied, "It's getting harder to *breathe!*" A girl next to me, who couldn't have been more than fourteen, began crying as her chest compressed, which didn't help her situation at all as she struggled to suck in air while sobbing. She appeared in such distress that I instinctively maneuvered the girl against the wall, put my arms around her, locked elbows and splayed my hands on the barrier. Just then, the place went dark. The intense pressure on us actually seemed to double as a wave of bodies surged forward in an insane mission to penetrate closer to the stage. Some folks up front bailed out, piling over the wall to be spirited to safety by security, but somehow we hung on stubbornly, *dangerously*, as Neil Young walked out onstage alone.

Looking somewhat disheveled with a wreck of long hair and his soon-to-be-trademark flannel shirt, Young was nevertheless clear voiced as he sat down at center stage, chose an acoustic guitar, and lightly strummed his way into Buffalo Springfield's "On the Way Home." The hooting and hollering from the crowd through the entire song appeared to annoy the musician as he finished up, ignoring the applause before beginning the delicate "Here We Are in the Years" from his first album. If anything, the noise only increased, with Young's acoustic submerged even more deeply under the mayhem. Ending the song, he looked out on the crowd with barely concealed disgust, mumbling into the mic that he'd bring the band out, then stood up and simply walked off the stage without a wave or a smile. As an excited mass, the audience had become a beast, impatient and intolerant of anything other than the hit songs it had come to hear. In that state, the gentle acoustic set, part of a musical personality that should have been obvious to people who'd listened to any of Young's albums, particularly *Harvest*, just didn't fly. It was too bad—not only had we missed some great songs, now we'd get a shorter show.

When the Stray Gators appeared with the star a few minutes later, the crowd ramped back up and bellowed a noisy welcome. Young smiled wickedly, walking directly to his amp and turning it up. He seemed determined to chastise the audience with a volume level so merciless it sounded like jet engines on full throttle, where melodies vanished into a wall of cacophonous white noise. As Young punished us for our sins, he worked through some songs from *Harvest*, then veered off into several unknown, unrecorded tracks that were barely distinguishable in the din to his hits. "Don't Be Denied" and "Time Fades Away" were the standouts, perhaps only because actual choruses and words could be discerned through the racket. When the end came, seemingly days later, the applause echoed distantly and hollow in my ruined ears. I hadn't left because I wanted to see every moment, but as Young and his henchmen quit the stage, I actually felt a great relief that the sonic assault had finally died. My ears could have been bleeding; I didn't check. We were among the last to leave, no choice really, being up so close. As we picked our way through the trash left on the floor and headed for an exit, I was thinking furiously, conflicted that Neil Young had done his utmost to alienate me. Still, there was an almost perverse respect I felt for the man for saying what he wanted to say, and if that was a hearty "Fuck you!" because the crowd was out of control, then I could understand it.

We headed back out on the road to thumb to Miami with a whole load of new stories to tell our friends, but they'd have to wait. A passing state trooper took offense, busting us for hitchhiking, and we spent two days in a Kissimmee jail with our ears still ringing. It seemed Neil Young was just as lucky: he continued wobbling down his own ninety-day highway, beating up audiences, turning in crap performances, shooting tequilas and becoming, generally, a flaming asshole to everyone around him. The *Time Fades Away* live album was released in October '73, filled with warts and embarrassment, considering the care Young had taken on his previous work. "I'm not sorry I put it out," he explained to *Rolling Stone* in 1975, "I didn't need the money, I didn't need the fame. You gotta keep changing." Years later, he told radio journalist Dave Ferrin, "I think it's the worst record I ever made—but as a documentary of what was happening to me, it was a great record." When Young's roadie Bruce Berry overdosed on heroin and died in June, it sent the musician into a deeper tailspin that resulted in the darkest album he'd ever record: *Tonight's the Night.* You want to see what it's like to have one foot off the ledge? Go listen to that one; but it's not recommended for parties.

CHAPTER 3

TRAFFIC AND FREE

BALANCE OF POWER

West Palm Beach Auditorium, Florida, February 17, 1973

Listen to: Traffic, "Dear Mr. Fantasy," "Glad," "Low Spark of High
Heeled Boys"; Free, "All Right Now," "Wishing Well"; bonus: Spencer
Davis Group, "Gimme Some Lovin'"

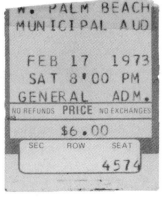

You would have thought we'd learned our lesson. Two weeks earlier, hitchhiking to see Neil Young in Orlando, my buddy Phil and I had been held up at knifepoint, then picked up by the state police and tossed in the cooler for two days. Believe it or not, we actually did get one phone call: "Hi, Mom! I'm in jail." Silence. "For hitchhiking!!" She promptly put Dad on. After delivering an obligatory army-sergeant dressing down, he actually laughed, told me to be more careful, and volunteered to send the bail money. "Thanks again, Dad." We were just about out of Cheech and Chong skits to regale the other prisoners with by the time we got out—"Dave's not here!" Upon release, we prudently marched down the road and out of sight from the Kissimmee police station before dropping our thumbs out to get the hell back to University of Miami.

Now we were back in the student routine, pacing in our cages. Luckily, Phil discovered another potential adventure in the campus newspaper: Traffic, Steve Winwood's arty, spacey, hyperintelligent group of jazz-rockers was scheduled to play in West Palm Beach with Free, the group that had scored big with "All Right Now" back in 1970. We agreed this was another must-see event, but, as usual, we had no wheels and no money. With recent history and painful experience poor tutors to desire, I still reasoned, "Not a problem! West Palm is only seventy miles north; hitching there will be a breeze!" Regarding the finances, after skipping a couple of pizza deliveries to the dorm, we managed to scrounge up the astronomical six bucks it cost for a general-admission ticket. Oh, those 1973 prices!

Traffic had been building a legend since 1967 when its first album, *Mr. Fantasy*, appeared. The band coalesced around Winwood, a wunderkind singer with keyboard- and guitar-playing skills, who had merely been in his mid teens when he scored a couple of pop smashes with the Spencer Davis Group ("Gimme Some Lovin'" remains part of wedding-reception playlists everywhere). He assembled the new outfit with drummer Jim Capaldi, flute and woodwind player Chris Wood, and guitarist Dave Mason, favoring a psychedelic mélange of rock and folk. The band soon amassed several hits while also becoming critical darlings on both sides of the Atlantic. But, the good vibes didn't continue: Mason split to go solo, eventually returning and leaving again before the remaining members cut their greatest album — *John Barleycorn Must Die* — in 1970. After a bout of successful touring in which Mason showed up for a *third* time, then left again, the band moved into a new and wholly unexpected phase — that of a jazzy jam band that had more in common with the Grateful Dead. Traffic released *Low Spark of High-Heeled Boys*, in which the original trio added three more players and wound out its songs to longer (and slower) lengths. Many critics blanched at the change; *Rolling Stone* journalist Paul Evans stated that Traffic "pushed jamming to the point of exhaustion." Nevertheless, the six-song album with its twelve-minute title track became Traffic's all-time best seller. As the expanded lineup toured and a new album called *Shoot Out at the Fantasy Factory* hit the stores just days before the

West Palm Beach show, Traffic seemed like a band sitting on top of the world. Or was it? Eventually we'd find out that this version of the group was already heading for a messy crash landing, but Winwood and company would manage to hold it together long enough to stage a spectacular and memorable night in southern Florida.

Free was having troubles of its own, resulting in a parade of musical chairs that changed so often that it seemed astonishing there was actually a band remaining to tour. Breaking onto the English rock scene in 1969, the teenaged band members, including Paul Rodgers on vocals, guitarist Paul Kossoff, Andy Fraser on bass, and drummer Simon Kirke, became a respected meat-and-potatoes rock unit with its first two albums. Then in 1970, Free's third record, *Fire and Water*, generated the worldwide smash "All Right Now." The single climbed nearly to the top of the English singles chart and raced out of nowhere to finish at number 4 in America. Now, as conquering heroes, the members reacted to their sudden fame in the usual ways: jubilation, paranoia, egomania, and excess. Guitarist Paul Kossoff, in particular, who had just turned twenty, fell victim to the destructive temptations easily accessible to a young rock star. As heroin and other drugs became part of his regular diet, Kossoff's imbalance and unreliability crippled the band's ability to handle the torrent of music-business demands. It was not all right now as the group blew apart in 1971. But, like the Hollywood gunslinger that'd taken several slugs but refused to kick as he wobbled down Main Street, Free miraculously reformed a year later. The reunion soon became troubled: by '73 Andy Fraser had left in disgust, and Kossoff was too drug-addled to perform. Still, even as Free meandered perilously close to its final breakup, the band unexpectedly crafted one of its finest statements—a powerful album called *Heartbreaker* and its magnificent single "Wishing Well"—before binging on this final tour, with Traffic.

So, the West Palm Beach show, the final stop on this U.S. visit, became a last hurrah for both bands in America. In Traffic's case, the six-member lineup (which added a seventh player on keyboards for live shows) would fall apart later that year after recording the *On the Road* live album in Europe. A four-man group would emerge for one more go-round in 1974 before retiring the name until a reunion album and tour twenty years later. Critical importance would always be generously lavished on Traffic, but greater fortune and fame would eventually be realized in the vast platinum success of Steve Winwood's solo career in the eighties and beyond. Free was saying goodbye for a final time; exhausted by the effort of maintaining the band's heartbeat, Paul Rodgers and Simon Kirke would depart within days to form their new venture Bad Company. That group would make them superstars, becoming a powerful force destined to sell millions of albums around the world and reestablish basic "four-on-the-floor" hard rock as the main mover and shaker of the midseventies.

What did Phil and I know about all this? Nothing, really. As mere ticket-buying mortals, we weren't privy to the unfolding melodramas of these Olympian rock stars dropping into town—we were just concerned with getting to the show. Our dormitory sat right on Route 1, so we simply walked out the front door, crossed the street to the northbound side and stuck out our thumbs in front of Burger King. It only took an hour and a half to reach the West Palm exit, and then it was less than a half mile to the auditorium. We walked on, soon spotting the squat conical building, which looked like a massive, concrete version of the Apollo moon capsules they were launching further up the coast at Cape Kennedy. Only a small crowd had arrived early, so when the doors opened, we had no trouble getting a spot close to the action.

Once Free took the stage, Paul Rodgers immediately started prowling about, mic stand in hand, in the cocksure manner we'd get to know well in Bad Company. Simon Kirke settled behind his drum kit and took a couple of ranging shots. Aside from those two, though, the other band members were rookie replacements. Even so, the latest (and final) version of Free killed it; we were rocking out from the first note. The big hits "All Right Now," "Wishing Well," and the monstrous slow-thump of "Fire and Water" sent the audience into dancing and head-banging fits. When the band quit the stage after an hour, the deafening applause and lingering shouts signaled a clear victory in what we couldn't have known was its swan song. If the crowd had realized the members of Free were taking their final bow, they would never have gotten away with just ending the set on a mere wave goodbye. But as it was, Free left us sweaty, happy, and satisfied.

Traffic took over and proved equal to the task of picking up the glove dropped by its tour mates. The enhanced lineup had so many rhythmic weapons available that the players could scarcely miss in the opening "Shootout at the Fantasy Factory" with Rebop Kwaku Baah's congas punctuating Roger Hawkins's drum blasts in a pulsing and infectious runaway beat. Jim Capaldi, once the drummer and now a percussionist roaming the front of the stage, sang "Rock and Roll Stew," which snaked in a slower groove and led into an extended jam. The long and meandering "Roll Right Stones" and epic "Low Spark" demanded dreamlike jazz improvisations, absorbing the greatest amount of time before Traffic's last encore brought the house down. The band had played brilliantly, performing a set mainly drawn from its three most recent records. After the encore, the clapping eventually faded and people turned to leave. "That was great," I shouted, "Let's get out of here." But a sudden squeal of feedback in the still-darkened arena prompted everyone to look back. There was commotion in the shadows onstage as flashlight beams darted about in front of the line of hot amplifiers with their glowing red power lights still illuminated. "What's up?" Phil shouted even as the stage lights welled up to reveal the answer. The members of Traffic had returned to their places, but they'd also brought the members of Free out to join them.

The distinctive six-note bass pattern of "Gimme Some Lovin'" burst out, bah-da-da-da-da—BOOM, prompting the audience to get right down to it—boogying, clapping, and singing along. Up on the stage it seemed like everyone jumped in to take a solo, and probably did because the song wound on and on and on as the musicians celebrated the end of their tour with this apt and spirited finale. It's hard to put a number on how long that version of the song went, but it surely breezed past fifteen minutes and might have even reached the half-hour mark. "This is so great . . ." the guy next to me began, but the words caught in his throat as the booming volume abruptly ceased, the final notes echoing off the back of the hall. "What happened?" he continued. The darkened amp lights testified to the reason. Power to the stage had been shut off, the guitars and keyboards falling silent and the microphones rendered useless. Obviously the soundman would never have done that; the jam must have gone on long enough to draw the ire of someone in charge. Loud boos and a few shouts of "Fuck the Man!" lifted from the audience and for a few nervous seconds it looked like the crowd would rush the stage as the front rows pushed threateningly into the wooden barrier. With the hated war in Vietnam still going on, a spirit of rebellion and resistance remained quite alive in early 1973. Certainly, the concert was no antiwar rally, but at this point in American history, it was not a good time to fuck with a young, worked-up crowd of several thousand that was quite aware of the power it had in numbers.

The very real possibility of a riot played dangerously on the moment as a wave of anger exploded throughout the arena. As shouts and boos reached an alarming intensity, narrowing, belligerent eyes locked on any policeman or usher who happened to be stationed on the premises. But, then . . . wait . . . listen! There was another sound in the arena, not as loud as the crowd, but definitely something else. The tumult from the audience dropped as people strained to hear. There were . . . congas and drums! The musicians had never stopped playing! They certainly weren't amplified, but they were still rocking. Rebop hammered on his array of Cuban barrels, Hawkins kept the beat on his kit, and Capaldi tapped on a set of bongos while Winwood and the others grabbed anything percussive they could find—cowbells, wood blocks, tambourines, drumsticks on mic stands—anything. Paul Rodgers and his mates got the crowd clapping again as the musicians who were accustomed to hitting things for a living continued to do so.

To hell with the curfew—this was our show! The vast drum circle throbbed on throughout the hall even as the houselights snapped on in full intensity. The police wisely stood down, and the audience stepped away from a confrontation, happily spending its energy, instead, on the music. Minute after minute the jam beat on and on, and it didn't stop until the members of Traffic/Free, or was it Free/Traffic, decided *they* wanted to finish it. Then the musicians hugged it out before waving a final goodbye as the pounding applause-filled flourish from the audience capped the night.

"Whoa! That was so good!" I enthused as we rode the wave heading for the exit, the smell of sweat filling the corridor until we finally got outside. What a great night—the people had had their say! In the scheme of things it was a tiny win, but a win nonetheless. The elation, however, soon faded as we remembered that we didn't have a ride home. The two of us stood at the parking lot exit. Many people offered us a lift, but they were either going into West Palm or heading north. We hung out till the last car left. Damn! Walking away from the auditorium, thankful that it was a warm February night in Florida, we considered our options, and hitching in the dark down to Miami wasn't a favorable one. Fortunately, the police might have tried to shut down the concert, but at least they didn't chase us off a pair of tired park benches we decided to snooze on till sunup. Power to the people . . . and also the God-given rights of two deadbeat college kids to earn a couple of stiff necks and take a few splinters in the name of rock and roll!

CHAPTER 4

B. B. KING

"I'VE BEEN DOWNHEARTED, BABY..."

Muhlenberg College Memorial Hall, Allentown, Pennsylvania, April 15, 1973

Listen to: *Live at the Regal* and *Live in Cook County Jail* (albums); "How Blue Can You Get?," "The Thrill Is Gone," "To Know You Is to Love You"

A quick visit from college brought me home to rural Pennsylvania for a few days, rubbing elbows once again with my close friends from the earliest days. With the edge of winter just departed, there wasn't much to do but catch up and walk outside in the pleasantly lukewarm April air. But the delight in observing the budding trees and farmers bouncing about on their tractors as they seeded in crops soon faded, motivating us to seek excitement in the nearby city of Allentown. Like prospectors digging through the mountains for months, then riding into Boomtown to cash in a few nuggets and go hog wild, we had money to spend and a weekend waiting. Someone mentioned that they'd seen an ad for a B. B. King concert at Muhlenberg College—a reasonable suggestion that would keep us out of some kind of adolescent trouble. A concert might be a lot more fun than launching fireworks at the neighbor's house or ringing doorbells and scattering into the darkness—or perhaps not—but on this occasion we decided to take the high road, of sorts. With Pennsylvania's drinking age at twenty-one, someone would have to embark on a supply run over to one of the many liquor stores that dotted the border of New Jersey just across the Delaware River. At the cost of four bucks for a concert ticket plus a case of Rolling Rock, it appeared this would be a fine evening at a reasonable price.

Thing was, I didn't really know much about B. B. King or the blues; I was a fan, particularly, of the Anglo-rock produced by Led Zeppelin, Cream, Deep Purple, and Ten Years After. I'd learn later that I was already hearing the blues in those groups without even realizing it, even though the English distillation of the style sat at the end of a very long evolution from the field hollers and Delta troubadours of America's past. Those enlightened Brits discovered the lessons from coveted sides of vinyl procured with difficulty from American record stores, often on "the other side of the tracks" in the (at the time) segregated black sections of towns. If an early English group embarked on a U.S. tour, they'd devote some free time to locating authentic "race records" completely unavailable in the musicians' homeland—and mostly invisible to me and my friends here. The Rolling Stones went much further by booking recording time at Chess Studios, Chicago's Mecca of the blues, in June 1964. There, the young devotees were astonished to witness Muddy Waters help unload their gear, Chuck Berry drop by, and Willie Dixon attempt to sell them a song. The environment proved immensely inspiring to the English acolytes, who ended up covering songs by all three blues giants. The Rolling Stones would also record an instrumental tribute to the modest two-story brick building housing Chess, titling it after the studio's address at "2120 South Michigan Avenue" and placing it proudly on its second U.S. album, *12 × 5*.

As I listened to *Best of Cream* and perused the album notes over and over, I wondered who the Robert Johnson who wrote "Crossroads" was, as well as the identity of Willie Dixon, who had penned "Spoonful." I dug deeper and learned about the former, a traveling Delta womanizer who wrote and recorded enough great songs in just two sessions to yield a couple of dozen cover hits forty years later. Willie Dixon, even more prolific, reloaded the Chess label's formidable songwriting arsenal on a daily basis, pumping out blues hit after blues hit: "Back Door Man," "Bring It on Home," "Hoochie Coochie Man," "I Can't Quit You Baby," "I Just Want to Make Love to You," "Little Red Rooster,"—and about a hundred others. Like so many Americans, I was suddenly redirected back to my own musical heritage by Cream and its many musical compatriots from across the pond. Now the blues legends who had nearly been lost to history received their just due, with Waters, Howlin' Wolf, T-Bone Walker, Lightnin' Hopkins, and dozens more stepping out of their juke joints to "cross over" racial boundaries onto college campuses, concert halls, and supper clubs with a sophisticated white clientele.

Riley B. King, an ambitious entertainer from Mississippi possessing great skill on the guitar and a fine voice that could effortlessly soar from a sexy growl to a sugar-coated soprano, found himself on the receiving end of this great change. Young Riley found early success as a DJ and radio performer in Memphis, his on-air handle becoming the "Beale Street Blues Boy," then "Blues Boy," and finally the B. B. who went on to international fame. In 1951 he had his first number-1 hit on the R & B chart with "3 O'Clock Blues," the first of many smashes on the American R & B sales survey. B. B. became a national sensation, and in 1956 the musician and his band performed an unbelievable 342 concerts. You better believe that group became tight onstage! The next step was King's crossover to the white audience, which he achieved on his 1969 mainstream hit "The Thrill Is Gone," with its restrained guitar work, inescapably gorgeous melody, and shimmering string arrangement.

I knew about B. B. King, but "The Thrill Is Gone" was about it. I'd heard an album he'd recorded two years later called *In London*, modeled in the record-biz fashion of the day to pair American bluesmen with their English rock-star pupils. A couple of those albums, particularly *The London Howlin' Wolf Sessions* with Eric Clapton, Steve Winwood, and some Rolling Stones, as well as *The London Chuck Berry Sessions*, were top-notch efforts (should be in every blues library). B. B.'s *In London* missed the caliber of those two efforts, but hearing him jam with

Ringo Starr, Gary Wright, and Peter Green of Fleetwood Mac, out-classing them easily, raised my respect for this southern bluesman even more. He kept his music fresh by adapting to the times, as well. In 1973, with much of the attention and success of black music centered in soul and funk, King immersed himself in those styles and added them to his repertoire. He sustained his momentum by releasing an album recorded in Philadelphia, the center of the seventies soul sound, featuring key assistance from Stevie Wonder. The white-hot Motown star had written and recorded the song "To Know You Is To Love You" with his wife Syreeta, but redid it with King, granting the blues star another mainstream hit. With twenty-two albums now behind him and a schedule of gigs stretching out far ahead, forty-seven-year-old Riley B. King was doing just fine.

We shuffled into Memorial Hall at Muhlenberg College, where I had first come to see the James Gang three years before. We found seats up on the hard, wooden bleachers that would, inevitably, get harder as the show went on. The acoustics of the place rang with the echoes and hollowness typical of an indoor basketball court, but you get what you pay for, and we'd only had to pay a few bucks. Sometimes, weird concert bookings were fun: you'd get to see someone totally outside of your realm of experience. And so it was tonight with the opening band Steeleye Span, an English outfit playing folk music and medieval explorations on fiddle, mandolin, dulcimers, and the like. They were probably very good, but not my main cup of Joe. I lapsed into conversation, exchanging beer breath with my buddies and missing most of the set. Shame on me, I suppose: Steeleye Span became a respected entity and continued to perform and record well into the next century. We barely noticed the group's departure from stage, merrily blathering away as our rear ends grew numb on the rigid wooden benches.

When the lights dimmed once again and at least eight musicians, including four horn players, walked onstage to find their appointed positions, we turned, now in rapt attention, and checked out the sharply attired arrivals in their dark suits and white ruffled shirts. Polite applause greeted the start of the show as the band fired up a sprightly instrumental and got swinging. This being my first experience with a show band, I looked in vain for the star of the night: where was B. B.?

I didn't have to wait long—he was introduced at the end of the first number and strolled into the stage lights cradling his big hollow-body Gibson, beaming broadly and turning to every point in the room to acknowledge those perhaps not seen, but certainly heard as a hospitable shout rose from the hall. Then he laid out a couple of warm blasts from his guitar, locking in with the shuffling rhythm from his fellow veterans and singing, "Every day . . . Ever-REE-day . . . I say every day . . . I have the blues!" Here we go!

There is a certain liberation in seeing a show when you know practically none of the artist's music. As those around you sing along, there's no shame in forgetting the words because you never knew them anyway! You don't have to berate yourself for not listening enough to the records or worry about your memory going south. With the exception of "The Thrill Is Gone," I knew none of B. B. King's tunes, great or small, and stood like a blank sheet of paper for the star to write on. Did he ever! The man purred the lyrics to "Every Day I Have the Blues," interspersing them with short and witty runs on his Gibson, bending the notes beautifully and pulling out a distinctive vibrato with his fret hand flickering as fast as a hummingbird's wings. In a flash, the song had ended, but the band eased on into the next, downshifting to an unhurried pace as the horn section put down its saxes and trumpet while King used the hushed moment to say hello to the audience. Then he continued on into the slow blues number (another signature tune, I'd later find out) "How Blue Can You Get?" The man's vocal gifts stole the show during this lament, "I've been downhearted baby, ever since the day we met." Eyes closed, King had already begun to sweat, the big drops just accentuating the pain in the song. Then the punch line: "I gave you seven children . . . and now you wanna give 'em back!" The crowd's reaction rose to a peak. This was not right! The woman had wronged B. B.! No one deserved this! I shook my fist mentally at the singer's faithless lover; real or imagined, it didn't matter. I had actually become angry! What the hell—it was just a song. I didn't realize it, but I'd just received a crash course in what the blues was all about.

It only took a few moments for this neophyte to realize that we were in the presence of a true master; King's talents were so prodigious and his band had the ability to play anything their leader asked. With fluid fingers flying and in utter command of his performance, King, nevertheless didn't settle into the humdrum of an endlessly rehearsed set of selections. He clearly worked himself up into a fit, throwing body and soul into those tales of lost love, dire need, fits of sobbing, and fading thrills, looking to uncover a deeper heartstring and move the audience toward real emotion. This was a professional entertainer for sure, but one who clearly enjoyed his work—every night. "The Thrill Is Gone" came near the end, its trademark strings absent, but the horn section picking up the slack. The crowd stood and cheered the hit single from three years earlier, the most recognizable track in B. B.'s arsenal. As far as I was concerned, though, he didn't even have to play it: he'd already had me since the second song. As a bunch of white, middle-class knuckleheads, we couldn't claim to have the blues at all, but on this night we surely learned what they were all about. King would have a long life exposing generation after generation to the essential American style by playing over two hundred shows a year nearly to the day he died in 2015. U2 would craft the song "When Love Comes to Town" around him in 1988 and immortalize the legend in the movie *Rattle and Hum*. It's a fitting memory: Riley B. King standing onstage with the young wide-eyed members of the already-famous Irish band, their roles as international rock stars reduced willingly to that of a humble and attentive group of students learning all they could from a true American master.

CHAPTER 5

DEEP PURPLE

THE FOUR-DAY RING

Allentown Fairgrounds, Pennsylvania, June 3, 1973

Listen to: "Smoke on the Water," "Highway Star," "Hush," "My Woman from Tokyo"

As a teenager, I was always right. After being introduced to rock by the matchless ingenuity of the Beatles, I thought my early forays outside of the Liverpool womb were pretty good. It was just my timing that sucked. Once I heard "White Room" with that wild Eric Clapton wah-wah guitar solo at the end, I was impressed enough to go out and buy the first Cream album I could find, which happened to be *Best of Cream*. I spent hours listening to it while trying in vain to figure out what the pictures of the assorted vegetables on the cover meant. I still don't know, by the way; I think it must have been a quick pick by some record-label hack desperate to get out to the Hamptons on a Friday. I also picked up the other album that Cream released in 1969, *Goodbye* (which was just another name for *Contractual Obligation Record*). Great! I discovered an awesome group and the members rewarded me by breaking up! There was a reprieve of sorts when Clapton and his drummer Ginger Baker immediately segued into a new group named Blind Faith. But, those guys split up before I could even get to the record store! Likewise, the James Gang rode off into the sunset after three fine studio albums and an impressive live one when its gifted singer and guitarist Joe Walsh departed for a solo career. Another favorite, Santana, mutated from that incredible Cuban/rock powerhouse we saw in the *Woodstock* movie into some sort of alien-jazz-meets-Sly-and-the-Family-Stone combination; as if Cupid, taking a break from his duties spreading love, had grown an Afro and shot Carlos Santana with a volley of Miles Davis–tipped soul-brother arrows.

Consistency wasn't necessarily a priority for young musicians. Before thoughts of a lifetime career ever took hold, players just followed their path wherever it took them, even if it catapulted them right out of a hit band. But, I craved consistency! Once I'd discovered a group, I wanted to mine its riches for as long as possible, not settle for one or two nuggets before getting kicked off the claim. Feeling somewhat cynical in this regard, when I discovered a tremendous band in the summer of '72, I naturally assumed it would break up within days. Deep Purple was the same English group I'd listened to four years earlier on Top 40 radio when it debuted with the worldwide hit "Hush." Since then the outfit had disappeared off my radar, but then Purple reappeared on the new FM "underground" radio scene. The band had shed some members in the wake of "Hush," gained new ones and now defined an explosive guitar/organ combination fronted by the screaming demon Ian Gillan, who would also nail the lead role on the original 1970 recording of Andrew Lloyd Webber's rock opera *Jesus Christ Superstar*. In 1972, exciting Deep Purple songs like "Smoke on the Water," "Highway Star," and "Space Truckin'" appeared from a strong new album entitled *Machine Head*. Plus — in a huge bonus — two more records that were nearly as good, *In Rock* and *Fireball*, had come out earlier and were also ripe for exploration with winning cuts like "Speed King" and "Strange Kind of Woman."

Deep Purple defined the new style of hard rock along with Black Sabbath, which was gathering momentum at the very same time. Although blues could be heard in the early recordings of both bands, for the most part they abandoned the time-honored constraints of that style to emphasize maximum volume and a thundering beat. One element that did survive from the blues tradition was the generous space allowed to each of the band's soloists: Ritchie Blackmore igniting a thousand fiery guitar breaks, Jon Lord pursuing both warm and incendiary Hammond organ tones for minutes on end, and Ian Paice rolling out his boundless excursions on drums. The high-decibel approach would only pick up steam over subsequent years, inspiring future generations and bands like AC/DC, Judas Priest, and Motörhead to keep the torch burning brightly through any conflicting musical climate that found favor with the mainstream. Nearly fifty years later, the stubborn presence of heavy metal shows no sign of retirement: it's as loud and shameless as ever!

The year 1973 unfolded as a complicated and wonderful fairy tale for Deep Purple. The English group began it in a strong position: *Machine Head* had received good airplay the previous summer on American radio, especially "Smoke on the Water" (the working title of which was "Durh Durh Durh!" for obvious reasons). A double album of earlier work from the "Hush" days entitled *Purple Passages* was in stores and selling respectably for an archival release. Plus, the group launched an album of brand-new songs called *Who Do We Think We Are?* in January, which zoomed into the U.S. Top 20 in three weeks. It stayed up there for another six, but like a rocket that had reached apogee, run out of fuel, and begun tumbling to earth, sales began to slacken rapidly. One of the reasons for the brief run in the charts was the anemic performance of its single "My Woman from Tokyo"; the other was that Deep Purple released *another* album less than three months after the previous one. *Made in Japan* had been recorded onstage in 1972 for the Japanese market, which had gone absolutely bonkers for the band. But, upon its release, so many copies were being imported and sold in America that the U.S. label, Warner Brothers, decided to put it out domestically to cash in. Soon, sales of the new double album had exceeded Purple's studio effort, and by June it was in the Top 10. In an inspired move, Warner released 1972's "Smoke on the Water" as a single with the live *Made in Japan* version on the B-side. It quickly became a Top 40 radio smash, one of the biggest of the summer. The single peaked at number 4, dragging the year-old *Machine Head* into the Top 10 and selling two million copies of that album in the process. The members of Deep Purple were now bona fide rock stars; with a tour of America already scheduled, the band arrived on these shores like heavy metal gods.

The old Pennsylvania burg of Allentown sat tucked up against the New Jersey border next to Bethlehem and Easton. Built on heavy industries like Mack Trucks and Bethlehem Steel, the tri-city area was surrounded by miles of cropland and dairy farms. Every summer since 1852, in the heart of the city, residents had celebrated their industriousness at the Great Allentown Fair. The expansive festival grounds included a dirt racetrack served by a spacious steel-and-brick grandstand that had hosted events from pre–World War I harness racing to a 1951 visit from General Douglas MacArthur. Concerts were also an attraction, but limited to the caffeine strength of acts like the Osmonds, Herb Alpert & the Tijuana Brass, or Liberace. That was about to change—big time. A local promoter convinced the managers of the venerable institution that the 14,500-capacity venue could also host some of the best-selling rock groups of the day, including that hip "new" band named Deep Purple. I'm sure the promoter failed to enlighten the founding fathers that the purveyors of "Durh, Durh Durh!" performed at a volume level somewhat greater than Liberace's. In fact, at a London concert, Purple's volume had been measured at 112 decibels: like standing next to a whining power saw and only 13 dBs shy of pain level. Now, that kind of enthusiasm interested my friends and me! We wasted no time grabbing tickets, for a whopping five bucks each.

As usual it was a general-admission show, so we waded down onto the racetrack through a crowd that quickly grew too densely packed to penetrate as we got closer to the stage. Still, we managed to infiltrate to within fifty feet. While we waited, there were several incidents on the far side of the track as gatecrashers hopped the pathetically inadequate security fence and sprinted madly toward us, bent on avoiding capture and melting into the swarm. This became great entertainment as we wagered the success or failure of each attempt, the crowd yelling en-

couragement and shouts of congratulations every time someone made it
through, then groaning its disappointment and booing the police with
each defeat. Despite the thrill of watching the members of Deep Purple
suddenly strut onstage, as soon as they peeled out into their opening
"Highway Star," our attention was commanded instead by the amazing
sight of *hundreds* rising from the perimeter and jumping the fence en
masse like an army of zombies bent on overwhelming us and munching
on our brains. They ran like hell, overwhelming the cops in a massive
human tsunami. A few of the rebels were collared as they sped by, but
the vast majority of the tide broke into the grandstand area and swiftly
blended in with the jeans- and T-shirt-wearing throng like nothing unusual had ever happened.

Despite the vast roars of encouragement from the crowd during this
dramatic incursion, Deep Purple's incredibly loud stage volume envel-
oped and absorbed the outside din, reducing our grand efforts at applause to mere mouse squeaks. Blackmore's guitar and Gillan's piercing
screams scythed through our ears while Roger Glover's bass and Ian
Paice's drum battery jolted our bones with tremendous shakes. At the
moment, Jon Lord's organ rode above it all with a churchlike calm that
belied the damage he could do, but later in the song he'd take a solo and
dangerously rock that Hammond back and forth on its legs to produce
a panoply of metallic groans and shrieks. Dazed by the sonic blast, the
people in front of each speaker column on the wings of the stage parted
as biblically as the Red Sea, allowing shock troops, like myself, the opportunity to brave the volume and get closer. Now up front, I could
scrutinize the action, even facial expressions of the members. As the set
continued, Gillan would smile as he worked the audience, but seemed
to scowl every time he looked over at his ever-irascible guitar player. In
fact, no one was smiling much onstage: grim looks and a businesslike
progression of songs with a lack of chatter or humor between the members seemed to betray an underlying tension. At one point, even the
imperturbable Lord had boiled over to the point that he angrily shoved
one of his keyboards right off the side of the stage where it plummeted
ten feet and impacted heavily into the grass. Ouch! Even as green as I
was going to rock concerts, I knew that couldn't have been a regular

part of the show. The instrument's mechanical guts surely must have been jumbled expensively by the violent crash.

In what seemed like moments, all the songs, solos, and goodbyes were over. In the startling, sudden quiet, from my ruined ears I could hear the rise of a distant noise which I recognized a second later as applause. It was joined by an unpleasant and persistent ringing tone that would become a faithful, if unwanted, companion in my head for four days. In another annoying development, I'd find out that less than a month after our show, this version of Deep Purple had performed its final concert in Osaka. I hadn't imagined the friction onstage in Allentown, as by that point Blackmore and Gillan weren't speaking to each other. The singer even made separate travel arrangements and stayed in different hotels to avoid the often-acerbic attitude of his guitarist. Also unknown to the public, Gillan had served the rest of the band with his intent to depart before the tour began, but stayed on to fulfill the group's upcoming run of concert commitments. The moment the trek finished in Japan, he was history, with bassist Roger Glover taking the opportunity to quit as well.

Deep Purple reorganized quickly with replacements, but no lineup of the band would ever be as creative and successful. Surprisingly, after the personal disagreements had dissipated and egos mellowed, this version of the group would reassemble eleven years later in the eighties. But even if I had suspected that the eventual reunion would occur, to a teenager in 1973, that event existed a whole lifetime away. Currently, I was just pissed off. I'd witnessed an amazing lineup destined to provide years of new music, but in the end, they'd only entered my gulag of groups that just seemed to implode into nothingness—Cream, James Gang, Santana, and now Deep Purple. But of course, even though that magical lineup vanished into classic rock's graveyard of heroes, "Durh, Durh, Durh" would never go away. Resolutely, it will still be on the radio, or whatever they use to play music on, even when someone cracks a bottle of bubbly on the prow of the starship *Enterprise*.

CHAPTER 6

TED NUGENT & THE AMBOY DUKES

THE CALL OF THE WILD

The Valley Theater, East Greenville, Pennsylvania, January 19, 1974

Listen to: "Journey to the Center of the Mind," "Cat Scratch Fever," "Stranglehold"

I grew up right off Route 29, a two-lane spike through eastern Pennsylvania woodlands and miles of farmland, skirting the eastern edge of Amish country and swinging south from Allentown toward Pottstown. Not much ever goes on there, other than the steady transformation of those fertile fields into acres of subdivisions, housing the white-collar workers that slowly supplant the farmers and feed their numbers into a growing local commute or a daily round-trip to Philadelphia fifty miles distant. If you lived in that area and were a farm boy, nothing hurt more than to see those grand old Pennsylvania barns fall into neglect, eventually collapsing into sumac-covered heaps of boards and slate roof tiles to be auctioned off, then bulldozed into streets lined with gleaming new mailboxes. Astride Route 29, just seven miles from my home, sat the sleepy village of East Greenville. Here, in the quaint locale of just a couple thousand, an event would soon occur that was destined to strike the townspeople like a compact thermonuclear device dropped from a B-52 into the streets below. Even now as the bomb plummeted, nobody at Ground Zero had any clue that a real-life version of Looney Tunes' Tasmanian Devil had been invited inside the town limits. "Gonzo" time had arrived!

You would say, "Of course, you idiot! You're talking about Ted Nugent: the 'Motor City Madman,' berserk rock star, passionate outdoorsman, expert bow hunter, stout NRA life-timer, and ultraright wing nut!" In the seventies, his frenzied guitar assaults and sophomoric songs of lust first connected in the Midwest with an army of mostly male teens, before going nationwide. Eventually Nugent would hawk over thirty million albums, earn six platinum discs, and sell out 20,000-seaters during the late seventies like gulping venison sausages at breakfast. Building his house on hard rock, the guitarist committed himself to the long haul, touring relentlessly — upward of 200 shows a year — and doggedly pursuing his dreams of stardom. The Michigan native's brazen constitution and considerable intelligence made him a domineering and astute opponent in any interview or debate, of which there were many, considering his open ridicule of animal-rights activists, gun-control advocates, and liberal political pundits. Given the opportunity, Nugent would happily pontificate on his views of a cracked, crippled, and impotent society that festered all around him and eroded the basic principles that founded America. In a word, he was *driven*.

But this was before all of that. "The Nuge" possessed all of those larger-than-life personality traits we came to be outraged at and/or loved, but in January 1974 no one had even heard of the guy yet. He was an unnoticed tiger prowling in our midst, a star in his own head still shooting clay pigeons instead of the real thing. The only thing I knew about Ted Nugent was one song that had briefly been on Top 40 radio five years earlier. That song, "Journey to the Center of the Mind," recorded by an obscure Detroit group named the Amboy Dukes, possessed an incredible sustaining guitar riff and solo that emerged feebly from my tiny, laughable, transistor radio, but punched right through the outdoor clutter and noise of a summer day. The song got to number 16 on the U.S. singles chart, but was impossible to find in any record shop. Despite that, the guitar riff stuck in my head for years until finally in 1972, I stumbled on a copy of the record at a farmers' market, of all places, and discovered the musician who played that unforgettable guitar. Then, just a year later when I was home from college during January break, the local FM "underground" radio station started playing a new song from Ted Nugent and the Amboy Dukes entitled "Call of the Wild." *The band was still alive!* The DJ also announced that the group would be performing a couple of concerts at the Valley Theater in East Greenville. *Really?* At this point I was convinced that some cosmic jigsaw puzzle had surrendered its final piece: clearly it was my destiny to see Ted Nugent.

On the strength of two songs and my conviction (plus a ticket price of three dollars), my best friend Bob and a few high school buds agreed to go. After all, it was a Saturday night, and what else could top a hard rock show practically in our backyard? We sufficiently prepared our minds and bodies with some beer and a bottle or two of the infamous and ghastly-tasting Mad Dog 20/20 (Mogen David wine). For better or for worse, the thick, sickly sweet Mad Dog, if it could be kept down, did wonders for eliminating teenage inhibitions. Tonight the effect was for the better: no one had gotten "the whirlies," and the four of us arrived at the theater in high spirits. We were immediately allowed inside and realized with delight that we had the whole place nearly to ourselves, front row ripe for the picking. The four of us moseyed down to a set of seats directly in front of the chest-high stage and stared in surprise, then anticipation, at an actual buffalo head mounted behind the drum kit. A hunting triumph turned into an imposing blank-eyed stage prop? No longer roaming the range, but now commanding the stage, the buffalo offered another clue as to just who this mysterious Ted Nugent was.

Over the next hour, folks trickled into the room. Opened in 1924 as the Grand Theater, the vaudeville and silent-movie house had been beat up more than a little bit, but when a group of local yokels named the Shimerville Sheiks got onstage to open the show, the sound system seemed decent enough. The musicians were actually quite good, playing jug-band style with bluegrass and country at the fore, odd considering the hard rock pummeling we expected from the headliner. We gave the Sheiks some hootin' and hollerin' during the set to encourage them, and once they finished, sent them off with our best applause yet. Alcohol-related euphoria aside, we reacted strongly, I suppose, because down in the front, there's a certain responsibility you feel when a musician is looking directly in your eyes. Years later, after I'd been in the music business for a while and emceed dozens of bands, I came to realize that usually the front row was *all* you could see, the blinding stage lights obscuring an audience certainly heard but rarely seen. Being in the front row was not a spectator sport; you had to be involved and earn your stripes down there. But I had no idea that just a few minutes after the Sheiks collected their instruments and politely left the premises, my friends and I would be struggling to prove ourselves worthy, hanging on for dear life as a mega-decibel, hard-rock safari stampeded boldly into the room. We would no longer be impassive judges of the talent, voting thumbs up with our applause or denying it if we didn't like the show; now we'd be the prey of a stalking wild beast. If we didn't react, we would *die*.

The theater hadn't filled up with much more than sixty or seventy people before the lights went down and we stood up to welcome the feature attraction. A bass player and drummer ambled out and settled in, kicking off a rhythm before a flash of brown suddenly scurried into view, animal-like, from the side curtains, stepping up onto a set of guitar amplifiers and hitting a massive introductory chord louder than we could have ever imagined in such a tiny place. Thoughts of falling plaster and crashing walls commanded my attention as I struggled to size up the outlandish figure who then hurled himself into the air, landing catlike and rushing forward to the lip of the stage while raking his guitar back and forth across the audience like John Dillinger spraying the cops with lead. Ted Nugent stood five feet away, eyes blazing into mine with a predatory fire. He was nearly naked, sporting merely a leather loincloth and full Indian headdress with wild tangles of hair tumbling under the feathers and past his shoulders to drape over a big hollow-body Gibson. He shook his eyes off the audience, bent over and commanded the guitar strings, then homed in on the microphone to begin belting out the words to the first song.

Nugent had chosen his game strategy well, proving that the best defense against an untested audience's possible apathy was an unexpected and overpowering offense—shock and awe. Like a unit of seasoned Rangers dropping out of the sky and taking out their target before any return fire, the guitarist wheeled about, headdress feathers swinging in a grand arc as he slammed into the chords of a second song. It was useless to try to talk; the waves of metal blasting forth rendered even shouting inaudible, so I gaped over at Bob, disbelieving eyes communicating all. It seems obvious now why I have absolutely no further recollection of the other two players—Nugent's warrior presence riveted all my attention. When the song ended, our quartet exploded with as loud a response as we could muster, but all our wild clapping and shouts sounded pitifully meek and ineffective in the wake of that powerful opening salvo. I turned to look at the people behind us. Some stood in isolated spots, joining us in applause, but most just sat in their seats, eyes glassy and faces blank with shock, minds still failing to process what had just happened.

If Nugent was disappointed at the half-empty house, he didn't show it, reaching up to take off the headdress, then plowing into the opening of another song. We didn't know the names of any of the selections except "Call of the Wild," but it didn't matter: Nugent had a flair for making every unknown piece of music memorable, from extended episodes of howling feedback to more gimmicks like taking his ax off and beating it relentlessly with the guitar strap while it shrieked and moaned. Who could have expected that the warrior would grab a bow and arrow from his box of stage tricks, threatening us like we were pheasants scattering in a field? In a few worried seconds the weapon had traversed the audience, then trained on a Styrofoam head placed on an amplifier. Nugent let the arrow fly and the skull split apart, plastic chunks flying all over the stage. *This sure wasn't Crosby, Stills & Nash!*

The music was heavy stuff, representative of Nugent's formative years in the midsixties Detroit scene that fostered some of the heaviest garage rock heard in America at the time. That style preached a do-it-yourself attitude, using whatever limited gifts young players possessed on their instruments to blaze away gloriously with devil-may-care rock-and-roll abandon. The scene in the Motor City begat a crop of high-decibel, in-your-face rockers including the Amboy Dukes, the MC5, and the Stooges, whose music would help to inspire the rise of punk rock a decade later with the Ramones and Sex Pistols. Nugent's aggressive wail on guitar and loud rhythm accompaniment also typified the hard-rock direction of late-sixties bands like Humble Pie, the James Gang, Mountain, and Grand Funk Railroad, with his playing comparing favorably to other skilled axmen of the period including Joe Walsh, Peter Frampton, and Leslie West. All Nugent needed were some hits, and within two years of the Valley Theater shows, he'd get them. "Great White Buffalo" off his next album, *Tooth, Fang and Claw*, became a concert showstopper, while "Stranglehold" and "Hey Baby" from his first solo album, *Ted Nugent*, in 1975 gave the Motor City Madman traction into platinum territory.

So, it wouldn't be long before Ted Nugent went nationwide and helped lead hard rock through a decade of dominance, but in early '74 a handful of people got a chance to see a spectacular preview of things to come. There was a late show that night in East Greenville, but for some reason we didn't go (three more bucks too expensive?), but I do remember that Nugent invited anyone in the audience to come around to the band's trailer behind the building and say hello between shows. We briefly considered it, but then headed off to our car. Onstage crazy was good, but in-person crazy seemed way too intense, at least for four kids just out of high school. As we shuffled off to our car, laughing about concert memories that would burn brightly for many years, I could swear I spotted a shadowy figure tracking our progress from the front yards across the street. Was Ted Nugent stalking us? It couldn't be; I must have merely imagined the outline of a bow aimed unerringly in our direction, its string trembling perceptibly as the heavy metal hunter considered letting another arrow fly.

CHAPTER 7

YES

SETTING SAIL IN A TOPOGRAPHIC OCEAN

Miami Baseball Stadium, February 8, 1974

Listen to: "Roundabout," "Siberian Khatru," "And You and I," "I've Seen All Good People"

After I'd headed to my usual table in the school cafeteria, probably loaded down with some government-surplus pasta product—spaghetti or mac and cheese—the excited chatter from my friends got my attention. A few of them had seen a band named Yes at Kutztown University the night before. I'd heard of the group because its single "Roundabout" was all over the radio and seen the *Fragile* album in the stores. Recurring statements like "They were amazing!" and "I've never seen anything like them!" didn't help to pin down what the show was like, but all the enthusiasm stirred my interest. On blind faith I bought a copy of *Fragile* and immediately discovered that the album version of "Roundabout" ran four minutes longer than the single, restoring a huge chunk of fine keyboard and guitar improvisation I never knew existed. The rest of the album combined rock and a classical-music inclination with dazzling musicianship, cosmic lyrics, and extended performances that we came to know so well, but were novel ideas back in early '72.

Yes released its next album, *Close to the Edge*, the week I left Pennsylvania and started school in Miami. A cool thing about college in the pre-Internet era was how roommates and dorm buddies from all around the country would bring their regional tastes and opinions to the table. We'd share our record collections in smoke-filled rooms and discuss the merits of what we'd heard rather than cram for our chemistry or physics classes. I remember one long session during which our coven vigorously debated the meanings of the six implicitly detailed Moody Blues album covers and why the band's subsequent *Seventh Sojourn* featured a monumentally dull painting of sparse, windblown rock formations in the desert. What was *that* all about? *Close to the Edge* became a particular object of our fascination: a record with only three songs on it, including a title track that took up all of the first side. No band we'd ever heard about had done that before; the ambitious artistic scope and superior performance were unmatched by anyone at the time. Unfortunately, the *Close to the Edge* tour went through Miami even before I unpacked my suitcases, so I missed Yes for a second time. Eventually, in May of '73, I'd get the next best thing, a sprawling three-record live set entitled *Yessongs*, decorated with more elaborate and beautiful Roger Dean artwork that could be scrutinized during the couple of hours it took to listen to the mammoth collection. Still, it was like giving a hungry dog a rubber bone—I wanted the real thing!

I only did one year at University of Miami, heading north to New Hampshire instead for my sophomore year at New England College. During Christmas break, all the students were informed by phone that the school's board of directors had decided to extend the normal winter vacation for a month on account of the ongoing Arab oil embargo, which had driven worldwide crude prices to astronomical levels. The college would save at least a hundred thousand dollars on the cost of heating its dormitories during the coldest part of the year, then make up the month of classes at the end of spring, an inspired logical move, I thought, even if part of my summer vacation had just vanished. Suddenly there was a month to kill. I decided I wanted to spend it in warmth, so with a hundred bucks in my shoe (good place to hide it), I stuck out my thumb and arrived in Miami two days later. Jay and Buddy, a couple of friends who had hung in there at U of M, knew I was coming and had invited me to stay as long as I liked. I found my way across campus to their two-bedroom apartment and knocked on the door, waiting next to the big Impeach Nixon sign in their window. Jay whipped open the door and grabbed me in a swift man-hug; after two days of accepting rides from pleasant-enough strangers on the interstate, it was great to finally see a familiar face. Buddy appeared a minute later with a big smile. "We have a surprise for you," he exclaimed as the recently released *Sabbath Bloody Sabbath* album howled away on the stereo behind him. "Yes," Jay agreed excitedly. "This is going to freak you out!"

"What?'

"We have tickets to see Yes—tonight! You couldn't have timed it any better!"

I stood there stunned as Jay handed over a copy of the brand-new Yes album, *Tales from Topographic Oceans*. "This just came out! Before we go to the show, you have to listen to it. We want to know what you think." I smiled because I'd always enjoyed my musical debates with these two and certainly looked forward to another one. He added, "You're going to have to cram, though—it's a double album with only four songs!"

"Really?" I muttered, looking at the extensive lyrics and song notes on the inside cover as Jay and Buddy gathered their things and took off. I began reading singer Jon Anderson's rambling dissertation about Paramahansa Yogananda and the Shastraic scriptures that had inspired this work. My eyes glazed over a bit, but the music would be the deciding element, so I put on side one, "The Revealing Science of God." Like the title track to *Close to the Edge*, the extended work resembled a symphonic movement of contrasting themes, a build and release of energy and recurring melodies. I was studying classical music in school and realized that the structure of the entire record and its quartet of album sides fit neatly into the typical four-movement form of the classical-period symphony. There was a dynamic and forceful opening, gentler and contrasting second movement, rhythmic scherzo for the third, and finally the recapitulating last segment with its big and memorable themes. This was, by no means, a three-minute pop song! By the time my friends returned, I felt like I was back at New England College in my music theory class.

For one recently arrived from the frigid north, standing outside in the baseball stadium with only a light jacket in February was, in itself, a pleasure. It was a general-admission show, so we gravitated toward a spot in the front of the grandstand, looking across the field to a stage adorned with translucent blobs of green plastic and a fiberglass or plastic canopy resembling a couple of primordial fish over Alan White's impressive drum kit. We were left to ponder the mysterious forces that would create such visual accoutrements as well as the ability of the players to reproduce their complex studio music when suddenly the familiar crescendo of Stravinsky's *Firebird Suite* welled up majestically through the speakers. The strobe-like flashes from a field full of cameras and pencil-thin beams from the roadies' flashlights revealed lightning glimpses of figures moving about in the darkness before the stage lights blazed on and Yes hurtled into the beefy rock-and-roll-driven "Siberian Khatru" from *Close to the Edge*. Spotlights caught Rick Wakeman behind — no, *surrounded* by — his keyboards in a semicircle, each hand a blur on a different instrument and a glittering silver cape reflecting the beams of light as hundreds of embers dancing into the audience from a human mirror ball. Bassist Chris Squier and Steve Howe on guitar flanked Jon Anderson at the center as the band immediately launched into full flight and quickly reached cruising altitude. Since this song was an FM-radio staple and one of the band's most familiar, the audience erupted in a roar, responding likewise to the following ten-minute "And You and I" before Yes completed the entire *Close to the Edge* cycle by performing the title track.

Deliriously happy at hearing Yes perform our favorite album, just to start the show, we awaited the second phase of the concert. Jay had heard on the radio that Yes would perform *Close to Edge* followed by the entire new album. "All four sides?" I replied incredulously. "The audience will never go for that." *Tales from Topographic Oceans* had been released barely a month earlier and was still largely unfamiliar to most of the crowd. If the idea of a four-sided, nearly eighty-minute studio work wasn't challenging enough, now the band had to sell its brand-new concept album live onstage. Although classical orchestras presented fresh and unfamiliar works in concert on a regular basis and jazz players improvised for minutes on end, few rock bands ever took the gamble of avoiding its obvious hits to unfold a complex new composition in its entirety. Yes was asking much of its audience: Would the fans respond, or give up in frustration? I prepared myself for the sight of droves of disappointed people leaving through the gates and Yes finishing its album recital in front of a half-empty house.

With the grandiose sweep of the music nearly approaching the depth of an orchestral score, much of the heavy lifting was done by Howe, who played an assortment of electric and acoustic instruments that his guitar tech patiently prepared and handed to him in the nick of time. Wakeman proved equal to the image cultivated in the music press of a towering keyboard god whose fingers flew with incredible speed and unerring accuracy over the ridiculous number of keyboards in his arsenal. Squire pounded his bass like a lead guitar and Anderson didn't sing a bum note all night.

But this was to be expected in the burgeoning world of what had become known as progressive rock, the antithesis of the do-it-yourself attitude that had inspired a hoard of garage bands to plug in and bash away on two or three chords. Many of the players in this new movement had morphed from their days as formal classical-music students and were already brilliant enough musicians to perform with perfection, tossing out half-hour concertos from memory and showing mastery of the most intricate musical scores. Perhaps the Beatles' explorations on "A Day in the Life" introduced the idea, but the Moody Blues' *Days of Future Past* album in 1967 fully mated a rock band with an orchestra and pointed the way forward. Major champions of the style included King Crimson, which mimicked an orchestra with its use of the mellotron, a keyboard that replicated the sound of a full string section, and Emerson, Lake & Palmer, who performed orchestral-style music as a high-energy three-piece rock band. Yes, though, had eclipsed all others in popularity, its five members finding chart success and using it as fuel to expand further into its album-sized masterworks. Unlike many, this band had mated a highbrow virtuosity with an underlying spirit of rock and roll; the members of Yes were certainly cosmic, *but they rocked!*

Somewhere during the performance, the reddish eye of the moon rose on the infield seats and soon cast a bright glow as it reached higher over the Miami skyline. Someone near me gushed in lysergic wonder that it must be a blessing on the concert from the goddess Luna. Meanwhile, below, with sheer artistic determination, the members of Yes powered their way through their entire new double album. Jon Anderson offered the final words, "*Nous sommes du soleil*" (We are of the sun) and the music ebbed to a close. The ovation that followed went on and on, a deafening response as the band members, backs soaked in sweat, clambered out of their positions and lined up in front. It had been over two hours of nearly nonstop and challenging music, yet it appeared as if no one had left the stadium. The expected encore, "Roundabout," took on greater significance as a sign of gratitude from Yes, the monster hit meant as a huge thank you for allowing the musicians to indulge themselves so deeply on this night; but that's a big part of what progressive rock was all about—indulgence. This sort of thing could not go unanswered by critics, who almost universally dismissed the new album in frustration and butchered the tour with a sea of poisonous reviews. Yet, the fans remained undaunted and accepting of the colossal amount of new music the English group insisted on presenting undiluted and unedited night after night in concert. Critics be damned! Elated audiences would fill the arenas and even stadiums Yes chose to play as the group sailed boldly through its *Topographic Oceans* night after night in 1974.

CHAPTER 8

ERIC CLAPTON

TRULY SLOW ... HAND

The Spectrum, Philadelphia, June 29, 1974

**Listen to: "Crossroads," "Can't Find My Way Home," "Let It Rain,"
"Why Does Love Got to Be So Sad," "Mainline Florida"**

Eric Clapton had occupied so many of my formative hours of listening through a piece-of-crap plastic record player, reading LP sleeves, and cramming rock and roll into my teenage/young adult skull, that when he finally walked out onstage I just stared in disbelief. After being weaned on Top 40 singles, the first albums I bought were *Sgt. Pepper's Lonely Hearts Club Band* and *Magical Mystery Tour.* But, intrigued by the fabulous wah-wah guitar solo I'd heard on the radio on a song called "White Room," I grabbed *Cream's Greatest Hits* on blind faith (no pun intended), and received *Wheels of Fire* as a present from my (way-cool) parents. The hunch paid off handsomely: not only did I get the longer, uncut version of "White Room" with an extra verse and more guitar, I discovered the awesome musical talents of Cream and its fantastic guitarist; plus I was introduced to a wondrous music called the blues.

Clapton and his mates Ginger Baker and Jack Bruce became so important to me in those early record-collecting years that I was dismayed to realize that I'd discovered them just as the band broke up. Cream released only four albums plus that hits package before 1970, and I collected them all. Eric Clapton, of course, became the most famous of the trio, going on to cofound Blind Faith, tour semi-anonymously with Delaney & Bonnie, and from the same spotlight-avoiding impulse form Derek & the Dominos, which perversely made him most famous of all when the *Layla and Other Assorted Love Songs* album became a huge hit. All the while that Clapton insisted he just wanted to be a blues musician, he continued courting megastardom in a series of major rock bands. He was famously inconsistent, yet his fame grew steadily, and no one knew about his inner demons of alcoholism and heroin addiction. It was with the latter that Clapton could control his anxiety; but predictably enough, it wasn't long before the solution took charge and began dictating the terms.

The star disappeared almost completely for over two years after the first and only Derek and the Dominos tour, the story emerging that Clapton had merely gone home and, with rare exception, refused to come out. The musician's wealth permitted him the luxury of avoiding work, gaining access to a steady diet of drugs and wallowing about, elegantly wasted in his suburban London mansion. But I didn't know about any of that; celebrity secrets were far more easily kept in the pre-Internet world. I was just mystified at the silence, since after 1970 there was . . . nothing. Just leftovers appeared: two live Cream albums, a double-LP career retrospective, and a Derek and the Dominos concert release, plus Clapton's very low-key appearance at the August '71 Concert for Bangladesh organized by his friend George Harrison.

Then, early in 1973, the rock press buzzed about an Eric Clapton "comeback" concert that had been held at the Rainbow Theater in London in January. Assembled by his friend Pete Townshend and including musical mates like Steve Winwood and Ron Wood, the show was intended to drag the recluse out of his house and back into the stage lights. During the promotion of the concert and eventual album that appeared in September, Eric Clapton's drug addiction became public knowledge, but word of a successful rehab tempered the troubling news. Despite Clapton's less than stellar performance on the Rainbow stage, Townshend's effort to help his friend succeeded: the former hermit was coaxed into putting a solo band together and entering a studio in Miami to cut a new record. No one could have predicted the results. Aside from a couple of rockers, the rest of *461 Ocean Boulevard* featured laid-back, blues-based ballads and a surprise monster of a hit single called "I Shot the Sheriff." Delivered in the Jamaican reggae style still mostly unfamiliar in America, the Bob Marley cover zoomed to number 1 in the summer of 1974 and sold a million copies. That a white blues guitarist pulled off the feat mystified all, but a hit was a hit, and Clapton bounced back on the road for his first series of dates in four years — a jaunt inevitably referred to by everyone as his comeback tour.

"I Shot the Sheriff" had just begun to heat up the airwaves with Clapton's new album not even scheduled to come out before the guitarist's summer excursion reached the Spectrum in Philadelphia in June. Too young to see him in his earlier bands, I wasn't about to let this opportunity slip by. My buddies and I picked up our tickets; they were nothing-special balcony seats, but we didn't care — we were *inside*. It was a good thing we motivated quickly because the concert sold out fast, and future shows would sell out even faster when "I Shot the Sherriff" dominated the airwaves and the album reached stores. Even though we had assigned seats this time, we stood in line long before the arena entrances opened. As soon as the bored-looking security staff unlocked the doors, we dashed to our section faster than the ushers could reach their posts. Then we waited and waited as the rest of the audience began arriving slowly, and we deemed them all unworthy because of their tardiness. A band named Ross warmed up the show, its music mostly forgettable, but the diversion from the endless minutes of hanging out was sorely welcome. Lights up, my excitement began to simmer just watching the stage crew remove the support group's equipment and begin assembling Eric Clapton's gear. Visions of lightning fast guitar solos like the ones on "Crossroads," "Let It Rain" and "Tell the Truth" began crowding my mind as the time crawled by and most of the audience hit the concourse for soft drinks and hot dogs. The arena didn't sell beer, but many of the folks around us had smuggled in nips or even flasks. There was very little toking going on; security prowled about uncomfortably close and they had easy view of any revealing smoke signals. Then, suddenly, the houselights winked out.

Stage lights revealed that a couch, some chairs and potted plants had been set up in the middle of the stage as the riot of welcome reached an astronomical level. "Slowhand" (the nickname given to him in 1964 when he was a member of the Yardbirds, was an ironic comment on his blazing finger speed yet slow hand at changing guitar strings on stage —it stuck) had finally returned after three interminable years! And there he was, an ant in my field of view; and he'd remain that way because the huge video screens that brought close-up images of the stage action to even the furthest recesses of a concert hall were not standard touring hardware in 1974. It would be a few years before that innovation made concert going a more enjoyable experience for everyone in the cheaper seats.

Clapton shuffled to the front of the stage and acknowledged the Spectrum audience with a nod before his group, which had filed in behind him, eased into a cover of a laid-back Johnny Otis song from the fifties called "Willie and the Hand Jive." Built over a lazy Bo Diddley beat, the song would appear on Clapton's upcoming album. This was not quite the opening I expected. I thought the guitar god would level the arena with one of his biggest hits, branding his territory with a fiery solo to set the tone for the night to come. "White Room" or "Why Does Love Got to Be So Sad" could have done the trick, but this song was not only unfamiliar, but a painfully restrained opener. The tempo loped along as Clapton's backing singer Yvonne Elliman stepped up to chime in on harmonies. Her previous credits included playing Mary Magdalene on Broadway and in the film version of *Jesus Christ Superstar*; now she brought a fresh dynamic to the band as she filled out what was, so far, a set of timid vocals from her boss. It could only go up from here, right? Wrong. The song segued directly into a nearly identical original entitled "Get Ready," another sleepy selection that also featured very little in the way of lead guitar work.

In between her singing duties, Elliman sat down on the couch and relaxed. That was kind of cool: why not chill out right there in front of everyone? But it seemed like Clapton had joined her on the sofa; for all the licks he was playing, the musician could have been sitting there holding a TV remote instead of a guitar. On "Blues Power" things finally began to heat up, but the legendary player, looking a bit unsure in his skin, abdicated much of the solo space to the band's second guitarist George Terry. "Man, I don't think he wants to play," my buddy remarked. "Yeah, maybe you're right," I replied as Clapton counted off the beginning of Freddie King's slow blues "Have You Ever Loved a Woman." "But he can't do this one without taking a solo; it's impossible." I was right: Clapton and Terry did some nice back-and-forth challenges. But the energy gained on that song and a new rocker called "Mainline Florida" quickly drained from the room on the completely unexpected "Smile," a thirties' Charlie Chaplin song, of all things. The vigor in the set would not return until later, when the star pulled out his warhorses "Layla," "Presence of the Lord," and "Crossroads" to end the night. By then, I didn't even care that the show had been embarrassingly short at only ten songs, with half of them no more than bluesy lullabies—I just wanted it to end. Clapton's mojo was definitely not working; perhaps a rock-and-roll vampire had surprised the guitarist, sunk his fangs in, and drained the essence from one who was once referred to in London as "God." We left the Spectrum supremely disillusioned, grumbling as we joined a similarly reserved crowd exiting into the parking lots. There was some serious consideration among my friends that Eric Clapton had sent some sort of stunt double out on the road in his place.

When the extent of Eric Clapton's heroin addiction and rehab became widely known later that summer, we realized the musician had still been in a state of tentative recovery when we saw him. But his manager and handlers had clearly erred: with Clapton out of action for so long, it's certain that an easier reentry through smaller venues would have been a much better decision. Emotionally, Clapton wasn't ready to undertake the arduous six-week, twenty-eight-city arena tour his manager dumped on him. Plus, the star admitted that he had grown tired of the "guitar hero" tag and just wanted to escape into his band—and he succeeded! But, Clapton must have soon realized that he'd never dodge that image and managed to resolve the conflict in his head and down in his fingers. As the *461 Ocean Boulevard* tour progressed, the guitarist emerged more and more from his three-year fog, stepping up and flashing the brilliance that had made him a worldwide legend while still in his twenties. The live album *E.C. Was Here*, recorded later that year and released the following summer, would show a revitalized artist on a more defined path to many years of continued greatness. Plus, as the summer of '74 passed into the fall on September 20, I gave Clapton another shot at the Boston Garden, witnessing an exciting and masterful performance filled with six-stringed majesty by the guitarist and a band that had grown to love playing with each other. Happily, the struggling stunt double I'd witnessed in Philadelphia three months earlier had been sent packing!

CHAPTER 9

CSNY/ SANTANA

"TIN SOLDIERS AND NIXON COMING"

Atlantic City Racetrack, New Jersey, August 9, 1974

Listen to: "Carry On," "Ohio," "Woodstock," "Southern Man" (live from _4 Way Street_)

Protected in the womb of college life, with no more responsibility than getting good grades to justify my parents' great expense, I reached out of my comfort zone and took a summer job to earn spending money for the upcoming school year. But, three days into working as a seasonal laborer for Pennsylvania Power & Light, I was astonished when the union took a strike vote and walked off the job. In a supreme moment of amnesia, I considered crossing the picket line for a shot at the exorbitant wages P, P & L was offering to maintain operations, totally overlooking my father's prominent history as a former president of Local 3048, United Steelworkers of America. His wasn't the shop involved in the strike, but that small fact didn't register to a die-hard union veteran. His line in the sand was a wall, a very high one with barbed wire on top: "You cross the picket line, you don't come home." I pled temporary insanity and came up with another plan: as a minor part-time worker with no stake in the union, I'd hitchhike around to visit my college friends while regularly checking in to see if the strike had been settled. Nine weeks later, after I'd hung out with many of my buddies around the Northeast, the walkout continued with no signs of resolution. Discouraged at having no job, but also elated to have summer days free, I decided to buy a ticket to see Crosby, Stills, Nash & Young in concert with Santana warming up. The price was higher than any I'd ever paid before, but I bit the bullet and slid my ten bucks over for a general admission ticket to the August 9 show.

As musical and political firebrands, the headliners had been prime standard-bearers for the late-sixties and early-seventies counterculture in America, pied pipers who rallied a massive popular opposition to the policies of the Nixon administration and its continuing support of the Vietnam War. May 1969 had brought together David Crosby from the Byrds, the Buffalo Springfield's Stephen Stills, and former Hollies member Graham Nash on a million-selling debut album of impeccable harmonies and exceptional songs. By August they were performing their second concert *ever* in front of the multitude at Woodstock and had added Neil Young to the lineup. Although already instant stars, adding Young to the mix brought a second lead guitar in to duel with Stills's formidable talent (he had played nearly all the instruments on the band's debut) and toughened the sound considerably. Young was also a prolific songwriter of great confidence and depth, his work challenging the artistic efforts of the other three. The second album *Déjà Vu*, with Young as an equal shareholder, bettered the first and drove CSNY to iconic status. Their renown only increased when, soon after the album was released in 1970, Illinios National Guardsmen fired on a group of protesting students at Kent State University, killing four. Neil Young's spontaneous reaction, the song "Ohio," was rushed out as a single and instantly became a "Battle Hymn of the Republic" for the emotionally charged antiwar movement.

But, relations within the "supergroup," so dubbed by the media, were always stormy, and after a 1971 live album, *4 Way Street*, the band blew apart. As seasoned stars, each with solo releases outside of their group efforts, these musicians could easily stand on their own, so inordinate amounts of ego and a jealousy to protect personal artistic prerogatives often led to squabbling. The tension scuttled repeated attempts to produce a new album or even a tour, but after three years CSNY finally found traction within their uneasy democracy to embark on a series of live dates during the summer of '74. It was the biggest tour yet by any band, and a sign of the concert business boom to come: a nine-week trek that would visit only the largest venues available — racetracks, stadiums, and if no larger place could be found, mere 20,000-seat arenas.

As the most popular political spokesmen for the entire Woodstock-era generation (Bob Dylan was more legendary, but wrote very few political songs as time went on) CSNY were counted on to carry the "question authority" spirit of the sixties into the less-idealistic and more pragmatic decade. Were they succeeding? Night after night, the quartet presented a concert usually longer than three hours, drawing an average of 50,000 fans, so it certainly seemed so. In his 2013 autobiography *Wild Tales*, Graham Nash wrote, "No doubt CSNY was branded a political band. We wanted our songs to make people think, and over the years we'd given fans a whole smorgasbord of them: 'For What It's Worth,' 'Long Time Gone,' 'Chicago,' 'Military Madness,' 'Immigration Man,' 'Ohio,' and 'Teach Your Children' to a certain extent." As the tour progressed while the infamous Watergate scandal investigation kept President Richard Nixon's administration squirming in the crosshairs, patriotic passions burned brightly at every concert.

I was always more into the music than the politics, but you couldn't run away from the issues that summer. Presaging the drama of reality TV over thirty years later, the daily broadcasts from the Senate subcommittee hearings combined long periods of humdrum with unbelievable moments of revelation, the determined legislators on camera methodically picking their way closer to the truth of an illegal White House cover-up. My mom kept the television on the hearings constantly, and as the first full week of August passed its midway mark, the legal maneuverings in Washington reached a climax. Facing certain impeachment by Congress, Nixon made a speech to the nation Thursday night,

August 8, to announce that he'd resign his position the next day. With all this American history unfolding (or unraveling) at the moment, being at a CSNY concert surrounded by thousands of like-minded individuals watching a group that wore its politics on its sleeve was about the best place you could be. The group happened to be playing Roosevelt Stadium in Jersey City for 30,000, and when Graham Nash announced the news of the president's decision, the place erupted. David Crosby mentioned it was the most memorable moment of the whole tour for him, and how could it not be? Here was an arrogant public servant in the highest office of the land caught abusing his power and trampling democracy. For once, real justice had been meted out, even if it had been a long time coming.

The next morning my friend and I barely spoke as we drove down from Allentown to Atlantic City, listening instead to the historic chain of events booming from the car radio. Nixon had announced he would resign his presidency just before noon. I couldn't see the famous parting wave and bitter countenance of the ex-president as he stood in the doorway of the Marine helicopter that would whisk him into private exile, his familiar game face attempting, and failing, to deflect the supreme shame of the moment. The reporters described it, though, in detail, followed shortly after by the swearing in of Vice President Gerald Ford as chief executive. Of course, Nixon couldn't be held responsible for all of the evils that had befallen the current generation in flight, but his departure felt incredibly uplifting, as if a cancerous tumor had been ripped out of the body. Humming happily along in my buddy's black Barracuda, I didn't even notice that the sunshine near home had disappeared into a canopy of gray shortly into the drive. "Hey, who turned out the lights," I joked as the sudden charcoal pallor of the sky announced the swift and dispiriting arrival of a thunderstorm. "Maybe we'll drive through it," my companion observed. We had no idea, really, since we'd forgotten to research what the weather would be like near the New Jersey shore that night. But, our youthful hopes remained high for a dry evening as we pulled into the racetrack parking lot.

Guys with Day-Glo vests beckoned us onward and then quickly through the far side of the main lot to other guides who redirected us into overflow parking, which meant bouncing along a rutted dirt access road, occasionally scraping the 'Cuda's bottom before arriving at a distant meadow. "It must be totally sold out if they're putting us out here," I complained. A path was indicated by well-worn signs and we trudged the quarter mile or so to the massive old racetrack, entering through the turnstiles just as a rain shower squeezed in behind us. Moving through the main building only took a few moments before the two of us emerged outside in front of the grandstand, gazing at the stage erected inside the racetrack. Slipping through a gateway to head across the dirt circuit proved difficult since people were packed in like sardines; later we'd find out that the place bulged with an official head count of 42,000. The sudden drizzle did have one positive effect, though, as the crush down in front to see Santana melted away when hundreds retreated to the grandstand to get under cover.

We made our way forward as the band blew on some jazzy new material. But, later when Santana began playing some of its familiar music from *Abraxas*, the polite sprinkle suddenly transitioned into a full-blown squall. Wet clothes rapidly became soaked before my buddy and I surrendered, finding refuge in a cavernous room underneath the grandstand itself. Closed-circuit televisions hanging liberally about the area to serve bettors watching their favorite horse pound around the track now helped us keep pace with the show going on outside the building. But, as more arrived to escape the storm, their clamor drowned out the tinny sounds emerging from the TVs. The isolation became complete: it felt like we were trapped at some airport with all flights cancelled, staring blankly at the distant arrival/departure screens.

Santana finished up and the drizzle relented, so we returned outside just as CSNY took the stage and began rocking with Stills's "Love the One You're With." The skies had pulled a fake, though, for as soon as we were in position, the heavens opened again. Just as Santana had been the warm-up musical act of the night, the previous shower served simply as an introduction to the heavier deluge now pounding loudly on the ground and off thousands of miserable figures. As if the clouds had received heavenly instructions to park overhead and punish all 42,000 below for their sins, the cold rain refused to relent. The terrible conditions forced many to flee, abandoning spots that they had held for hours in front of the stage as the entire track transformed into one vast quagmire. Those who remained behind sank deeper into the morass like torpedoed ships slipping slowly beneath the waves. Worrying flashes of lightning were about to convince me to turn tail, but then the band announced, for those who might not have heard, that Richard Nixon had, indeed, resigned and quit Washington. That moment, plus the emotional version of "Ohio," that followed held me riveted in the muck, singing and clapping along as crashes of thunder competed angrily with CSNY's vocals. Perhaps unfairly, I thought that the blood of those four dead at Kent State had been somehow avenged by the president's abdication. There was a resounding cheer all around me in response to the song and a vast crescendo from the grandstand behind us as we stood, pathetically sodden and shivering in the storm, yet wonderfully elated.

In the end, some accounts would report that the intense weather assault was the real story of that concert; in fact, one man died after being electrocuted by a bolt of lightning in the parking lot. The conditions were so deplorable that the quality of the singers' performance couldn't really be debated, but Neil Young's voice had rung out strong and true on "Ohio," and the others wore obvious joy on their faces all night as they performed song after song despite the frightful conditions. There was tremendous gravity in that moment of seeing the ideal troubadour spokesmen at a perfect intersection in time, as if they had been created for this very purpose. CSNY would continue to craft many more years of fine music, but never as emotional or essential after this culmination. For a brief instant, perhaps only that night and the morning after, the rain had washed us clean. All too soon, our cynicism would return: there would be autocrats to replace Nixon and wars to follow Vietnam, but like seedlings being watered, on this evening on the New Jersey shore we'd carry away renewed hope for a better world.

CHAPTER 10

GEORGE HARRISON

TOURING IN THE MATERIAL WORLD

Boston Garden, December 10, 1974

Listen to: "While My Guitar Gently Weeps," "What Is Life," "My Sweet Lord," "Give Me Love (Give Me Peace on Earth)"

I couldn't believe it: there he stood on-stage in the flesh, greeting the adulation from the crowd of 15,500 rapturous souls at a completely sold-out Boston Garden. Decked out in white long-sleeve shirt with those oh-so-seventies plaid pants and hair shorn just above the shoulders, George Harrison cut a very different fig-ure from the mystical monk-in-rubber-

boots (or stoned gardener) look he'd presented on the cover of *All Things Must Pass.* He paused in the spotlights with guitar hanging off the shoulder, beaming broadly and clearly enjoying the moment. A couple of songs later Harrison would be locking arms with Billy Preston and his magnificent Afro, doing leg kicks to the beat, so how could he not be having a good time? The group that had walked out onstage, includ-ing Preston, sax player Tom Scott, guitarist Robben Ford, bassist Wil-lie Weeks, and drummer Jim Keltner, just finished their introductory instrumental "Hari's on Tour (Express)," performing with the assured confidence and ease earned from six weeks on the road and thirty-one shows under their belts.

With the band's opening fanfare finished, the crowd took over, an uproar of response that nearly drowned out the delicate guitar figure announcing "Something," Harrison's number-1 hit from five years earlier. At the sound of one of the Beatles' most famous numbers, the Garden seemed to actually lift a few inches off the ground, as if in a sudden earthquake, then settled quickly as everyone strained to hear his first words. They emerged beautifully—no, they were barely croaked! It was only the second number and his voice was already shredded, punished by weeks of steady performances and rehearsals; the ruined remnants were barely able to convey the delicate love story found in the lyrics of his *Abbey Road* standout. Dismayed for the briefest instant, I resolved that it didn't matter. The one and only George Harrison stood on the Garden stage, and with his positive, "the-show-must-go-on" spunk bonding with the energy of his sidemen I overlooked the injured voice and continued to be swept up in the moment. I guess that most others agreed, because the end of "Something" brought a thunderclap of applause that couldn't possibly have been any louder, until the commotion was broken by the following "While My Guitar Gently Weeps." Then it got *really* loud!

I still don't know how we managed to get those tickets, because *everybody* wanted in. Harrison's was the first full-blown tour of a Beatle in the United States since the band had played its final show in San Francisco in 1966. Too young to see a concert back then, especially by that group of mop-haired vagrants my parents' generation rejected and vilified, now I finally had the opportunity to glimpse part of the genius that had altered no less than the entire course of pop culture. The group clearly towered as a sum greater than its parts, but even so, the talents of each individual were still quite formidable. John Lennon, Paul McCartney, George Harrison, and Ringo Starr stood poised potently in the afterglow of a career that had knocked the earth off its axis. Harrison, the quietest member, although quite vocal about his spiritual Hare Krishna religious journey, surprised everyone by being the most prodigious out of the gate, releasing his sprawling *All Things Must Pass*, pulling off the Concert for Bangla-Desh benefits at Madison Square Garden in 1971 and performing on solo efforts by Lennon and Starr. His next solo offering *Living in the Material World* went to number 1 in 1973 and aroused within him a desire to tour for the first time since his black-Edwardian-suit days.

We'd heard rumblings and rumors throughout the year, picking up "Harrison tour" bread crumbs from magazines and newspapers desperate to publish any tidbit dropped from whatever "source" available. The trail of possibilities finally led to an official announcement in September, revealing a challenging fifty-show North American visit (it would end up as forty-five dates) set to begin November 2 and end on December 20. The production, also starring Ravi Shankar with a troupe of Indian music performers plus Harrison's high-profile backing band, would land at the Boston Garden on December 10. I figured that the show would easily sell out before my friends and I could get in on the action, but we decided to give it a shot anyway. At the ticket outlet, the clerk informed us that all the seats were gone for the evening show. "Evening show? You mean there's another?" Yes! A matinee performance had also been scheduled and there were still seats available for that afternoon show. I gleefully plunked down the $9.50 for each ticket, and we were in! Plus, the seats weren't half bad—right off the main floor in the rear.

After the deafening applause following "While My Guitar Gently Weeps," Harrison handed over the spotlight to Billy Preston, who had come to fame as a Beatles sideman (he was featured in the *Let It Be* movie and the band's legendary rooftop concert) and had become a significant solo star since. A much more assured stage performer than his benefactor, Preston worked the crowd expertly and belted out the vocals to "Will It Go Round in Circles," his chart-topper from the year before. Harrison didn't appear to care in the least that his band member's performance eclipsed his own; at the very least it gave his ragged vocal chords a breather. He reclaimed center stage and continued with "Sue Me, Sue You Blues," a cynical comment on the ludicrously expensive war of lawyers that had marked the unraveling of the Beatles' mythical partnership.

At that point, the rock-and-roll band retired, and with it the accumulated rush of energy and excitement amassed so far ground to a screeching halt. The segment of the concert that would prove to be the most divisive for fans and, especially for the critics, had arrived. Platforms in the shape of semicircle with a central dais were quickly wheeled out and cushions placed upon them, then Ravi Shankar's troupe appeared with their exotic Eastern instruments to alight and sit facing the audience at stage center. Shankar, who had been ill from exhaustion to the point of suffering a heart attack in Chicago, appeared onstage to apologize that he was still too weak to perform. He handed the responsibility of conducting the group over to his sister-in-law, acclaimed Indian classical vocalist Lakshmi Shankar. During the set, which continued on for at least forty minutes, Harrison introduced each member of the Indian ensemble by name and many around me grew frustrated. "Hell with this! I'm getting a hot dog!" But a surprising number remained, mesmerized by the exotic rhythms and, in my case, the tabla and other percussion instruments, whose players challenged the talents of Western rock-and-roll drummers in their complex solo duels. Harrison's label Dark Horse Records had released the *Shankar Family & Friends* album that previewed much of the music featured in this set. Harrison and Tom Scott had played on those sessions, so they joined the Indian musicians on a couple of the songs. I found the experience stimulating, and applauded Harrison for assuming the risk of avoiding a simple "greatest hits" concert to open a window to this form of music that had been an important part of his art for nearly a decade.

What seemed acceptable and courageous to me, though, would annoy or even anger some fans and nearly every critic who witnessed a concert. By the time the rock and roll resumed with "For You Blue" from *Let It Be* and the solo hit "Give Me Love (Give Me Peace on Earth)," it was already too late for these people. How dare Harrison rob his fans of hearing those precious gems he'd unearthed over the years! They would be resentful for the remainder of the show and perhaps, forever afterward. But, there were reasons why the Beatles had been such a force of change in popular culture: along with the members' uncanny knack for writing catchy pop songs was their determination to take risks and follow various personal, musical, and spiritual muses throughout their celebrated career. Not all of those explorations had resulted in brilliant steps forward, but so many had. Why, then, wouldn't fans expect to experience at least some experimentation at a George Harrison concert? For those skeptics, the final third of the show favorably tracked back onto familiar ground: a surprising cover of Beatle John's "In My Life," more solo hits, and some additional shenanigans from Billy Preston. After an expected "My Sweet Lord" for an encore, the band waved goodbye and we sat back down, exhilarated while the ushers barked like border collies trying to herd us out the door. They did, after all, have another show starting in a couple of hours.

As the days passed and George Harrison released a new album called *Dark Horse* (the title track had already been on the radio as a single), I held good memories from the Boston Garden show and hoped that maybe he'd double back in the spring. How unprepared, then, was I when the negative reviews began appearing in the wake of his tour. The press delightfully pounced, savaging not only his concerts and albums, but also the man himself for wearing his spirituality on his sleeve and also incorporating Shankar's music in the program. They spoke of disappointed crowds, obsessed over Harrison's blown voice, and infamously labeled the concert swing as the "Dark Hoarse" tour. Almost gleefully, they castigated the man for trying to rehearse a band, record an album, and mount a major expedition in just a matter of weeks. They dredged up accounts of backstage cocaine use to explain his strained singing, while some of those same reporters, no doubt, carried their own tiny brown vials with the black screw top and spoon attached. What was the problem? The press jumped on George Harrison like a football team trying to recover a fumble on the one-yard line. And even after all the players were pulled off the guy crushed on the bottom, they still wouldn't end it. History remembers the 1974 tour as ill fated, dazed, confused, and at best, mediocre. The harsh criticism affected the "quiet Beatle" profoundly: he became even more reclusive, poking his head out to the media only when forced to promote a new release, and would only tour once again, in 1991. But, as we'd learn, Harrison was on a far more important quest to find a meaning in life apart from that thing that he'd labored in for so long called show business.

The whole debacle was really a preview of daily life today. The presence of the Internet and its instantaneous routes of access and exposure allows endless inquiry by thousands of eyes and ears reporting the barest shred of relevance in daily blogs and gossip websites. It's a world in which editorial has become fact, and targets are pronounced guilty before proven innocent. But, most observers don't hang around long enough to hear the defense state its case because they're already on to the next trend. Celebrity has always been a dangerous place to be; the image of what one does or what has happened is always more important than the reality. But in a cyberspace world, character assassination and misrepresentation are no more than just a few clicks away. In 1974, the critics, outraged at George Harrison for crimes against the Beatle legacy, used their angst to peddle a few extra magazines and newspapers. Now, it's all about selling banner space and running up the number of clicks on a website. We're still living in a material world, only now it's become a hell of a lot more efficient.

CHAPTER 11

THE ROLLING STONES

THE BEST STUFF IN TOWN

The Spectrum, Philadelphia, June 30, 1975

Listen to: "Monkey Man," "Midnight Rambler" (live), "Can't You Hear Me Knockin," "Loving Cup," "Doo Doo Doo Doo (Heartbreaker)," "Fingerprint File"

During the sixties British Invasion, if the Beatles were the biggest band on the planet, the Rolling Stones had to be the baddest, although you'd always end up debating those Kinks fanatics to say that. You were never too far away from a jangly Stones single blaring out of the radio, and in that regard, the band took its place next to pop acts like the Monkees and Tommy James & the Shondells. But when my sister took off for Vassar, temporarily abandoning a booty of albums including *Let It Bleed*, that's when I discovered the Stones' higher calling. Leaving the 45-rpm adapter behind, I took over the stereo in her bedroom and listened for hours to long-players, something I'd never really done before. Soon, the Moody Blues, CSN, John Mayall & the Bluesbreakers and the Beatles *Abbey Road* had swept me out of my diminutive 7-inch orbit and into deep space. Suddenly it wasn't all about the catchy A-side of a single, now there were multi-song masterstrokes with brushes of melodic paint and swaths of tone, spinning at 33 rpm and allowed to dry slowly, even over the course of an entire album. *Let It Bleed* revealed a musical sophistication only hinted at in the Stones' earlier-sixties single output and a lyrical ambition that was frightening in its subjects: drug addiction, loneliness, betrayal, and violence—then finding love in the midst of all that.

I started seeing a lot of groups in concert, but the Rolling Stones always existed on a level above, wielding the maturity and legendary status of being one that had actually helped forge the music that so many now emulated in the seventies. How many groups could claim to transport someone from teenybop favorites like "Get Off of My Cloud" and "As Tears Go By" to a seasoned college playlist including "Midnight Rambler" and "Fingerprint File"? The Stones, however, didn't tour America that often; as established international superstars, the group's presence was coveted all around the globe. The three previous U.S. visits had been separated by three years each: 1966, then the 1969 visit that ended in violence and infamy (as chronicled in the *Gimme Shelter* film), and a 1972 tour that featured music from that year's *Exile on Main Street* album. The record had generated two Top 40 hits, "Tumbling Dice" and "Happy," but most of the double album plunged deeply into the blues, so the band's concerts were rife with passionate American southern roots music delivered by a bunch of its greatest fans. Critically, the performances blew away the bad vibes of '69 while the fifty-one-concert tour became a tremendous popular success. Although it doesn't seem so much by today's standards, the Stones' paycheck of $4 million for the 1972 visit made it the biggest tour in history up to that point. They were true superstars now—crisscrossing the country in their own rented Boeing, commanding top dollar from promoters everywhere, and drawing the cognoscenti of culture backstage at each gig.

Three years later, right on schedule, the Rolling Stones announced a major summer visit. The "Tour of the Americas '75" would commence the first of June with two shows in Baton Rouge and wrap up August 8 in Buffalo. Demand had only increased, so some of the gigs were in stadiums, and ticket prices went up. Compared to the 1972 tour, this one had fewer concerts (45), but would make more than twice as much ($10 million). Tickets for two June shows at Philadelphia's sports arena, the Spectrum, went on sale after only a brief announcement on a few local radio stations. The *Philadelphia Inquirer* mentioned that the promoter, Electric Factory Concerts, hadn't wanted "crushing lines or hordes of campers" if advance word had been given. "By the next day, all 38,000 seats for Sunday and Monday nights [June 29 and 30] were sold out."

At that moment I was 360 miles away in New Hampshire at New England College, although it might as well have been on the moon, since by the time I heard about it, the Philadelphia sellouts were ancient history. Boston might have been closer, but tickets to two Garden shows had vanished just as fast. So much for that. I submerged into my preparations for final exams and promptly forgot about seeing the gods of rock and roll. After the semester, I stayed up north rather then return to my native Pennsylvania, and life in New Hampshire settled into a lazy cycle of work, party, and sleep. With the Rolling Stones tour completely off my radar, I have to say that when Jeb, one of my college buddies, approached one day and let slip the almost unfathomable truth that his dad had scored tickets to one of the Spectrum concerts, I was astounded. "Your *dad?*" I blurted doubtfully. Jeb was from the Philadelphia area, and he said something about a connection his father had to someone down there, but the stunning revelation remained: there were four tickets up for grabs. "You in?" he asked.

"Hell, yeah! When is it?"

"Monday." It was Friday, almost no time to figure out a way to skip work, but I'd do it.

When you're twenty, you'll do something crazy like drive six hours straight, then go to a concert, which is what we did, only detouring to get the tickets at Jeb's family's home in the suburbs. Then we shot over to the arena, where we could have easily cashed out our seats at great profit to any of the thousands of the un-ticketed desperately milling about. Fat chance. It was *the Rolling Stones!* We showed our tickets to an usher inside who turned his monumentally bored countenance our way while merely pointing up. Arriving one level higher we faced another equally bland attendant who waved behind him. "Take the steps." The seats were high off the floor of the balcony with only a few rows between them and the ceiling. Jeb was not positive. "Heck with this; I don't even want to go up there; let's get closer." Heading back down, we actually managed to infiltrate the first section of the loge without being detained, but had to keep angling downward toward the floor since there were no empty seats to disappear into.

Looking from the aisle I could see the Stones' much-ballyhooed custom-designed six-pointed stage directly below and to the right of us. The roadies who had been rushing all over it just a few moments earlier were now waiting at their duty stations, showtime imminent. We continued down the steps leading onto the floor, but our path was resolutely blocked by a man genetically designed for his job. In a walk-way that allowed two people to slip past one another, this behemoth's shoulders dominated the entire width, with beefy arms walling off the flanks. We were staring at the real life version of a "Rock 'Em Sock 'Em Robot," who gazed back with an immobile plastic scowl. The giant didn't even talk, just held a hand out for our tickets, which confirmed for him that we were just two additional losers off course. Waving a flashlight irritatingly up the aisle, he was about to inform us of what we all knew, when the arena turned pitch black.

Pandemonium! People boiled down the stairs behind us, thrusting toward the robot barricade, who decided that he didn't get paid enough to be trampled, and stepped aside. The cascading bodies propelled us into another stream of figures racing up the right aisle of the floor, hur-tling forward with white-water fury. In seconds, we were swept up and deposited directly against the security barrier between the front row of seats and the right apex of the stage. We were as close as you could get. Unbelievable! But would we quickly be rooted out and sent pack-ing back to the nosebleeds? It sure didn't seem likely as people swiftly packed in around us in an impenetrable mass, and security backed off to concentrate its forces behind the barrier between the audience and band. We were here to stay! Threat removed, I now concentrated on the shadows moving about on the darkened stage. Smoke generators clouded the space as a massive overhead lighting rig burned slowly into brilliance, revealing the group standing in a green spooky haze. The lights blazed hotter and details swam into view: Mick Jagger in light, loose-fitting pants and shirt began to jerk with his inimitable dance as

Charlie Watts snapped into the rock-steady rhythm of "Honky Tonk Women." Keith Richards appeared in stoned majesty, leather pants and T-shirt his simple rock-and-roll uniform while brand-new Stone Ronnie Wood, with rooster hair and the first of many cigarettes glued to his lips, snapped into synch alongside. Meanwhile, right in front of our section of the stage stood the nearly immobile bassist Bill Wyman, who gazed back at the hysterical audience with all the emotion of one staring at a baloney sandwich.

"All Down the Line," "If You Can't Rock Me" and "Get Off of My Cloud" breezed past before Jagger led the band into "Star Star" with its twelve-F-bomb chorus leaving little doubt what that song was about. Underscoring the sentiment, the girl next to me licked her lips, reached down for a while and came up with her panties, which she promptly whipped toward the singer. A surprise ten-foot fabric penis was inflated from a trapdoor onstage, and Jagger straddled it as a bull rider might, without the spurs, of course. The unisex rodeo segment led into deadly serious versions of the *Let It Bleed* classics, "Gimme Shelter" and "You Can't Always Get What You Want," which sent the crowd into a near riot. "You Got to Move" and "Ain't Too Proud to Beg" paid tribute to Mississippi Fred McDowell and the Temptations, respectively.

During the long dance groove of "Fingerprint File," we began to shout at Wyman, trying to get some reaction from a man who was playing great, but still staring at that sandwich. Within an easy ten feet from the Stone, we kept it up whenever a quiet break ensued. "C'mon, Bill! Crack a smile!" Then it got loud as the hits started whacking us: "Happy," "Tumblin' Dice," "Doo Doo Doo Doo Doo (Heartbreaker)," and "It's Only Rock and Roll (But I Like It)." The mellower "Angie" and "Wild Horses" gave us time to venture some more friendly harassment at Wyman, but it wasn't until an hour and a half into the show, when the band gave special-guest keyboardist Billy Preston an unprecedented two-song solo showcase, that we finally got a laugh and a glance down from the stone-faced bassist. Jeb and I slapped five. "He noticed us, he noticed us!"

The rest of the set was a salvo of the band's biggest hits in a punishing broadside that left us shattered. What group could possibly match the majesty of "Brown Sugar," then a jam of swaggering proportions on "Midnight Rambler," followed by the sheer adrenalin jolt of "Jumpin' Jack Flash"? Jagger remained the helpless dancer to the end, Richards and Wood wrote, typeset, and printed the book on how to mesh a pair of guitars, and Watts and Wyman shoveled serious rhythm coal in the band's boiler room. They made it look easy, but we knew better. The Stones were introduced at the start of *Get Yer Ya-Yas Out*, their magisterial live album from the '69 tour, with the words, "The greatest rock-and-roll band in the world, the Rolling Stones!" I suddenly understood why one, perhaps two, generations of Stones fans before me had made this "their" band, how those original followers were probably here tonight and wouldn't think of missing a show. This towered as elemental rock and roll; it was as close to the bone as I was liable to get this side of actually seeing Elvis Presley, Chuck Berry, or Jerry Lee Lewis. It was the real deal with no artificial ingredients (except for, perhaps, that renegade inflatable). The entire audience, including the folks in back inhabiting our real seats, stood on its feet, bellowing with Neanderthal glee. So this was the legend of the Rolling Stones, shamans of the back-beat and emissaries for the authentic rock-and-roll spirit — uncut and straight up.

It was a heady summer of mammoth album releases: Paul McCartney and Wings put out *Venus and Mars*, another number 1 in a lengthy string of chart-toppers for the former Beatle; in August Bruce Springsteen stepped into immortality with *Born to Run*; the Bee Gees brought a new dance craze called disco to the fore with *Main Course*; and Led Zeppelin minted more musical gold on its sprawling two-record *Physical Graffiti*. The Rolling Stones would patiently craft their next album in Munich with Ronnie Wood's appointment finally made official. *Black and Blue* appeared the following year, its mostly R & B and reggae flavors tracking a quick course to the top of the U.S. charts to become the next in a series of *eight* consecutive number 1 albums in the States. As expected, three years after the "Tour of the Americas," the band rolled out on another visit to the new world. Well on its way to establishing a decades-long dynasty, the Rolling Stones clearly had the best stuff in town — and they knew it!

CHAPTER 12

THE GREAT AMERICAN MUSIC FAIR

TEAR GAS AND TOILET PAPER

State Fairgrounds, Syracuse, New York, September 2, 1975

Listen to: America, "Horse with no Name"; Doobie Brothers, "China Grove"; Jefferson Starship, "Ride the Tiger"; Beach Boys, "Good Vibrations"; New Riders of the Purple Sage, "Panama Red"

The empty champagne bottle arched high in the air, somersaulting slowly as it traveled on its path. The longhair behind me who had thrown it darted back into the ragged mass of shouters and fist pumpers who taunted the two policemen in their cruiser beyond the sturdy chain-link fence. As the car inched forward, the bottle with its thick green glass sailed in a perfect arc, impacting with a thud directly on the front windshield. I fully expected the heavy missile to shatter the glass in an explosion of fragments certain to injure the occupants, but amazingly it bounced off to the side and burst apart on the asphalt. As if a call to arms had been sounded, the mass surged forward to the fence with a collective yell and dozens of hands began tugging at the wire. One of the cops got on the radio and within moments reinforcements arrived in force, a company of men wearing shirts with SECURITY emblazoned on them. The fence came down and the people rushed through the gap, clawing and kicking at the defensive line as if in one huge football play. There were no referees to blow the whistle on penalties here: the invaders battled their way in while the defenders blocked tenaciously. Dozens of gatecrashers penetrated through the melee and onto the grounds of the New York State Fair, losing themselves among the exposition buildings and eventually into a massive crowd waiting in front of the grandstand. We stood well back of the battle, not prepared to participate, but observing in amazement. Still, if we could just walk into the festival without paying, then why not? But, by the time we got close to the fence, a squad of state police wearing riot helmets and holding nightsticks had arrived to plug the gap. This opportunity had passed.

The Great American Music Fair in early September 1975 personified the best and worst aspects of the "rock festival" phenomenon that had arrived in the previous decade and found its greatest expression at Woodstock, six years earlier. Promising stellar lineups of talent, promoters counted on attracting hundreds of thousands to vast and often remote locations, usually racetracks, fairgrounds, or (in the case of granddaddy Woodstock) a farm. The scenes that followed always hit front-pages: miles of clogged highways, abandoned cars on the freeway, and small towns of horrified residents staring in astonishment at the flood of humanity urinating in their yards. Like refugees from a war zone streaming in the wrong direction, the festivalgoers kept coming, stretching the resources at the site to depletion. The basic needs of water, food, and shelter had often vanished even as the initial bands took the big stage. Plus, it seemed that in Mother Nature's "how-to" handbook under the heading of "rock festivals" her instructions promised one dash of sun and two of rain, guaranteeing bone-chilling overnights, even in the dog days of summer. Then, how about that mud? Thousands would abandon their sleeping bags and blankets rather than launder out the formidable amounts of soggy real estate they'd soaked up. Yup, you might have seen the Dead at Watkins Glen or Hendrix at Isle of Wight, even Green Day at Woodstock '94, but I bet you remember the taste of the mud even better.

The Great American Music Fair began with the same promise of a tremendous lineup. Headlining an afternoon set would be Jefferson Starship, on a roll with the classic Airplane front line of Grace Slick, Paul Kantner, and Marty Balin. The San Francisco band had a major hit single "Miracles" riding the charts (it would eventually get to number 3 in October) and a smash album *Red Octopus* heading toward double platinum. Supporting Starship would be Top 40 hit maker America plus the Stanky Brown Group. The evening set packed the punch of the Doobie Brothers and surf-rock legends the Beach Boys with a warm-up from New Riders of the Purple Sage. A one-day affair right in the middle of Syracuse, not some distant clover field, with interstate highways in every direction, meant easy access and space for a multitude.

The young twenty-five-year-old promoter John Scher needed to sell 60,000 tickets to break even, a goal that, given the talent and prime location, seemed easily attainable. Two factors, though, would prevent this from happening. The first was the same "two dashes" of rain that often soaked upstate and turned lush meadows into mushy morasses. Two days before the Syracuse concert, even as some early arrivals pitched camp in a parking lot across the street, the storms arrived, perching overhead until the morning of the show. Despite ending shortly after the gates opened at 6:00 a.m., the showers would resume throughout the day, squelching the attendance plans of thousands of fair-weather fans. The second sign of impending failure was perceptual, based on the history of rock festivals up to this point. At nearly every mega-concert, when the crush of new arrivals began to overwhelm the security resources in place, embattled promoters had declared a "free festival," throwing open the gates to avoid trouble and counting on advance sales to pay the bills. To the hordes milling around the State Fairgrounds, why spend $15 on the day of the show when the Great American Music Fair would soon be free of charge?

My two friends and I arrived just as that champagne bottle heralded the beginning of a day of pitched battle. With the breach sealed, we moved down to one of the two main gates to see if the festival had been declared open and complimentary. However, the presence of sixty grim-faced police officers equipped in riot gear with shields at the ready stand-ing in formation behind the ticket takers at their turnstiles, indicated that a free lunch was not likely. Now, fifteen bucks may not seem like much, but among the three of us we barely had enough money to cover the gas to get home. So, we hung out, biding our time, surprised at the belligerence of the huge crowd that had gathered in front of the gate to face the police. Shouting and badgering soon turned into rock throwing, the officers raising their shields to deflect the projectiles hurtling their way. Considering the show of force inside, the mob's sudden stampede toward the gate startled me. As the workers scattered, the police wasted no time, moving their wall of shields forward while others fired tear-gas canisters in our direction.

Tear gas? I'd seen it used on TV during the antiwar riots; now I was shocked to be on the receiving end of it. The shells burst among the rabble, but some of the awful smoke drifted over to those of us on the periphery, the gas clawing its way into my eyes and nose and sending unstoppable tickles into spasms only relieved by violent coughing. We struggled out of the cloud and off to the side of the gate just as the riot police charged the crowd. A nightstick came down squarely on the head of a kid three feet away, the squirting blood startling me more than the victim as it stained his brown fatigue jacket. The kid dropped like a stone and I followed him down into the mud; not only could I help the guy out, perhaps the police would leave me alone as I tended one of the wounded. But they weren't looking for me or my friends: the squad kept heading out with the help of some K-9 units and their German shepherds, targeting the ringleaders.

The bloodied kid was okay; he got up, muttered thanks, and staggered off as the battle raged on behind us by a set of railroad tracks. Enough local cops remained at the gate to prevent an incursion, but they all stood in rapt amazement watching their heavily armed comrades fire more gas into the brawling throng, some of those canisters picked up and angrily hurled back at the officers. Suddenly it clicked—*everyone is distracted, now's the time.* Using two halves of some spent ticket stubs we found by the fence, my buddies and I walked boldly up to the turnstiles where the workers stood with mouths agape at the melee behind us. My guy didn't even look as I faked ripping the ticket in two and handed him half. We stayed cool until finally walking deep enough into the concert crowd to know that no alarm had been raised. "We did it!"

America had just gone onstage, playing to a huge muddy lake that some people didn't mind standing ankle-deep in. The audience responded warmly, digging the tunes they'd heard so often on the radio, before the heavens opened up yet again. Some stubborn folks held their positions, but most headed back to the grandstand for shelter. The three members of America abandoned the stage and all went quiet. After a few minutes of soaking wet, a surprise appearance by festival veteran John Sebastian warmed the crowd. Sporting only a harmonica, he serenaded us with a ditty he composed on the spot called "The Stuck-in-the-Mud Syracuse Blues." Then, America reappeared inside a massive bubble of clear plastic that kept the band safe and dry, and hopefully contained enough oxygen to sustain the musician's lives, at least until we heard "A Horse with No Name."

An eighteen-wheeler parked behind stage, its trailer splashed with the Starship's famous *Dragon Fly* logo, acted as a perfect backdrop for the group's appearance, during which the sun finally burst through the clouds. The sight brought the day's first standing ovation, although technically, everyone had been standing anyway, unless sitting half submerged in a bed of soggy New York muck. The mood brightened considerably as the band's "Summer of Love" vibes permeated the festival's afternoon set. By 5:00 p.m. the New Riders of the Purple Sage opened the evening concert with the same good-time hippie spirit. Accustomed to finding no food at rock festivals, we decided, nonetheless to give it a shot and actually found plenty of choices at the concession stands. The hot dogs provided the energy to dance through the Doobie Brothers entire high-class boogie set filled with hit after hit and capped by the recent number 1 "Black Water." The final band, the Beach Boys, seemed out of place in the festival lineup, but I wanted to at least see them for a few songs. The wait, however, dragged on and on as "technical difficulties" plagued the sound crew. The band didn't start surfing until nearly midnight, but still, the breezy sixties singles quickly erased our fatigue and lightened the mood.

The good, the bad, and the ugly — every rock festival had, and has, all three. The good at the Great American Music Fair was the music: despite challenging conditions, every group played at its peak, even if one of them performed inside a ziplock bag. The bad: John Scher lost his shirt when only an estimated 30,000–40,000 people made it to the event, costing the fledgling promoter at least a quarter million dollars. He'd make out okay, though: in a more than a forty-year career, Scher would build the New Jersey concert business into a wildly successful competitor to nearby New York City. Still, if I ever run into him, I should probably give the millionaire those fifteen bucks I owe him. The ugly: violence at the gate comes to mind immediately, and in upcoming festivals for future generations that lesson would, sadly, never be learned. Four years later, eleven people would be crushed to death or asphyxiated while clawing their way into a Who concert in Cincinnati, leading to a widespread ban on general-admission seating. Eventually, though, that safety constraint would be phased out, so the danger of calamity and violence is still as real now as it was in the seventies.

But, we found another instance of ugly in Syracuse while picking our way through the utter darkness away from the spotlighted vicinity of the stage, the sweet harmonies from the Beach Boys fading behind us. A cold breeze had stiffened the nighttime air, and with the State Fairgrounds still employing permanent wooden latrines, concertgoers had taken to dismantling the old structures for firewood. Bonfires blazed around us, as if a bivouacked army were warming its hands in readiness for the next day's battle. This wasn't the ugly part though; that arrived in the shouts of surprise and disgust from the darkness as wobbling figures, just trying to pick their way through the night, suddenly discovered the open holes where the outhouses had been. Yuck!!!

CHAPTER 13

FLEETWOOD MAC

AN AFRO AND A FINE SKYLARK

Boston Garden, October 18, 1975

Listen to: "Black Magic Woman," "Hypnotized," "Rhiannon," "Monday Morning"

When I say my college town in New Hampshire cleared out in the summer, I mean it. The two-thousand-odd students and faculty bolted from their homes as if Martian tripods had arrived over the nearby hills, leaving tiny Henniker deflated and quiet, probably the way the locals preferred it. But if you stayed there for the summer, like I did in 1975, eventually you'd be recognized as a village regular. With my temporary "townie" status in hand, I passed the time sweltering in a local paper mill before reactivating my numbed brain cells each evening at the campus radio station. Long before the Internet became a household window to the universe, WNEC-FM was the primary means of connecting my isolated summer home to the busy world beyond. A couple of times every week, relief packages containing the latest records and music magazines were dumped in the front lobby. As music director, I had the enjoyable task of listening to those new platters, and even though WNEC existed in what many might consider the backwoods, we were as up on the latest music as any city tastemaker. Early summer hits included Wings' *Venus and Mars, One of These Nights* by the Eagles, Frank Zappa & the Mothers' *One Size Fits All,* and *Red Octopus* from Jefferson Starship.

On a scorching July afternoon, after vainly trying to shower the mill's disgusting chlorine scent away, I dropped in at WNEC and tore open the mail. The first package contained the brand new album from Fleetwood Mac, simply titled after the band's name. The group had limited exposure on the station: the early material was featured on the weekly blues show, while the laid-back soft rock that the band migrated to in the early seventies could be heard occasionally in regular programming. Steady and reliable, Fleetwood Mac had released album after album that sounded great, but didn't attract much attention. As on the bigger FM commercial stations, the song "Hypnotized," from '73, received the most requests and airplay. I examined the white-and-black cover, with its distinctive photo featuring the two remaining cofounders of the band, Mick Fleetwood and John McVie. Further examination revealed that their guitarist Bob Welch had left, replaced by two newcomers, Stevie Nicks and Lindsey Buckingham. I couldn't tell who was who, though. Was Stevie the tall gentleman with moustache and Afro, chest hair prominently visible through an open shirt, while Lindsey the cute brunette pictured in a flowery, fringed blouse to the left? "That must be it," I thought as I placed the vinyl on a turntable. "Monday Morning," leapt from the speakers. Buckingham's song had a breezy country-pop influence, a definite flag that some things had changed. The Fleetwood Mac trademarks of luscious melodies and easy tempos, along with stalwart Christine McVie on vocals and keyboards, were still there, but focused into a more alluring canvas of tremendous songs and honey-sweet harmonies. The other DJs agreed: within a week, nine of the album's eleven cuts had been featured on the air with "Rhiannon" an early favorite. And, by that point, I had learned that Stevie Nicks wasn't the one with the moustache or chest hair.

The story of Fleetwood Mac meeting Buckingham and Nicks has put on the armor of legend, platinum-engraved by the enormous success that resulted. The rags-to-riches romance of the story can't be overstated either, for by the end of 1974, both the group and its soon-to-be new members had reached career dead ends. The members of Fleetwood Mac had changed their base of operations from London to Los Angeles, but that fresh start was marred early in the year when their former manager, claiming he owned the band's name, audaciously assembled a bogus group named Fleetwood Mac and sent it out on tour. Blindsided, the authentic musicians won a restraining order before beginning work on their twelfth album, *Heroes Are Hard to Find*. The imperious manager struck again, attempting to block release of the new record and even a tour to support it. The members of the "real" Fleetwood Mac stood their ground in court, successfully arguing the case to confirm their right to exclusively use the band name. A celebratory three-month string of concert dates followed, but all the legal wrangling and an ambitious tour schedule drained the musicians of their inspiration, energy, and cash. Meanwhile, the new album stalled out at a disappointing number 34 on the U.S. sales chart, and just before New Year's Eve, Bob Welch announced that he'd had enough. Fleetwood Mac was in shambles.

In a parallel Los Angeles universe, the gifted, but unknown singer-songwriting duo of Lindsey Buckingham and his girlfriend Stevie Nicks struggled to put food on their table and cover the rent. He picked up sparse money on session gigs while she waited tables in Hollywood and cleaned houses. The pair had gotten a big break two years earlier when they scored a record deal and released the often-brilliant *Buckingham/Nicks*. That album revealed that the pair had a lot more going for them than the thousands of other hopefuls clustered around the record industry epicenter looking for a break. But the album, as excellent as it was, hadn't sold much, and Polydor Records passed on its option to record another. Frustrated, but not giving up, Buckingham and Nicks kept writing, adding daily to their large closet of music. It didn't seem to matter, though; the songs were all dressed up with no place to go.

Then, the big bang. When Mick Fleetwood found himself in Van Nuys checking out Sound City Studios as a possible location to record, engineer Keith Olsen, who had also produced the *Buckingham/Nicks* album, responded to Fleetwood's request for a studio sound check by blasting "Frozen Love," the record's dramatic finale, through the speakers. Since the song had also been recorded there, it would aptly demonstrate the room's acoustics. Building from the acoustic entry and the duo's urgent vocal interplay into an enormous electric and orchestral beast, rivaling the build of earlier warhorses like "Stairway to Heaven" or "Free Bird," the song gloriously filled the space. Fleetwood was impressed, both by the acoustics of the studio and also the guitarist on the song; he made some mental notes, thanked the engineer, and left. Later, with his band falling apart around him, the drummer called Olson and asked about the guitarist whose name he couldn't recall. Buckingham was stunned when Fleetwood contacted him; even so, he insisted that he'd only join as a team with Nicks. The parties met and got along famously, cutting a deal and cementing their commitment by entering Sound City with Olson at the controls only two weeks later. Nicks already had "Landslide" and "Rhiannon" written and demoed, Buckingham his "Monday Morning" and "I'm So Afraid." Fleetwood Mac rerecorded "Crystal" from *Buckingham/Nicks*, adding those to four of the best songs Christine McVie ever wrote. Mick Fleetwood called it "Magic. The undeniable sensation of rightness. . . . Merlin himself could not have cast a spell more perfect."

In July 1975, *Fleetwood Mac* began a fourteen-month climb to number 1 in America, one of the longest slogs to the top in chart history. Three Top 20 hits drove that success: Christine McVie's "Over My Head" in January '76, "Rhiannon" in June, and "Say You Love Me" in September. The band would work hard to push those songs up the chart, spending most of 1975 and '76 on the road. Stevie Nicks told *Trouser Press*, "Four gigs in a row, one day off. No limousines. We just never stopped; we played everywhere. We sold *Fleetwood Mac*. We kicked that album in the ass." Since the Mac had a long history of playing Boston, going back to their earliest stateside gigs at the Tea Party with founder Peter Green on guitar, a New England appearance was only inevitable. Word arrived that the new lineup would make its area debut at the Garden in October warming up for Jefferson Starship, which was having quite a summer of its own with a number-1 album and the single "Miracles" sitting at number 3. Since quite a few of my friends were huge Airplane/Starship fans, rounding up a posse to head to Boston didn't take long. To them, though, having Fleetwood Mac on the bill was nothing earth-shattering, just a fine appetizer to the evening's real treat.

After morning classes on October 18, too many of us piled into a car for the ninety-minute drive south to the Boston Garden. We walked into the venerable old barn in awe, Bruins and Celtics championship flags hanging regally from the rafters above. Like the out-of-towners we really were, we gawked upward like Dorothy and the boys shuffling into Emerald City. We didn't have too much company, though, because we were (as they say in Boston) "wicked" early, presenting our general-admission tickets and strolling out onto a barely-occupied floor. I sat down on the plywood and was surprised at how cold the surface was. "It's the Bruins ice under there," my friend Bruce marveled. The team was away facing the Islanders that night, but would return the following evening to host Toronto. Bruce might have been impressed, but I was just annoyed; my legs had already fallen asleep on the chilly surface. I stood back up, enduring the pins and needles, to survey the stage. Behind Fleetwood Mac's equipment hung a backdrop painting of the full moon illuminating a tangle of bony tree branches, the eeriness of that nighttime image complementing the iciness of the plywood tundra we stood on. While I shivered, the Boston Garden gradually filled up, but many people still hadn't arrived before the lights died and the members of Fleetwood Mac walked onstage without fanfare.

The group began on familiar ground with three Christine McVie vehicles: an old pre-Mac boogie called "Get Like You Used to Be," "Station Man" from 1970, and (a "should-have-been-a-hit") "Spare Me a Little of Your Love." It was typically good Fleetwood Mac, and generous applause rewarded each song, veteran fans obviously pleased with the classic choices and also the enhanced vocal firepower that the new three-singer lineup added. Most people probably hadn't heard her song about a Welsh witch before Stevie Nicks introduced "Rhiannon" for the first time in Boston. Softly strummed guitar and McVie's cool blanket of electric piano provided a gentle bed for Nicks's distinctive voice, pulsing and sensual for a few minutes, even pleasant, before Buckingham suddenly ratcheted up the intensity by howling into a furious solo. Nicks shot back, matching him ferociously with an extended rant on her lyrics, singing, shouting, and shaking, shredding her voice in a series of unnerving primal yells. Whoa, what's this? Everyone in the audience, no matter how distracted a moment earlier, focused their attention on the singing nymph in her flowing chiffon dress, now transformed into a raging enchantress casting musical incantations and hurling them down from the stage. I shook my head in amazement: a singer couldn't do what she was doing without damaging her delicate instrument. Yet, the song had captured her so completely that she attacked it with an almost out-of-body catharsis. Stunned, the entire Boston Garden audience snapped out of paralysis to rise up in one massive roar of response as "Rhiannon" crashed to a mighty finale.

It would remain the most intense performance I'd ever see a female singer give. She wouldn't be able to maintain that intensity for her entire career, but by then Stevie Nicks would already be a star for many years and could find other ways to dazzle. For the moment, though, everyone in the audience shared the knowledge that a great talent had just been revealed, and they would surely tell their friends (the seventies version of social media). For the record, later in the set when the other rookie with the Afro tackled his centerpiece, "I'm So Afraid," every guitar fan in the place stood slack jawed. Fleetwood Mac had always been a respected guitar band, and obviously that hadn't changed one bit. After the set ended with an encore of "Hypnotized," people couldn't stop talking about it, as if we'd witnessed the miracle of birth. As I massaged life back into my cold and numb feet, compliments of the NHL, we chattered excitedly about those two new members of the group. Heroes are always hard to find, but I think Fleetwood Mac had just found a couple.

CHAPTER 14

LYNYRD SKYNYRD

SWEATIN' BULLETS

Orpheum Theater, Boston, April 7, 1976

Listen to: "Gimme Three Steps," "Tuesday's Gone," "Saturday Night Special," "Free Bird"

It's eerie to think about seeing Lynyrd Skynyrd just a year and a half before the day the music died. Here was a band on its terrible road of fate, destined to board a two-engine commercial prop plane in October '77 that the members had already decided to get rid of because it gave them the creeps. A couple of weeks earlier, the same thirty-year-old bird had been examined by Aerosmith's flight crew and rejected because neither the aircraft nor pilots appeared safe. JoJo Billingsly, one of the ladies in the Honkettes, the backup singing trio traveling with the band, had a terrible nightmare in which she foresaw the plane crash. She conveyed the images of her terrifying premonition to her fellow musicians, but, the twenty-four-member Lynyrd Skynyrd entourage hadn't taken her warning and their own worries seriously enough to avoid the doomed flight, as she did. In the aftermath she would become a born-again Christian and a preacher, convinced that only divine providence had saved her. The rest were partying high in the skies over Mississippi by the time one of the engines started sputtering. Looks of alarm and panic must have shot between the passengers—and then the other motor quit. Complete terror while strapping in and grabbing hold, the wind rushing past a now-silent craft gliding earthward, the flight crew realizing in astonishment that they had run the Convair out of gas. The crash into a wooded swamp near Gillsburg killed six, including the pilot and copilot. Three members of the band including lead singer Ronnie Van Zandt, the spiritual core of the group, died from the impact. It would take ten years before the remnants of the mighty platinum-selling powerhouse pulled themselves together enough to perform again as Lynyrd Skynyrd.

The Lord's justice fell hard upon seventies southern rock. The style's three most important bands all experienced arching fame and catastrophic loss, in the kind of story that reached all the way back to the myth of Robert Johnson encountering the Devil at a midnight crossroads and signing a contract without bothering to read the fine print. The Allman Brothers Band experienced the death of its founder Duane Allman in an October 1971 motorcycle crash just after breaking through to a national audience with its live *At Fillmore East* album. A year later, founding bassist Berry Oakley perished in a similar accident on his own two-wheeler, hitting a city bus only three blocks from Allman's pileup. Then, in a truly Shakespearian piece of stagecraft, drummer Butch Trucks suffered a car wreck a year later in the same vicinity of Macon, Georgia, and luckily just broke a leg. South Carolina's Marshall Tucker Band suffered a crippling loss that marked the end of its glory years when founding singer and bassist Tommy Caldwell perished in a 1980 Jeep accident. Uncannily, a month before that, Tommy's younger brother had died in a car crash with a garbage truck. The older brother, Toy, Marshall Tucker's gifted guitarist, passed away in 1993 from a heart attack induced by ingesting cocaine. Then there was Lynyrd Skynyrd, the last in southern rock's Triple Crown, taken out in the prime of its life. The subsequent mental traumas from the plane crash did not prevent the survivors from eventually reforming, but the disturbing memories allowed them no rest. The pills and the booze didn't help either; after guitarist Allen Collins' wife died in 1980 from pregnancy complications, his practice of self-medicating took a deadly turn when he cracked up a car six years later, killing his girl-friend and paralyzing himself from the waist down. After appearing with Skynyrd onstage nightly in a wheelchair, he'd die from pneumonia in 1990.

But warm up the time machine and set the controls for April 7, 1976, a golden day before the fall. Lynyrd Skynyrd was on the road support-ing its fourth album *Gimme Back My Bullets* when it came to Boston with fellow Florida rockers the Outlaws in tow. Famous for its relentless tour schedules, Skynyrd had hammered through nearly fifty gigs since November with scarcely a break for Christmas. I couldn't call myself a fan of the band and didn't even own one of its records; nevertheless, I was prevailed upon by two friends, Jeff and Bruce, to accompany them to the show. In those days a ticket didn't cost much more than a double album — you could afford to experiment, and take in a concert to see if you liked a band (unlike today, where misjudgments are expensive!). Oh, I liked Skynyrd's hit songs from its first two albums, even enjoyed the tough rock I'd heard from the new album, but the band simply hadn't made it onto my A-, or even B-list. If that sounds incredible, or even sacrilegious, remember that the group had only been around for less than three years at that point and were still working on establishing their true national breakthrough (which would not occur until later in '76 when the live *One More from the Road* album went platinum and Lynyrd Skynyrd was booked to play Madison Square Garden). The heavy mantle of history had not yet yoked the band's name famously to disaster; at the time, it was just another rock group on the road trying to make it.

We found our way to our seats, high in the balcony of the old the-ater. It was already broiling and humid in the upper reaches, with stairs that climbed at a crazy angle until the top row of seats ended just a few feet below the peeling cement ceiling. It felt as if the collective heat and carbon-dioxide exhalations of nearly 3,000 bodies had all risen up there. Since the Orpheum was one of America's oldest theaters, built in 1852 and looking like it had never been repainted, I could only assume that any air conditioning installed in the building had to also be sadly out of date. While we looked down at the distant stage, my friends' enthusiastic debate over the talents of Lynyrd Skynyrd's guitar players began to rub off on me. In the current lineup there were two lead guitar players, Allen Collins and Gary Rossington, and both possessed chops strong enough to power individual bands if they wanted to. The epic "Free Bird" with its grand fits of soloing had proven their advanced skills as far back as the first album. I might have felt unworthy to be among an audience of true fanatics foaming at the mouth as they waited for Skynyrd's guitar glory, but, I'd seen the Outlaws a year earlier and enjoyed them very much; so, if nothing else, I had that coinage to purchase my right to a valuable seat inside the old theater. The warm-up band from Tampa did not disappoint, demonstrating its own special fire with a rabble-rousing three-guitarist lineup that insured that a solo was never too far away.

When Lynyrd Skynyrd finally appeared onstage, the unbridled and inebriated shout that arose in welcome nearly blew my eardrums in. The band's concert production was vastly ordinary: no ornately-designed staging with lasers or strobe lights, flashy stage clothes on the band members, or choreography to speak of, except perhaps, for the rehearsed move of the two guitarists and bassist Leon Wilkeson to line up in a row with axes bristling during "Gimme Three Steps." By far the biggest dramatic accoutrement arrived when a huge Confederate flag backdrop unfurled during "Sweet Home Alabama." Gary Rossington handled most of the lead guitar and slide, clutching a Les Paul Sunburst and rarely smiling, just concentrating on the matter at hand while Allen Collins with his long and curly Robert Plant hair laid down the killer rhythms and some leads with his favorite Gibson Explorer and an occasional Fender Strat replacement. Ronnie Van Zandt didn't move around much at all, remaining rooted at the center with his hand on the mic most of the night. His vocals were right on target, though, and easily discernible even in the mushy acoustics of the upstairs cheap-seat area. There are no photos of Noah, but when that biblical hero climbed off the ark after a year, he must have looked like Artimus Pyle, wild hair and beard flying every time he whacked those drums. Leon Wilkeson, a stick figure with glasses, sang backups and did his job on bass, while keyboardist Billy Powell, whose sparkling piano work was an underrated Skynyrd weapon, also moved back and forth to the organ during a majestic "Tuesday's Gone." The backup-singing Honkettes lifted the band's harmonies into church, a classy touch that proved to be the main embellishment from a group that obviously preferred to let its songs and performance stand on their own.

By the end of the show, Skynyrd had invited Hughie Thomasson and Billy Jones from the Outlaws onstage to jam, marking a ridiculous number of soloists swiping their six-strings on extended solos and ful-filling the fantasies of even the most ardent of air guitarists in the house. A fiery quarter-hour romp on "Free Bird" was the natural closer, and then they were gone after nearly two hours of undisputed brilliance. I noticed my sweat-drenched clothes and aching neck for the first time once we sat down after vainly trying for another encore. But really, were they going to come out again after performing southern rock's na-tional anthem? Folks started filing out of the boiler room—I mean, the balcony—while the three of us debriefed. Lynyrd Skynyrd had deliv-ered a no-frills slab of blue-collar rock with some of the best songs and musicianship I'd seen in any band up to that point. Now I understood why the place had sold out and why everyone had been standing up clear to the back of the balcony (including the tall guy right in front of me, dammit!). There was honesty in the band that defied criticism and a strength in the songs that confounded doubters. But, Lynyrd Skynyrd wouldn't get much more time to prove itself. The band's final New England show rocked the Cape Cod Coliseum fourteen months later, in June 1977; then its best album yet, *Street Survivors*, was re-leased just three days before the disaster in October.

With the Allman Brothers band recently broken up (and inactive until 1979), this group had assumed the leadership role in the South's guitar army. However, to call Skynyrd the cream of that narrow genre was surely limiting because the group stood firmly among the finest in *all* of rock music. The image of some motley assortment of backcountry redneck hacks woodshedding it out on dozens of endless, disposable solos was a far cry from what I'd experienced. Now I understood that we had witnessed a band soaring in full flight, exercising tremendous and sophisticated powers in its performance. In 1976, Lynyrd Skynyrd was America's best—a band in position to usurp the dominance of the era's leading English groups like the Rolling Stones, the Who, and Queen. For want of some extra aviation fuel, it would have happened too.

CHAPTER 15

THE EAGLES

SIX-STRING OUTLAWS

Schaefer Stadium, Foxboro, Massachusetts, July 25, 1976

Listen to: "Take it Easy," "Already Gone," "Desperado," "Hotel California"

From the first time I first heard "Take it Easy" on the radio, I was never really fond of the Eagles. Raised on a diet of Led Zeppelin, the Who, Cream, and Black Sabbath, my appetite leaned toward meat and potatoes rather than the over-easy, cheesy omelet of country and soft rock this L.A.-based band served up. Years later, I can listen to those first four albums, chock full of their blockbuster hits, and appreciate the truly skilled musicianship and songwriting craft that went into them, but in 1976 the only country strains I'd allowed into my vernacular were pretty much limited to Neil Young's *Harvest* or *Workingman's Dead*. So, when I heard about a concert of American musical heroes featuring the Eagles, Beach Boys, and Boz Scaggs at Schaefer Stadium in Foxboro, Massachusetts, the news barely registered.

Elton John's Bicentennial concert three weeks earlier on the Fourth of July in the same venue intrigued me more. I thought there'd be a lot more excitement in the British superstar's red, white, and blue (plus, uh, pink) onstage celebration than seeing a mainstream hoedown. But, as a fill-in DJ in Concord, New Hampshire, I worked all the holidays, so I missed Elton's American lovefest and somehow ended up instead at the July 25 trifecta, shelling out the nine dollars for an advance ticket and embarking on the requisite road trip south.

By the fall of 1975 the unit of Don Henley, Glenn Frey, Bernie Leadon, and Randy Meisner had been playing for just over four years with recent addition Don Felder having joined a year earlier. The group had been immensely successful, selling millions of albums, placing eight singles in the Top 40, and clinching the cover of *Rolling Stone* magazine in September. The latest album, "One of These Nights," had gone to number 1, hastening the Eagles ascendancy to the throne and etching its name in history as the group most instrumental in establishing the country-rock style. The national dominance of country music in the new millennium owes much to the groundbreaking effort of the Eagles thirty years earlier. But, by the end of '75, founding member Bernie Leadon had called it quits. As a bluegrass-inspired guitar, mandolin, and banjo player, certainly the most country-styled, versatile, and talented musician among them, he'd decided that the band's frenzied pace just wasn't worth it anymore. The Eagles' carefully cultivated image of mellow, whiskey-sipping, good-time cowboys ran parallel with the coke-fueled, cutthroat, nonstop competition of the L.A. music business. The Eagles replaced Leadon almost immediately with former James Gang singer and guitarist Joe Walsh. Fans and critics hotly debated the move, seen as a threat to the group's core sound because of the new Eagle's unabashed roots as a hard rocker.

Up in the boondocks, I heard nothing of the transition until a few days after the Foxboro stadium announcement when I caught a Boston disc jockey commenting that the Eagles summer tour would serve to introduce its already-famous new member to the fans. The mention of the guitarist's name sent a jolt through me: although I was no more than lukewarm over the Eagles, I absolutely loved Joe Walsh. The James

Gang had been my first concert, and years later I welcomed his solo career, watching Walsh perform a stunning concert in Boston on the heels of his big hit "Rocky Mountain Way." Now he was a member of the Eagles? Suddenly I was interested! When the Beach Boys dropped out of the lineup on short notice and were replaced by Fleetwood Mac, I felt God had given me a confirming sign. "Go in peace, my child, and rock out!" Who was I to argue with that?

Because of the snafu with the Beach Boys, tickets didn't go on sale until June 29, just four weeks before the concert. A few of my friends wanted to go, so my red-and-white '68 VW Microbus became the designated shuttle. I'd had some trouble with the four-cylinder putt-putt that summer, so a screw driver was always on hand to jam into the carburetor for start-ups, plus some fresh sheet metal lined the floor where a scissor-jack had punched through the rusty undercarriage when I had changed a tire on the interstate. I'd poured some concrete into the floor to help patch the hole, so I wondered how my traction would improve in the winter with all that extra weight. But, rough ignitions, the inability to change a passenger-side rear tire, and a lack of auto insurance (not required in New Hampshire) — certainly deal-breakers at a later time in my life — were only minor annoyances when transportation to a concert hung in the balance.

No one in the entourage had ever been to Schaefer Stadium, home of the New England Patriots, before, but in my concertgoing experience any time the word "stadium" appeared, "traffic nightmare" always followed. Accordingly, we skipped church and motored south on a beautifully sunny and perfect Sunday. Previously condemned to an efficient German-engineered, but woefully uncool, AM radio, I'd anchored an FM converter into the metal dash, replacing the usual static-filled commentary with rock-and-roll tunes out of Boston. The DJ came on, mentioning that nearly all of the 62,000 tickets had been sold, making this the largest music audience in New England concert history. Despite the expected traffic snarl, we arrived early enough to easily park near the stadium, although the lot lay at the end of a lengthy dirt path riddled with killer potholes and enough dust to camouflage the VW's bright colors into dull hues of tan and brown.

Boz Scaggs had been kicking around for years, but had just hit the big time with *Silk Degrees*, its dance hit "Lowdown" taking the album up to number 2 and way past a million sold. We spent a lot of time playing Frisbee and getting sunburnt before joining the line of marchers heading over to the stadium. Once we got inside, half of Scaggs's set was over. I felt sorry we missed all the tunes because his band, ten pieces strong with backup singers and horns, had the audience up and dancing—not bad for being third on the bill. Since all the tickets were general admission, most people skipped the aluminum backless benches in the grandstand to squeeze as close as possible on the field, so it was as tight as any overflowing disco down there. After Scaggs took his final bow, I considered a strategy to get close enough to see Fleetwood Mac. Security wasn't preventing anyone from walking down the stands to the front of the field, but once there, bodies were packed in so tightly in front of the stage that penetration seemed impossible. But wait! The day and night before, Foxboro had received a half an inch of rain, leaving a huge puddle thirty or forty feet across directly in front of the stage. "How deep can it be?" I asked my friends. Would it be like the water-filled hole that Ringo Starr gallantly laid his jacket over in *A Hard Day's Night*? Unlike the hapless woman in the film who stepped onto the garment and plunged hilariously out of sight, I doubted that this muddy pond would rise much above someone's shoes. Like a duck, I ventured gamely into the center of the water hazard, taking some non-approving looks from folks around me, but earning a perfect front-and-center view for Fleetwood Mac.

This new version of the veteran group with Lindsey Buckingham and Stevie Nicks in the lineup had dazzled the previous October warming up for Jefferson Starship in Boston. Since then, the band's eponymous *Fleetwood Mac* album with its three hit singles had steadily hovered near the top of the charts for months, turning double platinum and well acquainting audiences with the look of this refurbished lineup. After an hour-long set and encore, the crowd of ecstatic Eagles fans only reluctantly allowed the Mac to leave the stage. Perhaps some of the many new converts at this show, and others along the way on the band's long summer tour would now head out to buy the latest album. It probably happened that way because *Fleetwood Mac* would jump to the top of the charts just six weeks later.

Now bring on the main attraction! The surrounding crowd who saw me wade into the puddle had chosen imitation as a form of flattery moving in to dance and stomp the muddy water relentlessly into soggy earth. The pressure up front became enormous; so tight that I could barely get my hands up above my head. We decided to retreat, finding respite up in the stands as the members of the Eagles took the stage around 10:00 p.m., playing their first hit, "Take it Easy." The final lineup of Lynyrd Skynyrd and also the Outlaws had made the triple-guitar format famous, and most wouldn't think of the Eagles that way, but there they were: Joe Walsh and Don Felder flanking Glenn Frey as he sang the 1972 smash with Randy Meisner tucked in alongside on bass. A huge smile beamed under Walsh's oversize Pete Townshend nose and a gypsy bandana covered his noggin while offering backing vocals and a Strat solo as naturally as if he'd helped form the band years earlier. Frey with his long tousled hair, stoner eyes and bushy moustache looked rumpled, like he'd just tumbled out of the sack, but the hippie troubadour's singing not only nailed the song, but improved on the studio original. Felder, also with long wavy hair, moustache, and beard took a solo turn in this opener too. Don Henley powered the drums in back; his teased Afro ball bobbing up and down with the effort, except when he had to hold steady at the mic. I had to admit that the Eagles rocked a lot harder than I expected, satisfying my tastes and also sending the crowd around me into early hysterics. The members liberally rotated on vocals and instruments for different songs: Frey taking over keyboards as Meisner sang "Take It to the Limit," Henley leaving the drum stool to play guitar and croon "Best of My Love," and all five front and center on the often a cappella centerpiece "Seven Bridges Road."

Within five months, the band would release its landmark *Hotel California* album, but at this point no material from that forthcoming release had entered the set. The band, instead, leaned heavily on its last two records and generously added some Joe Walsh solo songs to the mix. Sure, there were some countrified and mellow moments that bored me to tears ("Doolin-Dalton" and "Lyin' Eyes"), but each of those songs was rewarded by a massive outpouring of warmth and appreciation, the same mighty response heard and felt every time the Patriots scored a game-day touchdown in this place. With all that adulation flying toward the stage, it sure didn't seem like many of the band's original fans had been offended much by the tougher rock stance. But even if the Eagles had lost some purists, further debate didn't matter; the band had just negotiated a tricky point in its career by selling out the biggest venue it could book in New England while introducing a key new player. Now the members could go home confident in their new direction and concentrate on finishing *Hotel California*, which would prove to be a blockbuster of mythical proportions.

While the band headed for a Lear jet, we trudged happily back to our parking lot. Unfortunately, some jerk had smashed a small side window to break into the Microbus, a pointless act since the driver's door didn't lock anyway, and tried to remove the FM converter. Bolted firmly, though, it had resisted all efforts at liberation. So there! The plastic knobs might have been gone and the black case cracked, but the music came in loud and clear as I turned the key. "One of These Nights" boomed from the speakers while everyone found a soft place to land, and then . . . silence. Damn! Now where did I put that screwdriver?

CHAPTER 16

TALKING HEADS

A NEW ARCHITECTURE

The Rat, Boston, January 22, 1977

Listen to: "Psycho Killer," "Take Me to the River," "Life During Wartime," "Burning Down the House," "Once in a Lifetime," "Road to Nowhere"

Even before 1977 my musical emotions were under attack. The progressive rock and seventies mainstream bands I'd enjoyed for years seemed to be stuck in a rut, or maybe I was the one in the rut. But, now that I'd moved to Boston, an entirely different circle of friends introduced me to a fresh range of possibilities in music. The style taking hold in the nightclubs of the city had been labeled punk rock, a black-leather niche of culture that I'd hardly suspected, except for former dalliances with glam rockers like Ziggy Stardust, T-Rex, and Lou Reed. The primer coat on that alternate universe had been painted in sixties New York City from a radical new palette of colors presented by Andy Warhol's Velvet Underground, which introduced lurid, back-alley soundscapes and striking visual performance art. While the hippies chased peace and love by day, Lou Reed and the other Velvets offered a more pragmatic and darker vision born in the shadows. Their approach directly influenced Bowie, Bolan, and the entire English "glam scene," then inspired later hometown acts like the New York Dolls to gob smears of rouge on their faces and the Ramones to slam home fourteen songs in less than a half hour on their 1976 debut album. It was a new age, to quote the Velvet Underground song.

Big Apple sentiment then found fertile ground in London's discontent and also made it to Boston, where the center-city clubs bred an underground circle of aggressive rock bands and a cabal of devotees. I bought my leather bomber and wore it like a badge of honor, spiking out my hair (I hated when it was flat anyway), and sporting a really cool zipper earring. Then I tried to look tough enough so nobody would mess with me as I walked to rock-and-roll refuges like the Rat in Kenmore Square (a glorified basement that was punk HQ in Boston), Cantones in the financial district (an old-school Italian restaurant with decent eggplant parm by day), and the Club in Cambridge (the smell of Necco Wafers wafting over the place from the candy factory down the street). Inside those places I was surrounded by an intriguing and stimulating circle of fellow fans, disciples like me who were never as threatening as they might have looked; what they mostly wanted to do was just dance (and mate).

My mission in moving to Boston, to find a job in journalism or radio, failed magnificently for a long time (much longer than it takes to starve to death). I found more menial work to survive while taking the advice of a friend who studied at MIT to volunteer at its noncommercial radio station WTBS-FM for some artistic fulfillment. I started out playing the progressive rock and mainstream selections I loved, but soon heard fellow DJ Oedipus featuring his edgy new records and tapes on a program called the *Demi-Monde*. He'd eventually be feted as a punk-rock pioneer, because, at the time, nobody played this kind of music on the radio; indeed, most people didn't even suspect the style existed, certainly I hadn't. Oedipus became the conduit to discover and experience these new sounds; his airplay provided the kindling to ignite a local punk scene and arouse a coterie of like-minded musicians in the area. In the beginning, the anti-stars of CBGB in New York journeyed north to do most of the heavy lifting, and we got to know them all because they inevitably dropped in on the *Demi-Monde* with new tapes and vinyl in hand. The Ramones, Blondie, Patti Smith, Television, the Dictators, the Shirts, Richard Hell, Johnny Thunders, and the rest all found a paying gig in Boston, not necessarily the case outside of a small network of clubs in America's northeast. It wouldn't be long before their example fostered a strong home team including Willie Loco Alexander and the Boom Boom Band, the Infliktors, Nervous Eaters, DMZ, the Real Kids, Third Rail, and Marc Thor. Most of those bands were featured on *Live at the Rat*, a September '76 double album that set the template for the new generation, a blaze of energy that would soon make the Boston local music scene one of the most prolific in the nation.

The radio station was a small place, so it wasn't long before I got to know Oedipus, who continually encouraged me and some of the other jocks to visit the Rat sometime and check out the local scene. We listened to the pink-haired visionary in his bright red glasses, wondering what we'd gotten ourselves into, but there was only one way to find out. He suggested we check out a major event for the Rat, a three-night stand from the Talking Heads, a young trio from the Big Apple. This group perched alone in left field, about as far from the four-on-the-floor assault of the Ramones as one could get. The members had met in New England at the Rhode Island School of Design and then moved south. Although the group didn't play anything close to punk rock, it had become an integral member of the avant-garde scene fostering that style, making its stage debut at CBGB in June 1975 warming up for the Ramones. Talking Heads' art-school fascinations were most evident in the spectacled office-clerk persona of lead singer and guitarist David Byrne, whose unsettling vocal spasms (like karaoke night over the Cuckoo's Nest) were matched by the band's fitful, yet skillfully tight rhythms. In late '76, Oedipus began playing an advance copy of the band's first single "Love > Building on Fire," which wouldn't officially come out until early the following year. It was the most messed up assortment of stammering vocal phrasing and taut, italicized offbeats I'd ever heard, but, *why did I like it?* All the goofiness of a teenage love infatuation typified a giddy early section of the song that gave way to a dramatic build in energy with spirited horn arrangement elevating the whole feeling. Love *had* turned into a building on fire by the time the single finished.

On a small tour of colleges and the occasional nightclub, punctuated by regular homecomings to CBGB, the members of Talking Heads were gearing up for the release of their single in February followed by spring sessions to record a debut album on Sire Records. The band's unique style had drawn me in, and obviously I wasn't alone in my fascination; with a trio of nights booked in Boston even before any of its music had been released, Talking Heads commanded *someone's* attention. The band's spare, deceptively simple lyrics, phrasing, and arrangements opened up on examination to reveal music of surprising intelligence and power. The Heads appealed to a broad swath of freaks, geeks, criminals, and intellectuals with their combination of punk attitude and smart design, perhaps revealing the secret of why this group had appealed to so many so quickly. Essentially, they were a musical Rubik's cube, generating so many questions with an endless puzzle of possibilities. Perhaps seeing the band live would answer some of those questions.

Walking onstage unceremoniously behind drummer Chris Frantz and bassist Tina Weymouth with her fashionably short hairstyle, Byrne introduced the group simply: "This band is Talking Heads," before pushing off gently into the set. Accustomed to seeing musicians either work within a structured stage show designed to help explain their concepts or cloak themselves within character masks while performing, I was surprised by Byrne's complete disregard of swagger or bravado. Indeed, he came off as some kind of anti-star, a Clark Kent to so many I'd seen trying to be Superman. There was no macho, power-chord persona leaping from the stage here. No, Byrne's authority came from his words: ostensibly unsophisticated lyrics about love coming to town and books he'd read, among other deceptively simple subjects. I found myself trying to work out the riddles by first figuring out if there was a puzzle at all. What was the mystery or majesty in a song like "Who Is It?" which spent a couple of minutes just asking that basic question before answering " . . . it's you!" But, why did a song have to be more than that anyway? Was an image, a haiku, sufficient for rock and roll? I guessed that it must be, because here was a band intriguing us by doing just that. Everyone around me applauded each song unreservedly; it was an unusually attentive and appreciative gathering. So much for the popular image of punks being hooligans and reducing rock-and-roll clubs to rubble. I liked this new crowd: I had the feeling I'd be seeing the inside of this basement, dark and musty as it was, a lot more in the future.

Through the first set and into the second, I knew none of the songs except for the single I'd heard, but later learned that Talking Heads performed as many cuts from its forthcoming first album, due in September, as a distant second record in 1978. Despite Byrne's lack of stage drama and the benign presence of the other Heads onstage, the members did build the second set to a climax by wrapping it up with "Love > Building on Fire" and the inevitable hit "Psycho Killer" with its crazed yelping from the lead singer as he acted out the part. Then the group encored with "I'm Not in Love," pulling former Modern Lovers member Jerry Harrison onstage to join them. Already in the works, Harrison would join Talking Heads on guitar and keyboards within weeks as a permanent member of the band before the recording of its debut album. That debut would turn the heads of anyone in the scene who hadn't witnessed the band in concert, but it was the second release, *More Songs About Buildings and Food*, that introduced the group to the mainstream.

That collaboration with legendary producer Brian Eno would take the Talking Heads to both a new artistic level and also generate an unlikely Top 40 success in their remake of the 1974 Al Green hit "Take Me to the River." A surprise gold album was the result, but it proved to be no fluke as the record-buying public opened its arms wide to a refreshingly original group with the spastic lead singer and his cockeyed view of the world. Unbelievably to me, the Talking Heads would forge boldly into the popular sales charts, compromising not one iota, but selling millions of albums anyway, even a couple of double-platinum discs including the 1984 live album and film *Stop Making Sense*, which also signaled that the group had mastered the burgeoning eighties art form of creating memorable videos. By the end of the decade, when David Byrne sadly signaled the end of the band, it had assumed a leadership role, along with U2, in justifying all of those clandestine early nights spent in dingy, spray-painted punk clubs helping to rally a scene that would rise from the dark and eventually grow to a building on fire throughout the world.

CHAPTER 17

THE CARS

CROSSTOWN TRAFFIC

The Rat, Boston, September 9, 1977

Listen to: "My Best Friend's Girl," "Just What I Needed," "Moving in Stereo/All Mixed Up"

"Hey! You guys suck over there! Punk rock is for *loseahhs!*" The group of portentously drunk, apparently former wrestlers hung on to each other, laughing and pitching about on the sidewalk in front of the disco club. They gestured rudely across Kenmore Square toward a few of us as we talked, our leather jackets insulating us from the coolness of an early September night just after last call. "Didn't you hear me?" one of them taunted, his powder-blue leisure suit filled ominously with muscles as big as his vocal cords. "I said—you guys suuuuuuuuck!" His buddies howled, then began stumbling away while we profoundly ignored the outburst. "Punk-rock chicks are all sluts," he conjured up, "they'll do any of us over here for a quarter!" Again, we let it go by, but one stunner in a leather skirt, blue-jean jacket, and the stereotypical safety pin dangling as her earring did respond with a hearty "Eat shit!" Well, that was it: the group stopped in its tracks while Mr. Powder-

Blue feigned total outrage. "Did you hear that?" he shouted. His mates rejoined him, weaving slightly as they moved to cross the street. A rallying yell, "We're gonna kick your . . . !" was abruptly cut short as a hurtling cab blared its horn and nearly sent the wrestling squad flying into some suburban cemetery. Perhaps Stoughton, Billerica, or whatever woodland town they came from slept soundly at 2:00 a.m., but Kenmore Square in Boston still throbbed with activity. With two wide streets to cross and an MBTA bus station in the middle, it would take the drunks a little while and some determination to get to us, but the disco boys seemed bent on "clobbering time," so still they came on. This time around, though, they looked both ways before stepping off the curb.

We were standing on the sidewalk in front of the Rathskeller, Boston's preeminent punk-rock club. The place sat directly across the wide intersection of Commonwealth Avenue, Brookline Avenue, and Beacon Street from the glittery environs of Lucifer's, one of Boston's best-known dance clubs. Like a stone's throw across the Berlin Wall from one extreme to the other, the fashionably attired gaggles that stepped out of their limousines or poured in polyester finery through the front doors of a mirror-ball fantasy world couldn't, or didn't want to, relate to their neighbors in ripped jeans and leather across the square. To the latter, dressing down to a basic urban anti-chic proudly displayed a rejection of mainstream style, the punk attitude, exuding a fascination with the stripped-away essence and original rebelliousness of rock and roll. The gulf between these two coexisting cultures in 1977 seemed incredibly wide, but ironically, most of those punks were as middle-class as their flashy counterparts and probably drove into Boston from the same suburban neighborhoods. In fact, it was even possible that Mr. Powder-Blue over there lived only a few doors down the street from Miss Safety Pin, who had given him that quite audible "finger" from across the Square.

The sign out in front might have said Rathskeller, but to those who practically lived there, it was always the Rat. Sure, the punk club did exist in a cellar like a German beer hall might, but after that, most similarities ended. One descended a dark stairway into a room framed between a cement floor cushioned by a bed of rotting cigarette butts and a low ceiling crisscrossed by turn-of-the-(last)-century plumbing caked in layers of ancient dust. I wagered that the footprints of many members of species *Rattus norvegicus* could be seen dotting those pipes, express lanes for the alarmingly large critters often seen scurrying from wall to wall. That's why it was always a good idea not to look up at the Rat; occasionally, when a lead singer reached above to hang on the large-diameter pipe passing right over stage, you had to hope that he was current on all his required immunizations. Black paint on the walls, black paint on the ceiling (goes with everything, you know), the space was truly a lobby into Hades. But, you didn't go to the Rat for the décor: this place served as the prime meeting point for a whole local scene, while the do-it-yourself bands of a new Now Generation worked it out on a plywood square barely higher than the floor. That was the way it should be too: the punk-rock movement was a proletarian one — of the people, by the people, and for the people. No stars at the Rat, or so we thought.

The best place to watch a show at the Rat was right in front of either speaker cabinet flanking the stage. It was *loud* there, but if you stuck a finger in the ear closest to the noise, you could handle it. From this prime vantage spot that few reasonable people ever fought for, I watched the Boston band that all my really cool friends couldn't say enough about. The Cars were an up-and-coming local group that seemed to have a jet engine attached to its back. Since its debut on New Year's Eve 1976, the five-piece had played the Rat two dozen times, always drawing a long line of supporters waiting impatiently to get in. The Cars had warmed up for Bob Seger at the 4,000-seat Music Hall, and a demo tape of two songs, "Just What I Needed" and "My Best Friend's Girl," were getting heavy airplay on local radio. Rumors of major-label interest floated about continually, a whisper down the alley that would soon prove true when the ink dried on a contract with Elektra Records in November.

Drummer David Robinson displayed the most punk cred since he had played in Jonathan Richman's Modern Lovers, but most of the girls couldn't keep their eyes off the pretty blonde bassist and colead-singer Ben Orr. Ric Ocasek, a tall and gaunt stick dominating the stage in sunglass aloofness, also sang and wrote nearly all of the band's music. Left-handed guitarist Elliot Easton arrived from the very un-punkish world of formal education at Berklee School of Music, but could always be counted on for an inventive solo. Finally, the owlish dwarf Greg Hawkes bent over his keyboards, providing the bloops and bleeps that gave the Cars much of its identifiable "modern" sound. These five, so disparate in their appearance, still managed to project a singular customized look, jelling cleanly into a unit coordinated by their characteristic red, black, and white onstage color scheme. The Cars appeared as uncluttered as a Corvette revving up with a throaty and welcome roar; it was only a matter of time before this machine had to fly off the showroom floor, even a grimy one awash in nicotine and sweat.

The group launched into a set of songs that would eventually fill a multimillion-selling debut album with stories of cars, girls, rock and roll, and, did I say—girls? Ocasek's knack for writing an irresistible hook that stuck in your head like a McDonald's milkshake in your gut sold each and every selection. Even with that album ten months away, I still felt as if I was listening to a band play a set from its greatest-hits record—no duds, just hard-driving ear candy. I had to search widely for a negative, and only managed to find one while watching the five musicians stand stock-still in their places for the entire set. I would see the Cars a lot of times, from the Rat all the way up to a concert at the Boston Garden on its "final" tour in 1987 with the inevitable reunion a couple of decades later. In every case, when folks would ask what my favorite part of the show was, I'd respond with a chuckle, "When they moved!" And it was true: the band members remained rooted like molded toy soldiers with that tiny piece of plastic joining their feet. After watching *Toy Story*, you know how hard it is to get around with that annoying thing down there. Now, don't get me wrong: the band's onstage stiffness was not a big deal. In interviews the members even revealed that it was designed, going along with their look and presentation. Still, you sort of expected a blur of motion from a band named the Cars. The group concentrated, instead, on its cool blend of futuristic synthesized dance music combined with fiery, but economical, rock and roll. The Cars cruised on a tradition trafficked from Buddy Holly,

Elvis Presley, and Eddie Cochran, shaking hands with a celestial future dropped off by Brian Eno, Kraftwerk, or a visiting UFO. Perhaps that's why the band became so popular: as it bridged the gap between the seventies and the eighties, it also crossed the border between the fringes and the mainstream. *The Cars* would be one hit album that diehard punks always allowed onto their turntables, while pop music fans could risk a drive into punk territory for its catchy, yet edgy, songs. Of course, neither camp knew anything about that future agreement; at the moment they were as divided as the two sides of Kenmore Square.

The buffoons were still trying to cross the streets to kick our asses. Really? They couldn't know it, but the band I had just seen would probably be a regular part of their mental playlist in less than a year. The Cars recorded and mixed its debut album in twenty-one days; it came out in June '78, and by Christmas was heading toward platinum. You could not avoid a Cars song on the radio if you tried, especially in Boston. Maybe Mr. Powder-Blue and his cohorts would even shell out the ten or fifteen bucks to see the band headline a Top 40 radio-station concert at the Boston Garden in December 1978 with John Belushi emceeing the show. Perhaps they'd buy one of the Cars' subsequent six albums in the next ten years, helping to turn each of those into a million-selling milestone. Then, as fans, they'd rue the day that Ric Ocasek decided to leave the Corvette on the curb, his departure ending a storied career that had made the members wealthy stars and the group a respected Boston institution.

But, those guys across the square didn't know any of that yet (and, of course, we didn't either); so even if we were future comrades-in-Cars, right now the lives, or at least the faces, of the punk rockers loitering on the chewing-gum splattered concrete were in immediate danger. Careening traffic kept the invaders at bay for the moment, pumping fists and shouts demonstrating resolve as they waited in frustration for the parade of cars and taxis to diminish. Finally the flow eased and the ragged bunch ran across to the bus station, climbing a low wall to reach a surging wave of automobiles heading the opposite direction on the other side. "Screw you. We're gonna mess you up!" the ringleader shouted; but most of his buddies had already become weary of their mission. With the endless supply of honking vehicles darting by and drivers yelling for the fools to get out of the road, the group turned around and began walking back, one of them calming down Powder-Blue and pulling him along. The posse made it back to disco territory alive, and after one last glare back at us, disappeared up Beacon Street. Who knows, maybe I'd be sitting next to one of them at that Boston Garden show in a year. Hopefully, though, neither of us would be wearing anything close to that blue polyester thing.

CHAPTER 18

DAVID BOWIE

SOUND AND VISION

Boston Garden, May 6, 1978

**Listen to: "Space Oddity," "Rebel Rebel," "Suffragette City," "Fame,"
"Young Americans," "Heroes," "Let's Dance"**

I had moved ninety miles south from the calm seclusion of a one-intersection New Hampshire town into the blur of Boston city life, ostensibly to break into the music business. But, while sitting in bed at night, listening to the railroad cars couple with bangs and screeches in Allston's marshaling yard, I was just thankful that I could keep pace with the rent. I had a minimum-wage record-store job in Harvard Square that barely covered the bills, but most importantly I had scored a volunteer position as a morning DJ at a local radio station. WTBS-FM in Cambridge was so anemically powered that we used to joke there was more wattage in a kitchen toaster than our broadcast signal. But, even with the pitiful transmitter, WTBS still managed to cover most of metro Boston since its antenna perched atop one of the highest buildings on the MIT campus and, indeed, in all of Cambridge. A few of us joined forces to create a morning block of common programming from Monday through Friday called *The Late Riser's Club*, featuring music from the underground punk scene. Since few radio outlets around the country even touched this genre in 1977, *The Late Riser's Club* received a great deal of notoriety.

Despite the support and generous praise from the select scene of Boston punk fans, when I occasionally journeyed back up to New Hampshire to visit, taking the opportunity to spin some Buzzcocks or Ultravox songs on my old college radio station in Henniker, there was a sharp disconnect. "Take that garbage back to Boston," was the message from, well, nearly everyone. Despite its significance in the city, this music remained a relatively obscure urban art form in America and, in most cases, would not reach the mainstream until new wave, punk's younger and less acerbic child, strode boldly into the eighties a couple of years later. The popular rock stars of the period viewed the lurid punk scene with suspicion, most ignoring even the possibility of its influence and potential danger to their careers. Three notable exceptions were Pete Townshend, who appreciated the significance of the Sex Pistols, but worried that they had already rendered the Who obsolete; Bruce Springsteen, who allowed the N.Y.C. punk sounds he experienced to influence the recording of a tougher *Darkness on the Edge of Town* album; and David Bowie, who fled the glitz of his rock-star life in L.A. to guide proto-punk Iggy Pop out of his musical and personal slums. Bowie produced two albums and toured with the younger upstart in 1977, but that proved to be just the beginning for the most famous chameleon in rock, who created and discarded characters as if every day was Halloween: the glam of Ziggy Stardust, the sci-fi Diamond Dog, and the plastic soul of the Thin White Duke.

By 1976, taking his wild mutation as a rock-and-roll star to the extreme, David Bowie had become gaunt, even emaciated, from a regular diet of cocaine, appearing eerily skeletal and nearly vanishing within his ever-fashionable outfits. In a remarkable epiphany, however, he jolted to his senses, crumpling up the destructive lifestyle and tossing it behind him as he fled to Germany and the austerity of a simple apartment, shedding the ego he'd supercharged through five years of steady hit making. In search of a new canvas, Bowie embraced the minimalism of punk and the simplicity of electronic sound, renouncing what made him famous and entering—what rock historians refer to as—his Berlin Period. Along the way he discovered a conceptual travel agent, the creative specialist and musical recluse Brian Eno, who encouraged and abetted Bowie's artistic cravings. The pair crafted *Low*, a not-necessarily vendible combination of funky rock and cool electronics. Critically, the album pleased the music press, but sold disappointingly next to its predecessor *Station to Station* with its global hit "Golden Years." But Bowie remained committed to his fresh sound and vision, collaborating with Eno on a second Berlin album entitled *Heroes*. Similar in layout to *Low*, the album featured songs in a toughened rock stance combined with additional electronic pieces. The jagged overblow in "Beauty and the Beast" and "Joe the Lion," intensified by former (and future) King Crimson guitarist Robert Fripp, had roots in punk, while the title track aimed for a more refined ambient sound and scored respectable American radio play throughout the winter of '77.

By spring, plans were underway for David Bowie to introduce his new, unmasked, persona to the stage. Revealing the Berlin Period musings to a live audience would be challenging, to say the least. How much new music should be presented? Should the tour be scaled down into small halls and aimed at Bowie's core loyalists? Bravely, he decided to pursue the project at the same level established on his previous world tour of 1976, playing 20,000-seat arenas. There were challenges in this: Would Bowie's mainstream crowd tolerate a swing to the left? And how much new material could he get away with playing in those cavernous boxes? For the DJs spinning records on *The Late Riser's Club*, however, any concerns Bowie or his management might have had simply did not apply; both *Low* and *Heroes* were embraced with enthusiasm. Edgier Bowie tracks from the past, like "Queen Bitch," "Width of a Circle," or "Suffragette City" had mixed in well with the street punk we played, but his later and more commercial efforts just hadn't meshed. This Berlin Period music, though, came from a place analogous to our radio shows, agreeing with the darker energy, pugnacity, experimental élan, and commercial ambivalence. David Bowie moved from the periphery of a small, but vibrant, radio happening to being a reliable core artist, and it wasn't long before those two new records began to get scratchy from overuse. When he booked the Boston Garden for a show on May 6, 1978, there was no question that I had to go.

My companion at the concert would be Bruce, a New Hampshire buddy playing with the idea of relocating to Boston, who had journeyed south for a few days to reconnoiter the situation. We'd seen a lot of shows together over the years and he had not yet endorsed the punk bands I was discovering, but Bowie offered a career that appealed to many preferences, so he was in. Bruce offered to drive us downtown in his aging, somewhat-orange–sort-of-yellow Pinto, certainly a luxury to me since I'd been getting around the city on the trolley and subway for a year. We even found an on-street parking space near the Garden, reveling in the good luck as a favorable omen for the show. Just after the houselights faded we squeezed into our seats.

David Bowie strolled out in front of a stage-wide band of white, florescent-tube lights burning brightly into the retinas of those stand-ing on the floor. I felt as if I'd stumbled into a twenty-four-hour conve-nience store at 4:00 a.m. with every detail obscenely lit in a glare meant to discourage shoplifting. As the Boston audience filled the arena with an incredible racket, Bowie smiled, but other than that, barely acknowl-edged the applause while striding to a Chamberlain keyboard perched on a waist-high stand. Taking his place as a band member, he began with the purely electronic instrumental "Warszawa." The show opener was unusual, since most performers typically began a performance by blitzing the audience with one of their biggest hits. But I guess I should have known that Bowie wouldn't pander to the obvious: here was a shape-shifter to rival any, and he would have his show as he wished it. Surprisingly, the crowd quieted down respectfully during the largely unfamiliar six-minute Bowie-Eno collaboration. A stunning version of "Heroes" followed, Bowie's words expressed with seeming desperation as he told the story of sweethearts meeting at the Berlin Wall, kissing under the ugly snout of a guard tower and rusting rolls of barbed wire. Two more new songs followed before "The Jean Genie" dragged the crowd back onto familiar ground. It was a brief respite for those who desired a greatest-hits show since Bowie rolled fearlessly through five new songs in a row after that—some electronic, some propelled by jolts of distorted guitar, before ending the first set with his number-1 smash "Fame."

During the intermission, Bruce and I debriefed. The music from the two recent albums was somewhat unfamiliar, but magnificent in its brave new frame. I admired Bowie for being able to break out of his platinum cage, and yet still impress an arena-sized crowd with something that they couldn't have been expecting. Bowie as an artist had already prevailed, and the show was only half over. When he returned for his second set, he returned as Bowie the showman. As if we were being rewarded for our patience and attention earlier, he put the Ziggy Stardust mask back on for a sextet of hits from that lipstick-covered 1972 tour de force. From the first notes of "Five Years" to the delirious final chord of "Suffragette City," the Garden bounced up and down like a squeaky mattress exercised by two lovers. After the long applause, since he had barely paused between songs, "Art Decade" from *Low* and a cover of "Alabama Song" cooled the room before guitarist Adrian Belew launched into a dramatic solo of shrieks and whistles that announced the approaching locomotive of "Station to Station." Ten minutes later as the magnificently howling epic finally chugged down to a thunderous final chord, Bowie, fully ensconced in his Thin White Duke mask, took a bow and left the stage.

After an encore of "Stay," "TVC 15" and "Rebel Rebel," Bruce and I sat down wearily, sweating as we looked at each other. "Was that as good as I thought it was?" he said. Glancing at all the ecstatic faces around us, I really didn't need to answer, but I did anyway: "I would say, yes!" We trudged out with the crowd, walking through the claustrophobic exit tunnel that angled down back and forth to the street. Outside, the fresh air hit us like a blast of wintergreen, instantly refreshing and invigorating. We found the Pinto, jumped inside, and continued to chatter breathlessly. "How about that guitarist? He was amazing!" "'Beauty and the Beast' from the new album rocked!" "What a band!" Our nonstop exchange persisted as we glided up the entrance ramp onto Route 95 and accelerated northward. "Did you see Roger Powell from Utopia on the keyboards? How cool was that!" "I loved the electronic stuff; I'm going to have to listen to those songs on the albums again." The long drive through the darkness seemed to fly by. "I wish I'd seen him before this; I'll never miss a tour of his again." Across the border and off onto the secondary highway outside Manchester, we entered the darkness of farmlands and woods, broken only occasionally by streetlights.

I looked out the Ford's passenger window, peering contentedly at the blackness outside, when a thought slowly crystallized in my mind. I couldn't believe what I had just realized. "Umm . . . hey Bruce?"

"Yeah."

"You know . . . I hate to tell you this, but . . . I don't live up here anymore!" In our extended Bowie afterglow, we'd completely forgotten that our intended destination had been Allston, within sight of down-town Boston — a ten-minute ride. It was too dark to see his face, but I heard the surprise: "Oh, shit! All my stuff is at your place." I laughed loudly, "Unbelievable! We just drove eighty miles . . . in the wrong direction . . . to the wrong place!" It was true: we were nearly in Hen-niker, the town where we'd spent years going to college and Bruce still lived with a few roommates in a lake house to the north. He started chuckling; he wasn't even mad, just blown away by the absurdity of the moment. "I guess it really was a great show," he joked. "You know, we can turn around and go back. . . ."

"But we're already here."

"Okay. So let's see who's still up!"

CHAPTER 19

RAMONES

"HEY! HO! LET'S GO!"

**Buckley Recital Hall, Amherst, Massachusetts,
October 26, 1978**

**Listen to: "Sheena Is a Punk Rocker," "Rockaway Beach," "Cretin Hop,"
"I Wanna Be Sedated," "Rock 'n' Roll High School"**

THE RAMONES
AMHERST COLLEGE
OCTOBER 26, 1978

WAMH-FM CONCERT GROUP
presents
THE RAMONES
with THE REAL KIDS
Thursday, October 26th, 1978 at 8:30 pm
Buckley Recital Hall
Amherst College
ADMIT ONE $4.50
Doors Open at 8:00 pm

Nº   243

Punk rock showed up in a rusty old Plymouth in New York City and did a "drive-by" on the music scene, the Ramones emptying a machine gun into mainstream rock's swanky hotel bar loaded with the rich and pompous. Sporting uniforms of holed blue jeans and scuffed leather jackets, the band members stumbled on the radical idea of deconstructing songs into two-minute bursts of energy, then assembling them into an album shorter than the average length of an early Beatles concert: thirty-five minutes. I remember working at my college radio station in the spring of '76 when *Ramones* first arrived in a package from Sire Records. The stark black-and-white cover showing the band members standing in front of a graffiti-scarred brick wall appeared in defiant contrast to anything I'd ever seen except for

John Lennon's *Rock 'n' Roll* album from a year earlier with its photo of the pre-fame former Beatle in leather jacket loitering on a street in Hamburg. The comparison didn't stop with the cover either: Lennon had gone searching for his musical roots on that release, stripping away everything that had resulted from a decade of Beatles evolution, finding new inspiration in the 1950s hit singles of his adolescence. The players in the Ramones had embarked on a similar mission, stripping away the pretenses and excesses of the seventies music scene to replace it with just an essence. If people accused the group of being simplistic in its approach, well, that was exactly the idea! The members worked within their limited performance strengths to generate a singular and powerful preamble to rock's changing times.

I didn't get any of that, though, at least at first. Up in the wilderness of New Hampshire, I hadn't heard anything about the subterranean currents of energy coursing through the basements of New York City then climbing onstage at CBGB. *Ramones* featured fourteen songs — seven a side, unusual for a vinyl album with its limited space for sound information; but with a total duration of the music being only twenty-nine minutes, the grooves held plenty of room to spare. I dropped the needle onto song after song, hearing a similar chainsaw of sound screaming from each. Shaking my head, I placed the record into the new-release bin in the studio and washed my hands of it. None of the other DJs reached for *Ramones* either, and I'm certain that the vinyl remained unblemished for years without so much as a fingerprint or crackle ever scarring it. But once I'd gotten into Boston, becoming absorbed in the music of the local rock scene stirred by the shock waves of New York punk, I began to understand and respect the twenty-nine minutes of cacophony that I'd previously ignored. By then, Ramones had released two more albums, *Leave Home* and *Rocket to Russia*, the last featuring most of the songs and harmonies that would grab local radio play and gain the band an early following: "Rockaway Beach," "Sheena Is a Punk Rocker," "Teenage Lobotomy," and the covers of two sixties hits "Do You Wanna Dance?" and "Surfin' Bird." Instead of some high-speed metallic joke I couldn't understand, now I accepted this new band and their sound, something I likened to the Beach Boys on amphetamines.

But, I'd never seen the Ramones in concert, and it seemed that all my newfound punk friends hanging out at the Rat in Kenmore Square night after night had. I did spend a lot of time seeing the Real Kids, what some referred to as Boston's answer to the Ramones. That group released one of the best albums to ever come out of the scene, a 1977 eponymously titled album on Red Star Records. "All Kinds of Girls" became the local hit, but I lived for the album closer, "Reggae, Reggae," which at five-minutes lasted an eternity when measured on a punk-rock timescale. If the Kids played the track live, the challenge for the audience was in managing to pogo up and down relentlessly for the entire song, the only respite being a false end about three-quarters through. The guys in the Real Kids knew Joey, Johnny, Dee Dee, and Tommy Ramone well, sharing concert bills with their New York City neighbors in what I considered a perfect rock-and-roll matchup. Linda and Joanne, a couple of my friends who would always go the length of "Reggae, Reggae" on the dance floor, mentioned that there was a show coming up that actually featured my Ramones/Real Kids dream bill. The problem lay in the concert's location, two hours away in the western part of the state at Amherst College. However, one of the girls managed to conjure up a ride, and there was room for one more. Even better, as friends of the Real Kids, the band put us on their guest list. Now the show fit my budget!

It seemed odd to head out on a road trip with my punk friends; after all, as vampires roaming the streets of the city after dark and gathering together in black covens to commune nightly with the true spirits of rock, we'd surely perish if caught out in the light of day away from our "native soil." Even so, we managed to survive our expedition away from the safety of Kenmore Square well enough, driving west through a rural beauty of fading fall colors that I had so recently been well acquainted with. Amherst College seemed as similar in isolation and calm as my own alma mater in New Hampshire, with students walking in small groups about the broad lawns surrounding both colonial-style and modern brick buildings. As we steered onto the quiet campus, a hush descended in the car as if we had to keep our voices down to not disturb the students walking by, lost in their academic ponderings. Then I laughed, "The Ramones are playing here in a couple of hours—why are we being quiet!" That was true: it felt as if a flight of B-52s had taken off from some faraway airbase hours before and were now approaching the vicinity of their unsuspecting target, about to unload a carpet of bombs that would pulverize this entire campus. Instead of being silent, we should be screaming at the kids hauling their loads of books to the next class or back to the dorms: "Run while you can! Ramones are going to destroy this entire area! Save yourselves!" But no, the incongruity of a pastoral campus versus the imminent punk blitzkrieg only grew wider and weirder as we got closer to Buckley Recital Hall, an acoustically refined theater usually reserved for far more elegant events. Kudos had to go to WAMH-FM, the college radio station that sponsored the event and managed to get it approved by Amherst's administrators. It might be a bit intense for the room, but it *would* be educational!

We entered the hall with the earliest arrivals and swooped down along the softly angled slope of comfortable-looking seats to the front row. I looked around, gauging the place to have room for 500 or so, and by the time the Real Kids took the stage at 8:30, the place had filled up impressively. My preconceptions about the docile nature of this college crowd soon proved mistaken, as the small area between us and the stage filled with kids bouncing up and down, even during our friends' warm-up set. We'd have some time to say hello and thank the guys before the Ramones got onstage, so with just a line of explanation to a student ostensibly posted for security reasons, we slipped through a side entrance to backstage. Passing by an area with dozens of music stands awaiting the next classical program or stage production, we found John Felice and his Real Kids mates working off their adrenalin chattering excitedly with the four Ramones who were spooling up for the intensity of their coming set.

We were welcomed into the mix (always happens when in the company of a couple of ladies), talking with everybody before, at some point, I made off for a bathroom. Directed to the door, I pulled on it, apparently just as a figure behind had reached to twist the doorknob and push from his side. The panel flew open and the person tumbled out in a heap in front of me, right on his face! My God: it was Joey Ramone, all six-plus feet of him! The lanky lead singer got up without a word, replaced his glasses and mumbled something unintelligible before shuffling away even as I offered an apology to his disappearing back. Nice going, I berated myself. Way to make a good impression! I was horrified; and rather than go back to the staging room in embarrassment, I returned to the hall itself and regained my position up front.

When the lights went down and the Ramones appeared, the group hurtled into a nonstop blast of sound and relentless rhythm for just under an hour, still managing to hit twenty-five songs! Joey had lost all vestiges of awkwardness as he delivered the band's comic book impressions of punk, pinheads, brain surgery, shock treatment, love, beaches, sun, and Nazi thugs. Pauses between songs were measured in milliseconds. "Blitzkrieg Bop" brought on the "Hey! Ho! Let's Go!" chant, stirring even the most reluctant to join in on "generating steam heat." Up and down, we bounced crazily along to "Cretin Hop," and "Rockaway Beach"—the band keeping it hopping while we "chewed that bubble gum to the rhythm of the beat"—and "Pinhead," a self-effacing ditty uniting the room in cries of "Gabba Gabba Hey!"

Johnny Ramone stood up there in his rock-steady sawhorse stance pounding out the bombardment of guitar chords with an impregnable web of bass and drums shoring up the bottom. The elated sound blast made a ruinous mockery of the acoustic panels hanging on the walls; their critical role in accurately conveying the warm tones of a cello were not required on this night! Like a 110-decibel vacuum cleaner, the Ramones sucked all the pretension out of the room, sending Yes, Emerson, Lake & Palmer, Queen, and all the other dust bunnies into a collection bag while the punks put rock and roll back in its rightful place. Joey Ramone might not have been the most graceful and assured figure on- or offstage, and come to think of it, neither was I in my daily walk; but together as singer and fan, we made the music mighty once again. "Gabba Gabba Hey!"

CHAPTER 20

THE POLICE

"THERE SHOULD BE MORE DANCING!"

The Rat, Boston, October 26, 1978

Listen to: "Roxanne," "Can't Stand Losing You," "Message in a Bottle," "When the World Is Running Down," "Spirits in the Material World," "Every Breath You Take"

The room reeked of the fifties, with equipment held over from the Eisenhower administration and a stubborn layer of Korean War–era dust in the places the cleaning people couldn't, or didn't want to, reach. Despite the rising temperature of another late August day, the heating system in the basement of the Walker Memorial Building, a venerable concrete-and-steel warhorse on MIT's campus, hadn't gone on summer break like most of the student population. The hot, dry air surging out of the dirty vents ensured the arid conditions helpful in maintaining the school's midcentury broadcasting equipment, but it also sucked all the moisture and life out of anyone who had to work down there. Tucked away like an afterthought, the college's noncommercial radio station, WTBS-FM, was, nonetheless, beloved by those who ventured into its Saharan environment to man the control boards and broadcast a variety of music and talk shows. In 1978, weekday mornings featured a block of punk-rock and new-wave programming called *The Late Riser's Club*. I stood in the tiny control room with fellow "Riser" Dave Wohlman, a veteran of the station who had trained me a couple of years earlier with an album in one hand and a hash pipe in the other. On this occasion, we were changing shifts, Dave finishing up and my show about to start.

For a program based on the latest punk and early new-wave music trends, we both studied England's prime music weekly the *New Musical Express*, then visited a couple of favorite local record stores to locate the freshest vinyl. One of those discoveries had been the Police, a trio out of England with its import single "Roxanne," which we'd featured earlier in the spring. The promising track, though, hadn't gotten too far on the English charts after the BBC balked at playing a tune written about a prostitute. But now the band's next seven-inch single, "Can't Stand Losing You," had jumped off to a great start; everyone liked the catchy melody with its campy suicide-threat theme and high-pitched vocals from a guy named Sting. Dave turned on the microphone: "We've been playing this new single from the Police so much," he intoned on the air, "why don't we flip the record over and hear what the other side sounds like?" Turning around and eying me, he remarked, "Have you heard this one, Carter? It's called 'Dead End Job.'"

"Not yet." I yelled from five feet away, so as to be heard clearly on the air.

"All right then, let's go." Dave thumbed on the turntable and flicked off the mic. From the first drumbeat, the song rocked out at breakneck speed. "I don't want no dead-end job, I don't wanna be no number!" Sting yelled while another voice (which I later learned was the guitarist Andy Summers) read some newspaper want ads in the background. Dave turned the studio volume down and got his stuff out of the way while I moved in with my records and notes, all very routine as we made small talk. Taking my position in front of the control board, I turned up the volume again to hear Sting yelling his (un)employment mantra in long, repeating monotones, "I don't want no dead-end job, I don't want no dead-end job." Then suddenly, out of the driving rhythm and musical chaos, bright and clear as day: "Stuff your FUCKIN' dead end job . . . !" Dave and I stared at each other, shocked. I was about to say something, when four seconds later, Sting added a delightful coda to his sentence: " . . . CUNTS!"

I couldn't fade the career-ending song down fast enough, then segued directly into another selection. Although the FCC at this time maintained a lax posture on obscenity standards, MIT held a higher standard. The conservative station management had allowed the punk-rock shows to exist, but didn't necessarily enjoy hosting an underground scene stereotyped as a bunch of black-jacketed zombies wearing safety pins in their ears and pogoing endlessly till dawn. As such, we were determined to be on our best behavior. "We're screwed, man," Dave moaned. "If anybody heard that . . ."

"No man," I replied, exerting damage control with a smile, "You're screwed! That was on your show." He wore a sheepish grin while complaining, "Yeah, but you helped!"

But, nothing happened. No one on the WTBS board of directors heard the expletives or learned about the incident, and why would they? Our audience of rockers and punks never complained; for them, the edgier the music sounded and the grittier the attitude, the better. That's why the ascent of the Police seemed so incongruous. As the band's early singles began to gain traction, we learned more about this trio, finding out that they were recognized talents on their instruments. Summers had even played guitar for a later lineup up of the distinctly *old-wave* band the Animals. So, there was no learn-as-you-go bashing about on stage for these guys—they knew what they were doing. Plus, in a definite credibility spoiler, they'd dyed their coifs blonde, not as a small symbol in defiance to the Queen or such, but merely to imitate a punk band in a Wrigley's Gum TV commercial! The punks had every reason to label these three as poseurs and then move on, but somehow things were working out for the Police. "Can't Stand Losing You," gained enough chart action to lead to an album deal, with the debut *Outlandos d'Amour* released in England just as the band touched down in America for its first U.S. tour.

Playing America at this point seemed to be the most bizarre idea of all. Why would a group that hadn't released any music in the States come here to play? With only a handful of minor U.K. singles to the band's credit, how many Americans would even be aware of the Police, then go out and see a concert? There was also the annoying issue of how to pay for the ballsy endeavor throughout the eastern United States. Stewart Copeland, the drummer and third member of the band had two brothers: Miles, who essentially managed the Police for free at this point, and Ian, a booking agent who waived his fees to place the group in a three-week club tour that began in New York City at CBGB, journeyed as far west as Toronto, then returned to the Big Apple for two final gigs at CBGB. The group traveled from London on Freddie Laker's Skytrain, a new budget shuttle service, wrestling their instruments onto the plane as carry-on luggage. I always wondered if Stewart Copeland, cradling a drum or two in his limited personal space, had to plead with the person in front of him not to place his seat back in the resting position and right through a snare. Traveling in a beat-up van, the trio gleaned enough in meager profits from the series of low-paying club gigs to finance the ongoing tour and save just enough for a flight home. The Police performed ten shows in a row at one point to avoid any downtime, and it was during this particular marathon that the band visited Boston for four nights to play the Rat, the city's premier punk rock club.

Stepping down the sticky stairs and around the corner into the low basement, I could see the Reds, a recent major-label-signed quartet from Philadelphia working onstage. Moderately filling the club and modestly interested in the warm-up group, people in the audience mostly socialized. There was a definite buzz on about the Police, passed on by friends who had gone to one or more of the first three nights. Some, mightily impressed, had returned to this final Sunday night performance. Locally, "Roxanne" had rebounded; although the BBC gave the song a bad rap and tried to bury it, Boston radio now embraced the reggae-flavored track, drawing more of the curious into the club. I guess I hadn't prioritized seeing the Police, having waited until the last show, but I soon realized my folly. The three members walked on and plugged in unceremoniously, slamming into a punk-paced "Fall Out" to start the proceedings. Nobody had the album yet, so nearly all the material was unknown. It didn't matter; the band skillfully played tight and economical full-bore rock and roll on the opener, drawing people closer to the stage. The ladies noted in particular, that the three band members were quite easy on the eyes, certainly that cute lead singer, a blonde Adonis in the flesh.

Punk-rock introduction complete, the group dropped into "Hole in My Life," a cleverly syncopated stop-and-start beat revealing more musical sophistication than merely replicating a pounding jackhammer in three chords. "Roxanne," the hit, was next. Sting would opine this song to be a tango, but it sure sounded like reggae to me. Skanking Jamaica-style on the dance floor was always a lot easier than bouncing wildly up and down for forty minutes, so my friend Joanne and I got out there. Since the band barely had enough material to fill out a typical contract-satisfying set, the trio wound this one out to four or five times its original studio-version length. We moved easily along with the beat, but danced for a *long* time as they broke down the music and Sting vamped on the lyrics. Spying us down front, he announced, "There should be more dancing!" In what would become familiar in the future as a typical cockiness (some would even say arrogance), Sting's blatant ordering of the crowd to action actually worked. People shrugged off their reticence, leaned into the music and got involved. In less than a dozen songs, the band owned the room. Everyone was moving, even the bartenders, as the back-to-back speed demons, "Next to You" and "Dead End Job," sealed the deal.

The Police had everything: the looks, the moves, the songs, and the drive. As the three of them stepped off the stage leaving sweaty, delirious applause in their wake while huddling to consider what they had left to play as an encore, I thought about how this unknown band had just accelerated to cruising speed in the space of one brief concert and one short tour. Now, the wisdom of the Police's seemingly reckless guerilla visit to America seemed clear. The members had a confidence in their own live abilities as a group that proved potently accurate, swelling the ranks of their tiny following, but also energizing the U.S. arm of the band's record label to rush-release "Roxanne" as a single. The song quickly became an American hit (no thanks to the BBC), prompting a similar stateside appearance of a debut album in the spring of '79. Three albums would follow, roughly one a year, each selling more than the previous one, as the Police became world contenders and musical tastemakers. *Ghost in the Machine* in 1981 moved an impressive 3 million copies in the United States, setting up the worldwide blockbuster *Synchronicity* and its decade-defining hit single "Every Breath You Take," which completely dominated the summer of 1983. The Police became global stars, filling the largest venues possible—70,000-seat domes reserved for the NFL and going on to sell 75 million albums around the world. The band would splinter apart at the apex of this success, launching the enduring solo career of lead singer Sting, and leaving legions of fans bemoaning the group's sudden demise. But the trio would leave a permanent legacy as one of the world's biggest-selling and most influential rock and pop bands ever. On an October night in 1978, it was all just beginning: the group blasted out of that Boston basement and was now in hot pursuit of its future stadium-filling glory. To anyone who was at the Rat on any of those four nights it was quite obvious that the Police really had stuffed their [*censored*] dead end job!

CHAPTER 21

THE CLASH

"I'M SO BORED WITH THE U.S.A."

Harvard Square Theater, Cambridge, Massachusetts, February 16, 1979

Listen to: "I'm So Bored with the U.S.A.," "London Calling," "Washington Bullets," "Charlie Don't Surf," "Rock the Casbah"

Suppose we borrowed Dr. Who's Tardis and traveled back to 1979 to look around, maybe buy some ridiculously inexpensive concert tickets to a historic show or two, then bring back a couple of eight-tracks just to prove to the kids that the bulky plastic things really existed. Somehow in our haste to leave the past, however, an iPod bounced out of our time machine just as we shimmered out of that existence and flashed back to the future (oh, yeah, a power cord fell out too, or else my scenario wouldn't last more than a couple of days). Within moments, a leather-jacketed punk with spiked orange hair rounded the corner and discovered the great-great-great-great-grandson of his Walkman lying on the sidewalk. If it was possible for him to take the iPod home and input data from a record, cassette, or even an eight-track tape, into the device, what sort of playlist do you think he'd come up with? Well, it would depend a lot on where this transfer took place, because in 1979, the sweeping universality of the Internet hadn't been dreamed of yet. Even MTV stood two years away from spreading the leading-edge culture growing in America's cities to the vast wildernesses surrounding them. New music bands that arrived from England or worked their way up in Boston, Los Angeles, or New York might have swaggered about the city streets basking in the glow of another sellout or local smash hit, but go completely unrecognized just a hundred miles away. But some bands did manage to climb above provincial barriers, reaching ears across the nation and also overseas. Which of these would our young punk "download?"

Guaranteed he'd have at least a few Ramones songs in that list; after all, that band had provoked so much of the initial fuss as far back as 1975 with its machine-gun bursts of two-minute songs. Blondie, Television, the Dead Boys, DMZ, and Patti Smith would add some domestic muscle, and even mainstream crossover groups like the Cars and Tom Petty and the Heartbreakers should make the grade. As far as international selections, the Sex Pistols' "God Save the Queen" and "Pretty Vacant" would be required listening for any self-respecting punk. Even though that seminal bunch of rock-and-roll losers had broken up two years earlier, the group had dynamited open the door to England's charts with its caustic and perfectly offensive *Never Mind the Bollocks, Here's the Sex Pistols*. If the kid were like me at the time, he'd also have added some Adverts, Buzzcocks, Undertones, Damned, and Stiff Little Fingers to the mix, plus the most important of them all, the Clash.

While American bands spewed punk as a cultural statement, declaring their independence by spitting on a recent glut of music that had grown ponderous and conceited, in England the stakes were higher: there the punks openly rebelled against the political system, advertising discontent by taking to the streets and giving poshes the boot. When the Pistols lost their shelf life in just a year, the Clash inherited the hill because of their unbridled commitment to the power of the songs, jamming pointed social messages into intense three-minute anthems. That energy, sparked by outrage at the English government, violence in the streets of London, and European economic disaster, resulted in a bevy of the best singles of the period: "White Riot," "Remote Control," "Complete Control" and "(White Man) In Hammersmith Palais." Such was the devotion of the band to its ideals that many considered it to be the best damn group on the planet, or even rock and roll's last hope. CBS Records failed to grasp any of that; when the first Clash album came out in England in '77, the label didn't even release it in the States. Nevertheless, New England fans kept marching down to enlightened record emporiums, snapping up every overseas copy of the album that came into town. Eventually, enormous import sales of the U.K. record would prompt a domestic release (with some track changes), but it didn't happen until two years later.

In the meantime, the Clash's second album, *Give 'Em Enough Rope*, came out in England and America in November 1978, becoming, technically, the group's debut in the United States. To support that album, the Clash—Joe Strummer on snarling vocals and rhythm guitar, lead guitarist and singer Mick Jones, Paul Simonon on bass, and drummer Topper Headon—planned to make their first foray across the Atlantic in February. The announcement of the band's brief Pearl Harbor Tour sparked near hysteria in the Boston punk scene as a date at the Harvard Square Theater was announced. To those who cared, this was as close to the ethos of London street rock as they might ever get, like experiencing John Lee Hooker in person to divine the essence of the blues or John Coltrane to understand bebop. The Sex Pistols, a designer hand grenade on suicide watch, had inevitably exploded, but the Clash stood on active duty as "the only band that mattered," to quote a phrase constructed by their record label but quickly adopted as cultural currency. The Harvard Square Theater's 1,800 tickets sold out in an hour.

Great efforts were expended to be one of the lucky ones to snag a seat, and everyone, to a person, buzzed with anticipation while filing into the old movie house that cold night. I stood excitedly at my seat near the front and could recognize or knew just about everyone in the audience from hanging out at the city's rock-and-roll clubs. It seemed like the entire scene had made it; in fact, if the roof had fallen in, punk rock in Boston might have collapsed with it! Fascinated by American R & B like many English musicians, the Clash had invited legendary Chicago bluesman Bo Diddley out on the road with them to precede the headliners at each concert. But, the group also stipulated that the first band to go on in each city would be a local outfit, hopefully with at least one female in the lineup. The honor in Cambridge went to the Rentals, who'd scored some notoriety in the area with its single "Gertrude Stein." Admittedly, anticipation for the Clash made it hard to concentrate on the opening set from our friends, but everyone remained polite and supportive. After the briefest of equipment changes, Bo Diddley's thumping jams built around a soulful overblow on his trademark box-shaped guitar fared much better. But clearly, the expectancy of the coming event dampened reaction for the legend.

The Clash's backdrop, a huge curtain quilt of international flags with the words Unprovoked Retaliation stenciled in one of the squares could be seen at the back. To the uninitiated, a hint of the band's political concerns or the power of the music could be construed here; I read both. The electrical current of excitement sparking through the theater grew as the minutes dragged on after Diddley's set. This was it—the epicenter! There was no better place to be and everyone knew it. Your house might be burning down and you still would make excuses to the fire inspector: "I'm sorry. I'll be there in an hour and a half." This was a moment to confirm all the change that punk promised: a firebomb to level the landscape, but also raise up a new and better structure. Like the hippies, we were out to change the world, and the Clash would show us how to do it. Of course, it was wrong to saddle any band with that mantle of responsibility, but that didn't stop anyone from attempting it. I wandered from my chair and into the lobby where I was astonished to run right into—Joe Strummer? Folks were streaming past on their way to cokes, popcorn, and a bathroom as he voiced his fears about the sound quality of the theater to a tiny group of fans that had recognized and surrounded the singer. He'd been all over the theater, even upstairs in the balcony, disturbed that the acoustics sounded like mush up there. As Strummer returned toward the stage door, I headed to my seat, impressed that the singer cared enough to check things out for himself, and obviously had no qualms about mixing with the local natives.

Lights down! No shit. This was it! Everybody shot to their feet, and they'd stay that way all night. The Clash swung into position onstage,

Mick Jones bludgeoning the opening chords to "I'm So Bored with the U.S.A." Of course they would start with that! Strummer marched out to the lip of the stage with his guitar gripped in Tommy gun stance, the bass and drums kicked in, and the first of twenty songs began racing by in a blur, like a train flashing past a crossing. Jones, in blue tunic, galloped about and around Strummer, constantly moving and only slowing briefly to spit harmonies into his mic. Dressed in Johnny Cash black, Simonon with his bass in a death grip rarely rooted himself in one spot for more than a few seconds. Unfortunately, Strummer's fears about the challenging acoustics of the place proved to be correct: it was nearly impossible to discern the words to many of the poignant manifestos he spit out. But his sheer intensity and concentration, plus laser-like glares directly into the faces of those up front or dramatic expressions and poses illustrating moments in the lyrics created a figure I couldn't rip my eyes from. Even if the words were mush, we knew them all from the records, so the power of the performance still reinforced those messages. Into "Guns on the Roof" and the hard core up front were already sweating bullets. While punk rock was all about energy and meaning, not necessarily proficiency, this band could play! The members of the Clash were tight as hell up there, playing the loudest, most aggressive rock on the planet. A garage band from garage land; they'd spent their rehearsal time well.

"We didn't get time for a sound check and the hall sounded horrible," Headon complained afterward. "We'd rather play in a smaller place for the few hundred vibrant people who got off." The Clash, however, would never be able to fit into a smaller box again; and why should they? Clearly the members wanted to spread what they saw as truth, so even if fame (and everything that goes with it) seemed to be a career oxymoron for the Clash, the band was heading inexorably in that direction. The drummer's assessment, honorable as it was, limited his group, whose star burned so brightly by this point that mere technicalities like a room's poor acoustics didn't even register. The Clash transported everyone in the theater that night, confirming that the members did, indeed, give a shit about the crap condition of the world and were out there trying to say something about it — certainly a braver aspiration than what most groups attempted. The Clash would not live long, only another three years in its present and relevant form, but the groundbreaking and epochal *London Calling* glimmered only nine months down the road at this point with even more glories to arrive after that. Strummer, Jones, Simonon, and Headon would eventually collapse into dispute and implode like so many others. But for a short time, they tried to save the world, and best of all, inspired us to try to change it as well.

CHAPTER 22

JOHN COUGAR & THE ZONE

AN INTERESTING TABLE GUEST

Paradise Theater, Boston, August 18, 1979

Listen to: "I Need a Lover," "Jack & Diane," "Pink Houses," "Cherry Bomb," "Authority Song," "Wild Night"

I got my first big break in radio in June 1979, when I was hired at WBCN-FM to be a weekend DJ. At the time I was, arguably, still learning how to do it. Perched on top of the Prudential Tower with the streets of Boston stretched out below, the station had been a fixture in the city for over a decade, playing rock music and sponsoring new talent as it arrived on the scene. That's how my path crossed with an unknown singer-songwriter out of Seymour, Indiana, named John Cougar. These were early days for both of us; soon he'd dump the despised "Cougar" moniker foisted on him by an early manager, and begin using the Mellencamp surname under which he'd eventually enter the Rock and Roll Hall of Fame, collecting enough gold and platinum to sink a Lake Michigan ferry along the way. Raised in Indiana's open farm country, he'd had more time and space than any city kid to ponder life and pen lyrics about his bucolic existence. Those emotions went into hits like his first Top 40 entry "I Need a Lover," his first number 1, "Jack & Diane," "Hurts So Good," "Lonely Ol' Night" and "Cherry Bomb." A socially active spirit bred from growing up in a place where neighbor counted on neighbor led to edgier "message" songs such as "The Great Midwest," "Pink Houses," "Small Town," "Rain on the Scarecrow," and "The Face of the Nation." Eschewing both coasts and even Chicago, Mellencamp would continue to live in his beloved Indiana, pouring out his observations and concerns, renewed every time he headed back into the cornfields after a long concert tour. From that place came his founding involvement and continuing commitment to Farm-Aid, as well as so many other social causes and benefits. Four decades later, the successful pop star of the past would mature into one of America's true musical folklorists, taking a weather-beaten guitar and a headful of songs into the select circle including Guthrie, Dylan, Baez, Cash, Leadbelly, and Springsteen.

But in the summer of 1979, John Cougar was just an unknown singer-songwriter slogging it out on a small-club tour of the United States with his road band the Zone. The twenty-seven-year-old had already lost one record deal on MCA, but released an overseas album that found Australian chart success with the single "I Need a Lover." That small flame kindled enough interest for Cougar to secure a new U.S. label contract and generate a self-titled album of fresh material, with his previous Down Under hit added in hopes of sparking excitement (and sales) in his native land. The tour worked its way east; John Cougar was slated to perform his Boston concert debut at the Paradise Theater on August 18 with a live broadcast of the event scheduled on WBCN. With most of the full-time DJs enjoying their summer vacations, my boss volunteered me, the brand-new guy, to MC the show before I'd head downtown later for my midnight radio shift. I was happy to do it, even eager, as the record label had brought Cougar to town earlier in the year for a promotional visit, and I'd been blown away by the singer's extreme focus and sparkplug energy. The *John Cougar* album featured lots of inspired songwriting, especially the single and my favorite, "Small Paradise," with its familiar "you can never go home again" theme. Listeners seemed to agree: requests for "I Need a Lover" trickled in, and then redoubled as the date for the show approached.

A special low ticket price and generous radio plugs about the broadcast gave John Cougar & the Zone a full enough house and some great response to work with. I could tell as I did my introduction, seeing people crowded into most areas of the room and noting the explosion of applause as I brought the band on. The two-year-old Paradise was more of a club than a theater, its layout a long rectangle with the stage in the middle of one of the long sides. Although it would later become known as a general-admission venue, at this early stage there were still tables bolted to the floor with assigned seating around each. I made my way offstage and through an unseen labyrinth to return to the room, where Cougar had urged, "Everybody put on their seatbelts, okay?" before hurtling directly into his album's opener, "A Little Night Dancin.'" The radio station had one round cocktail table set aside in the front row, where my producer Clint and another buddy stood as I joined them. The infectious rhythm and distinctive guitar melody (which I still can't get out of my head as I write about it thirty-six years later) had everyone up hooting and hollering, with a natural boost from being live on the radio enhancing the excitement. The singer and his band, some of them friends in Indiana for years, had been on the road for a few weeks and radiated an easy affinity and confidence onstage. The show had been minutely thought out: scarcely a second passed before Cougar led the group into "Sugar Marie" followed by a rehearsed segue to "American Dream." A lot of people sat down at this point and we were faced with the question that always arises to anyone lucky enough to be up front at a concert: do you stand your ground and cheer the group on or sit your ass down to give the folks behind you a better view? We chose the former, but after just a few bars, some supersonic ice cubes bounced off the back of my head, hastening my decision to give in and let those people have that better view. No respect for the MC? I guess not.

John Cougar, the bandleader, whirled about like the Tasmanian Devil cartoon, dancing continually around his players, flailing arms and hands dispensing cues and setting the tempos. When the band's pace

laid back a bit, he'd speak breathlessly to the crowd, seemingly close
to losing his voice or even passing out. But, each time a song resumed
in full flight, he'd launch back into the lyrics with a renewed burst of
energy, as if a small nuclear reactor blazed hotly within that wiry five-
foot-eight-inch frame. I briefly entertained the thought that Cougar
might be self-medicated, but quickly dropped that speculation; despite
his winded bullet-speed chatter, the singer's voice never faltered, and
he spun out his lyrics with a clarity that required his complete attention. There was a lucidity there that I'd rarely seen onstage, perhaps
only matched by Neil Young, David Bowie, or Mick Jagger (I would
add Springsteen, but I hadn't seen him yet). Cougar continued his five-
mile jog onstage by leading the Zone into an eleven-minute medley
showcasing a couple of unreleased songs and the disco-esque "Miami,"
which would go on to become his second big hit in Australia. Nobody
seemed to be sitting down at this point, so without the risk of losing an
eye to some more ice, I leapt to my feet as "I Need a Lover" united the
house in a loud sing-along.

The music had continued uninterrupted for thirty-five minutes before the musicians finally allowed themselves a moment, although the
break lasted barely long enough to toss back a swig of water. Then they
bounded into the second, more wanton part of the concert. Cougar's
next selection, "Dream Killing Town," introduced a half-hour medley
of originals fleshed out into a jam including Eddie Cochran's "Nervous Breakdown," "Summertime Blues," "Honky Tonk Women," and
a goofy snippet of the summer's Top 40 rock rage, "My Sharona." This
wasn't the enhanced, more studied, "Americana" approach of a future
tour like 1987's *The Lonesome Jubilee*, with its roster of accomplished
sidemen including a fiddle player, accordion, banjo, and a percussionist.
No, Cougar had provoked a raw and sweaty rock-and-roll bender in the
Paradise with the spirit of Jerry Lee Lewis riding shotgun until perspi-
ration poured in torrents off of everybody in the club. Somewhere along
the way, the singer ended up on Mike Wanchic's shoulders, riding the
guitarist around the stage with his head narrowly missing the dangling
stage lights as the crowd howled. They closed the set with a cover of
the suitably hilarious "You Just Like Me 'Cos I'm Good in Bed" by the

Australian group Skyhooks. Cougar jumped off the front of the stage, microphone in hand and cable tailing off like a black king snake over the stage monitors. Stalking back and forth in front of the crowd, he spied an empty seat at our radio station table and dove into it, lounging in the chair as figures pushed in tightly around us. There was no air left to breathe as Cougar sang while eyeing the three of us across the tabletop as if we were playing poker and he held all four aces. He had the triumphant look of a man completely in control as he held swift counsel, then whirled away with a smile. That was the end of the set; delirious applause followed the musicians as they ran into the shadows and toweled off all that Midwestern sweat.

The tumult in the Paradise never slackened, so there was no question of drawing the band back onstage. Since no one had seen John Cougar & the Zone before this (unless there was actually a fanatic who, even at this early stage, had incessantly tailed the band across the country), everyone had become a brand-new fan, converted by the tremendous songs and a ridiculously tight and entertaining live show. Cougar thanked the crowd before the group eased into a stately encore of "Small Paradise" and quick reprises on "I Need a Lover" before degenerating wonderfully into a rollicking "Roadhouse Blues" and the irreverent, drunken-sounding, fifties lost-classic "Plastic Jesus" to end the night.

I had to get moving or I'd be late for my radio shift, so I hustled backstage before the crush of well-wishers and congratulated the still-sopping musicians. When Cougar appeared, I decided to be polite and invite him to come by the station after midnight. Of course he'd turn me down: the band probably had an overnight bus ride to some East Coast city to look forward to. He said as much, surely not knowing his own schedule (most touring musicians never do, relying completely on their road managers to get them where they need to go). I caught a trolley, got on the radio, and settled into the pace that would get me through till six in the morning. After enthusing early about the broadcast, I completely forgot about my invitation until the hotline in the studio intruded at 1:00 a.m. "There's a John Cougar here to see you," said the stern voice at the security desk downstairs. Really? Oh yeah—I remembered that

I invited him now. "Send him up." When the Tasmanian Devil arrived, he was still operating on stun, his fast-paced sentences peppering my laid-back responses. But it was okay; the "kid" from Indiana remained entirely respectful. I asked him why he stayed in farm country. Why not hasten his career by moving to L.A. or New York City? "I shoot pool and I ride motorcycles and nobody cares that I make records. I can be a human being there." With that, Cougar confirmed that he craved his music far more than rock stardom, setting the stage for artistic permanence rather than pop-culture instability. It's impossible to listen to *John Cougar* all these years later and not hear the talent percolating up from those songs. Plus, the John Mellencamp who later filled arenas with his tightly arranged shows and spectacular musicianship had his stagecraft completely together, even at this earliest phase. If you were at the Paradise on August 18, 1979, or anywhere else on that tour, you just knew that nothing was going to hold this guy back.

CHAPTER 23

TOM PETTY AND THE HEARTBREAKERS

EVEN THE LOSERS GET LUCKY (THIRD TIME)

Orpheum Theater, Boston, November 19, 1979

Listen to: "Refugee," "American Girl," "I Need to Know," "Running Down a Dream"

My buddy Clint and I waited for an inbound trolley, staring hopefully down the empty rails divided by crushed stone, wooden ties, and pizza joint litter. Fragments of glass glittered in the bright streetlight glare of a cold November night that forced us to shuffle about to keep warm. A Green Line train, if it ever came, would take us down the center of Commonwealth Avenue past the classrooms at Boston University, then plunge under Kenmore Square where we had witnessed many a punk-rock show at the already-legendary Rat. Heading downtown under the streets of Back Bay, we'd exit at Park Street, walk upstairs, and pop out in front of the Orpheum Theater, where the marquee tonight read Tom Petty and the

Heartbreakers. Of course, we were excited; the Gainesville native who had journeyed to Los Angeles to find fame and fortune in rock and roll had reached a high-speed career trajectory after punching through with his debut album a couple of years earlier. "Breakdown" from that release had been the initial American hit, and the meteoric, under-three-minute, scorcher, "I Need to Know" from a solid second album in '78 continued the upward thrust.

Right across the street from the trolley stop we were stomping around on stood the Paradise Theater, where Petty and his band had played an epic sold-out gig the previous July that aired on Boston radio powerhouse WBCN. Those that managed to get tickets were already believers, but the broadcast convinced thousands more who couldn't get in that this white-hot group was on to something—a fresh reboot of rock and roll straight out of a stack of Elvis Presley, Chuck Berry, and Buddy Holly 45s. I thought about how amazing that concert had been, so mind-blowing that I had never regretted laying out the extra cash for a scalper's ticket; in fact, I wish I could find that scruffy street capitalist and give him a big hug. Petty's band, especially right-hand man Mike Campbell on guitar, had stuck to their leader like glue, elevating his every move and forcing a worthy comparison to nothing less than the gold standard of Bruce Springsteen and the E Street Band.

A distant squeal of metal on metal whisked me back from a year and a half ago as an ancient trolley made the corner down the street and rumbled drunkenly toward us. The rusty doors swung wide with a screech and we stepped in. This car should have been retired years ago, but the cranked-up heat worked fine, so we weren't about to complain. My mind started wandering again: Petty had been away for a long time from what he and his management considered a key city during this early and critical period of building a success story. The new single, "Don't Do Me Like That" and songs from the third album *Damn the Torpedoes* that had just appeared on the radio had actually been delayed by intense music business drama for several months. We had no idea that was going on until interviews with Petty began appearing in newspapers just prior to his return. Instead of working on the road to promote his career, the rocker had spent a major portion of a year raising his right hand and swearing to tell the truth in court. Like a pantheon of young players before him, Tom Petty had originally signed a record deal that assigned him a paltry percentage of any profits and no ownership of his publishing rights. Then, his record label was gobbled up by industry giant MCA in 1978. Fearing he'd be lost in the shuffle at the corporation and also desiring a more equitable deal, Petty invoked a clause written into the original contract that allowed him free-agent status if his label was ever sold. Even so, MCA refused to let go, suing the band and locking the two parties into a legal struggle that forced Petty into bankruptcy. Recording a third album had already begun and continued during this process, but with MCA threatening to seize any master tapes and release whatever music it found, the group handed off the precious results of each day's work to one of its roadies, whose assignment was to hide the masters from the musicians and even Tom Petty himself until the next session. This arrangement shielded the musicians from committing perjury in court should MCA's lawyers demand the tapes.

The wheels of justice ground slowly, but Petty's tenacity remained strong. Eventually, when it appeared likely that he'd actually win the case, MCA caved in completely, giving the songwriter rights to his publishing, a better percentage of the profits, and a custom label for the band that the media giant would distribute. With this process, MCA gave Petty his freedom, but held the bright, young talent close in its corporate grasp. The master tapes were summoned back from their clandestine location and released as the album *Damn the Torpedoes*, which became a ticket to ride as it ascended to number 2 on the U.S. album-sales chart and sold millions. In November '79, "Don't Do Me Like That" hit the charts and eventually took Tom Petty to the Top 10 for the first time, followed early the following year by further hit singles "Refugee" and "Here Comes My Girl." Suddenly great demands were being made on the musicians' time and energy with scads of newspaper and radio interview requests and an invitation to guest on *Saturday Night Live*. The opportunity for the November 10 TV appearance could not be ignored even though it meant postponing his Boston concert at the Orpheum Theater the night before so that Petty and his group could be in New York to rehearse. They'd only perform two songs, but

it was critical to get them right; at the time, *SNL* was the foremost promotional vehicle a rock-and-roll band could get on American television.

We had our tickets for Friday the ninth, but got word that the concert would be postponed to the following Wednesday. Disappointing,
yes, but at least the Boston appearance hadn't been cancelled outright.
I had an excellent eight-dollar mezzanine ticket burning a hole in my
pocket; it would just have to smolder in there for another five days.
When Wednesday night finally arrived we jumped out of that train
and practically sprinted up the steps to leave the subway station. Right
across the street was the alleyway leading up to the front doors of the
old vaudeville theater. But as Clint and I rounded the corner, we were
practically mowed down by a wave of figures marching full tilt in the
opposite direction. What's going on? People should be rushing *toward*
the building at this point. But we kept bumping into bodies, struggling
upstream as if fighting a white-water torrent. I picked out words from
the fleeing figures: "I can't believe it," "What do we do now?" and
"This sucks!" We finally reached the front doors where several ushers,
wearily repeating themselves over and over again, yelled, "The show
is postponed because of sickness . . . hold on to your tickets!" Really?
Tom Petty was postponing a *second* time? Plus, it was at the last possible moment.

Mikal Gilmore, following the tour for a *Rolling Stone* article, sat
backstage at that moment. He detailed in his piece, published in February 1980, that Tom Petty had been under the weather for several days
and felt he had blown his previous night's performance in Philadelphia.
Gilmour wrote: "By the time of the group's sound check, Petty can
barely croak. With just an hour remaining before the doors are scheduled to open, he agrees to postpone the show."

We were certainly disappointed, but understood. It was obvious,
even at this early stage in his career, that Tom Petty was a perfection-
ist. Committed to the quality of his performances as much as he remained devoted to the craft of writing great songs, his meticulousness
was often overlooked, submerged by an enduring image as a laid-back,
long-haired stoner from Gainesville. But it was that attention to detail and driving ambition that had placed the artist and his band at a

perfect point in rock-and-roll history. After the punk explosion had driven a boot through the door a couple of years earlier, exposing a scene of complacent rock stardom and excess, a host of what became "new wave" bands piled through the hole, scattering the bloated occupants in the room beyond. Some star bands like Emerson, Lake & Palmer, Electric Light Orchestra, and Supertramp would never really recover; styles such as southern rock and progressive rock were driven into background roles while other groups, like Yes, took sabbaticals until some of their relevance to the mainstream returned. Tom Petty and other lean late-seventies rock and rollers such as the Police, the Clash, Elvis Costello, Talking Heads, the Cure, AC/DC, the B-52's, and (in England) the Jam and XTC had grabbed the flag and taken up the charge. It was a whole new field of battle out there, and the musical world was being remade in front of our eyes and ears—we wanted to be right in the thick of it!

The show must go on, and it finally did on November 19. The band walked triumphantly out on stage to a tumultuous reception, drummer Stan Lynch sporting a comical T-shirt with the three scheduled Boston concert dates written on it and the first two crossed out. Petty admitted he was recovering slowly and still on antibiotics, but you wouldn't have noticed it as the group accelerated into a breakneck two-hour show that left everyone in the house panting in exhaustion. All the new songs from *Damn the Torpedoes* that would soon become classics hit their mark, rising to meet and challenge the proven in-concert standards like "Listen to Her Heart" and "American Girl." In a monumental Tom Petty and the Heartbreakers performance, the band piled on three scoops of effort to compensate for the missed dates. But as I would discover in subsequent years, this was actually their standard operating procedure: punch the pedal at the beginning, kick in the nitrous about three-quarters down the track, and only take the checkered flag when the last fan had collapsed in a puddle of sweat or simply couldn't clap any more. We reached the peak when Petty tore into a cover of the Isley Brothers' "Shout." Anyone who hadn't heard the 1959 R & B classic in years past knew the song intimately because of Otis Day & the Knights' recent party version in the *Animal House* film. Petty made a party of it too — for ten joyous, rollicking minutes of pulsing dance fever. The playful call-and-response between the band and the crowd involved everyone, convincing even the last holdouts in the Orpheum to give it up and join in. As the final echoes faded on a night when Petty made losers feel like heroes and refugees taste home, he showed us what rock and roll was all about — giving it all and making us shout!

CHAPTER 24

PRINCE

BEFORE THE PURPLE REIGN

The Metro, Boston, March 17, 1981

Listen to: "Little Red Corvette," "Dirty Mind," "1999," "Purple Rain," "Controversy"

My friend Jimmy and his pals had impeccable musical taste and intuitively seemed to know the coolest new bands and what underground happenings were essential to attend. As a joke I guess, they once maneuvered me into their favorite hangout, Buddies, a prime gay bar in Boston's Back Bay, just to see how I'd react. No big deal, except for all the times my ass was grabbed. My scheming friends got a huge laugh out of that, but they affectionately hovered nearby, ready to dive in for the rescue if things became uncomfortable. For a kid who grew up on a farm in Pennsylvania, the sexually driven scene was incredibly eye-opening: there was energy, excitement, and a sense of the cutting edge of cultural and musical taste, which interested Jimmy in particular since he worked in the music department at the same rock-and-roll radio station I part-timed at as a DJ. When we got together in the office, he had a way of casually mentioning something he felt I'd be foolish to pass up, underlining its importance by staring at

142 | **THE DECIBEL DIARIES**

me until I "got" it. "Have you heard of Prince?" I'd only just heard the song "Dirty Mind" that we'd begun playing: a bass-heavy synth-track with falsetto vocals and cute hook that sounded more like the Cars than James Brown, but had elements of both. Other than the song, though, I knew nothing about the artist—Prince could have been a disco group from Paris for all I knew. "Prince is not a band. He's a singer on Warner Brothers with three albums out." Jimmy's eyes burrowed into mine; this was something I was required to understand. He held up a record sleeve. "This is *Dirty Mind*, the whole new album. He's coming to Metro in a couple of weeks; you have to see him." And just like that, I had received my assignment.

The Metro was a historic place: it was right across the street from Fenway Park and the final site of the famed Boston Tea Party concert hall at the dawn of the seventies. The place presented disco dance nights and also ballroom-sized concerts; tonight would be a mix of both. With the start of baseball season still a couple of weeks away, the commotion on the street couldn't be blamed on a Red Sox crowd openly blocking traffic as they so often did while wandering toward the gates into the park. No, the people filling up the sidewalk in front of the Metro to file into the Prince concert had been joined by a huge number of the ticket-less who were engaged in busy negotiation with anyone who'd offer. Inside, the 1,300 allowed through the front doors squeezed in tightly, elbowing through and staking claims as close to the stage as possible. It was a completely mixed bag of blacks, whites, gays, straights, males, and females—perhaps the most diverse concert crowd I'd ever swum in. The bouncers watched with particular keenness; it was, after all, Saint Patrick's Day, a usual night for high jinks in Boston. But, the ex-citing electrical charge running through the dance floor only united the crowd, as anticipation flew high for an artist that only a few had seen, yet all had heard rumors and tales of.

"It's only a matter of time," Jimmy pronounced, "he's definitely going to be a major star." True, he had two albums out already, but those R & B–oriented efforts had produced only a limited response, although the second one, *Prince*, would eventually go platinum years later. His new effort embraced the relatively recent wedding of punk and new wave with the dance-music scene. What had been separate camps shook hands and now met under the mirror ball, summoned together by genre-bending singles like Blondie's "Heart of Glass" (a disco hit from a N.Y.C. punk band), "Miss You" and "Emotional Rescue" (from rock royalty the Rolling Stones), and "Cars" by Gary Numan (an otherworldly U.K. new-wave alien). This new trend in dancing fever would only be exacerbated by the appearance of MTV in fewer than five months.

"He's only twenty-two, you know," someone mentioned as the lights went down and the crowd exploded. A generous supply of smoke had been loosed to cloak the stage as the band emerged and took their places. My buddies were already defying gravity, jumping up and down wildly before the music had even started. Then the lights welled up and the sound blasted out, a pastiche of mechanical electronic beats, darting synthesizer notes, twanging bass slaps, and swipes on rock guitar. Although I couldn't see him yet, Prince's clear and steady falsetto voice cut through the smoke as the crowd roared out their welcome. Everyone craned for a view of the wunderkind; and then the haze dispersed to reveal the figure at stage center wrapped in a leather trench coat, banging on an old Telecaster. The attractive black man in ebony high-heeled boots and leggings had curly dark hair and moustache, penetrating eyes, and a confident grin while checking out the crowd jammed from the stage as far back as the lights could reveal. Two other black musicians shared the front, guitarist Dez Dickerson and Andre Cymone on bass, while three white players, including keyboardists Lisa Coleman and Dr. Fink (in green scrubs and white surgical mask) along with drummer Bobby Z, held down the back line.

Tight and well-oiled, a necessary cornerstone for any successful rhythm-and-blues review, Prince's band nailed it from the start, sliding directly into the second song during which the human dynamo onstage uncorked a furious and extended guitar solo that ended in a glorious heavy metal crescendo and left the room slack jawed. Then, the guitar went around his back and he cradled the mike cooing out those Smokey Robinson–like vocals on "Gotta Broken Heart Again" from *Dirty Mind*. In fact, in the course of the concert, he'd perform every song from the latest release. Prince worked the Romeo angle — selling his tale of lost love with urgent pleading and sorrowful glances at the audience, falling to his knees and stopping, then restarting the group on a dime. With heartstrings tugged and their sexual heat aroused, the girls in the audience (my friends too) got in on the act, loosing a constant accompaniment of screaming and encouragement.

Only three songs in and the place was sweating and drooling! The combination of sexy soul singer with his choreographed dance moves right out of the Motown tradition clashed merrily with the guitarist's rocked out study of Jimi Hendrix, but Prince had clearly mastered both. His command of the stage, really just a mixture of self-assurance and bravado, plus the perfectly timed delivery of his "punch moves" dazzled, ranking him as a master performer. The word "genius" came to mind after a while; it was not a term to be bandied about lightly, but such a one appeared to be standing just a few feet in front of us, and each succeeding song confirmed that realization more and more. The trench coat came off, to a chorus of female shrieks, revealing a compact and lean frame. Then came "Head," the daring song about, uh, gratification, which, subject aside, made a fine funky jam that Prince expertly broke down into a pulsing skeleton of a beat on which he laid a delightful fingerpicking solo. Then, just in case you missed the tune's slant about wickedly waylaying a bride-to-be on the way to her wedding, Prince accented the taboo with an overtly obvious trick, also taken from the Hendrix playbook, crouching down on the stage and erotically working his guitar neck up and down. Outrageous and offensive, Prince dared the audience to prudishly react in protest and shout him out of the room, but we didn't. The sly smile confirmed that he knew we wouldn't, because everyone has a dirty mind somewhere, and he had just played to that place no matter how cloaked or denied it was.

Astonishing and overwhelming: that's a way to describe the multiple talents of the kid from Minneapolis, of all places—not New York City or Los Angeles, places you'd expect might be better suited to school him in these things at an early age. Massachusetts had just had its drinking age raised from eighteen to twenty the year before, so Prince would have only been recently able to have a beer (although I'd heard he didn't touch the stuff). These musical gifts seemed truly God-given, even if the messages delivered often strayed into the unquestionably carnal. But Prince was merely another traveler in an all-so-human pattern, displayed in the tradition of those Delta bluesmen from the thirties and forties who crisscrossed the plantations and towns of the South to offer songs about human wreckage and sexual release. Those same sinners who accompanied their battered six-strings with tales of the eagle flying free on Friday and going out to play on Saturday would also acknowledge the need to be in church on Sunday. After all, the spirit was willing, but the flesh weak—always will be. In the future, this "fallen" human condition would continue to run through Prince's music, romancing and "getting down" with the physical one moment, while appealing for redemption from God in another. Amen.

At the Metro, it was just a couple of songs from the end of the show. After removing the trench coat earlier, Prince had kept going: now he was down to a pair of black satin briefs and a guitar; that was it. If the audience was excited, well, we could tell that he was excited too. Jimmy looked over at me with a knowing glance that said, "Didn't I tell you?" And he was right. I had the impression I was witnessing a greatness that wouldn't easily be contained in a space this small in the future. But I'd heard other stunning debuts from bands like Derek and the Dominos and the Sex Pistols who had promptly wandered into an iceberg or vanished without a trace. As talented as he was, Prince could easily miss that magic combination of talent, luck, and fate that would certify his talent with lasting fame and fortune. That, of course, did not happen: major success waited just down the road with the *Controversy* album six months later going platinum, followed by his major pop breakout *1999* and Top 40 hit "Little Red Corvette in '82. After the *Purple Rain* movie and album with its four Top 10 hits, including two number 1s, you'd be hard-pressed to find anyone in America unaware of the boy-genius. As he demonstrated so powerfully at the Metro, blending the styles of rock and soul while playing a guitar hero equally adept at landing splits on the dance floor proved undeniable to the vast mainstream he would conquer. Prince was destined to become a giant on the short list of true superstars, an absolute reign until his untimely passing in 2016.

By the way, my buddy Jimmy died as a result of AIDS in 1986, the first person I knew to perish from the disease. Back then there wasn't much chance of beating it, so he knew he'd basically received a death sentence. But I never felt that he thought he'd wasted a minute. Borders and walls, whether musical or social, were never impediments to Jimmy—they existed in name only. It would make sense that he wanted me to see Prince, another traveler whose only regard for boundaries was to try to break through them.

CHAPTER 25 | AC/DC

"FOR THOSE ABOUT TO ROCK (WE SALUTE YOU)"

Providence Civic Center, December 4, 1981

Listen to: "Jailbreak," "Dirty Deeds Done Dirt Cheap," "It's a Long Way to the Top," "Hells Bells," "For Those About to Rock (We Salute You)"

I always loved AC/DC, from even before I received an assignment from the tiny Boston music publication *Pop Top* to write about the group's catalogue. That was 1978 and AC/DC already had four albums out in the United States. I got paid the four records. You can't put food on the table with wages like that, but I didn't care; the band's no-nonsense approach energized me then as much as it does gazillions around the world now. As far as the beat went, I never thought there was much difference between AC/DC's "It's a Long Way to the Top" and a disco behemoth like the Bee Gees "Night Fever." Both grooved forward inexorably in a steady, unchanging pulse that dragged dancers irresistibly to the floor, the only difference, perhaps, being in whether they wore polyester double-breasted suits and evening dresses or ripped jeans and leather bomber jackets out there. I watched AC/DC's steady rise with its wise-ass singer Bon Scott at the helm, cheering when the *Highway to Hell* album sold its 500,000th copy and went gold in December 1979. With the king of mainstream rock, Aerosmith, floundering under the weight of its drinking and drugging habits, here was a worthy successor to grab the baton from the ailing champ and press on. But just two months after its American sales milestone, AC/DC's future hit a probable dead end as Scott's lifeless body was hauled out of a car, alcohol poisoning (or "misadventure," as they called it) the cause of his tragic death.

Bon Scott had been the sparkplug of AC/DC, brainstorming songs and writing the lyrics. His antics in front of a crowd fed the equally visual and explosive performances of the band's schoolboy-garbed lead guitarist Angus Young. But Scott was gone, his body cremated, and the ashes left behind in the seventies. The early days of the new decade marked the most important decision the members of AC/DC would ever make: pack it in or continue. With Scott's relatives urging the group to soldier on, they turned the page with a new Scottish singer named Brian Johnson, his brute-force style certainly different than Scott's, but quite adequate for the job description. But would it work? Would AC/DC loyalists accept the new voice? The answer came five months later, confirmed in the incredible reaction to *Black in Black*, the magnum opus that blazed in sales for years to come, becoming the second-biggest-selling album in history.

AC/DC visited Boston on August 21, 1978, playing the Paradise Theater, the first and last time Bon Scott would perform in the city. Four days later, the band drove a short distance south across the border to do a show at Warwick, Rhode Island's, Rocky Point Amusement Park. This may evoke images of the infamous Puppet Show and Spinal Tap sign, but AC/DC was no over-the-hill memory searching for a comeback: this lean outfit hungered for stardom and chased it in a relentless tour schedule that took it around the world over and over. After Brian Johnson got his bunk assignment on the bus, AC/DC steered back out on the road, this time supporting *Back in Black*. It seems inconceivable now, but that tour began in small theaters, as the concert bookings had preceded the album's incredible rise. But, nine months later, the entire world spoke fluent AC/DC, the band reaching the mythical "top" that

Bon Scott had sung about back in '76. A follow up album, *For Those About to Rock (We Salute You)*, appeared in late 1981, hitting number 1 in America and spawning a huge hit in the title track. Augmented by cannon fire on record, the song inspired AC/DC to haul twenty-one "cannons" out on the road for its new tour, hanging them in pods above the stage for an encore salvo of explosions and pyrotechnics. In arena after arena, this became the sensational, over-the-top, tour production that all were judged by at the time.

AC/DC scheduled two nights at Boston Garden in December, and I made plans to go to at least one of those shows. Shortly after the announcement, though, city officials worried over a perceived fire danger, decided to ban the use of the climactic cannon fusillade. I supposed it was good to be cautious, but wouldn't a building constructed with concrete blocks tend to be fire-resistant? AC/DC retained its Boston booking, prepping for the occasion by bringing along a tape of its twenty-one-gun salute from the record and planning to add it to the sound mix at the appropriate time. "It's not right! We're going to miss the cannons!" My boss and the first confirmed AC/DC freak I knew, Tony Berardini, pounded his desk. He certainly had a lot of other things to think about, but he was genuinely pissed off about this affront to his favorite band's artistic integrity. I worked at WBCN radio in Boston, which featured AC/DC liberally, and Tony, as general manager, had some pull. It didn't take long to discover that the band's tour schedule took them to the Providence Civic Center, only fifty miles south, ten days before the Boston Garden shows. There had been no ban on the group's pyrotechnic display in that city. "We're going to Providence," he announced, ignoring the possibility of debate. "I'll make some calls." Just like that, an AC/DC road trip came together for December 4. Tony knew the band and worked on tickets and backstage passes, while Marc Miller, from the station's music department, talked the record label into hiring a limo to take us south. How different this was from the road trips to gigs that I'd embarked on as a kid, sometimes heading out on just a thumb and a prayer. No, this was going to be indulgent, cushy, and fun — a long way to the top, indeed!

But, the short jaunt ran into snags from the start. People were late;

we left Boston behind schedule and ran into an angry tangle of after-noon commuters on I-95 south. The decision to strike off onto local roads proved to be an unwise one, our driver doubling back more than moving southward, it seemed. In the back, drinking beers, we were constantly tossed about during the frequent and abrupt U-turns, be-cause who actually puts on a seat belt in a limo? We finally crawled into Providence and headed toward a fine Italian restaurant near the city center. Tony laid down the law, barking: "We're very late. We are leaving this restaurant in forty-five minutes, sharp!" Since his previous job had been as a tour manager for rock bands, no one doubted that if he needed to, Tony would surely leave someone behind to make sure everyone else arrived when they were supposed to. As the saying goes: the show must go on! Our schedule now demanded a quickly deliv-ered food option, but we were, nevertheless, committed to this stately sit-down establishment embodied by its slowly paced parade of wines, appetizers, and main course (we'd never get to the desserts and aperi-tifs). Plunked down in the middle of the room at a vast round table, our already-primed cast of characters loudly selected seats and proceeded to horrify all of our abutters and, I imagine, the proprietors, who some-how remained polite, to their credit. But they were not about to say no to a check from a half dozen diners and, especially, wine enthusiasts, even if we were flying low under the dress code. I mean, I'd dressed for an AC/DC concert, not an upper-crust Italian restaurant; the camou-flage tank top made perfect sense to me.

With Atlantic Records buying, we ordered freely from the impres-sive menu, and soon bottles appeared all over the table. Those vintages disappeared quickly, but the main courses took forever, even after Tony fearsomely informed the waiter that we were in a great hurry. With the restaurant packed, the kitchen did its best, the fine dishes finally ap-pearing forty-minutes after ordering. Do the math: we had five minutes to eat. Our tour manager decided to go easy: "I'll give you an extra five minutes. We're out of here in ten!" In a dead heat, I feverishly chowed down lobster Fra Diavolo, trying not to laugh so hard that some lobster meat might shoot out of my nose (bad table manners!). Six hundred seconds later, Tony got up and declared, "Okay, we're gone!" The record label guy had already paid the check, so those two started walking out. "Wait. What about the wine?"

"Forget about it. We got to go." I'm not sure how the bottle of fine red got into my pants, but when I got back in the limousine, it had been successfully salvaged. "They would have just thrown it away!" I rationalized. We toasted with that red during the five-minute bolt over to the Civic Center.

Even so, we were late. Expediting our arrival by flashing passes to the backstage security crew, we used the rear entrance to avoid any delays from the crowd streaming in the main concourse. Still, when Tony pushed open the final door and we emerged to the side of the massive stage itself, AC/DC had already launched into "Hells Bells," slamming out its first monstrous power chord while every single person on the floor stood at attention, clapping or fist pumping, the welcoming Rhode Island roar as loud as the music. Losing the critical opportunity to find our seats, we balked at the hassle of wading into that mass and bushwhacking to our designated destinations. "So what!" Tony yelled, "We can watch from here." Not a problem to me, as our passes permitted us to stand there, and we had clear view of the stage. Barrel-chested Brian Johnson in his simple black T-shirt banged the huge one-ton (hell's) bell the group's crew had laboriously hauled onstage earlier, and then worked the crowd with blue-collar efficiency, getting out in front of the band and making eye contact with the folks in the arena. Angus Young used a lot of his same moves, but most people hadn't seen them yet: the infamous schoolboy ensemble, mooning the audience during "Bad Boy Boogie" and piggybacking on his lead singer's burly shoulders for a ride around the vast stage while slamming out another solo. When Johnson nailed "The Jack," a signature Bon Scott slow blues, that sealed it for me. If he could pull that one off, he could do it all.

"You Shook Me All Night Long" thunderously closed out the set. Then it was cannon time. We knew when it was coming because a couple of stagehands directed us out of our area and back against the wall. "Sparks or embers possible, you know," was all one said. "For Those About to Rock (We Salute You)" had been reserved for the encore, and since most already knew that the cannons would be fired, there was a great sense of anticipation. AC/DC reached the chorus: "For those about to rock . . . we salute you!" The pods high in the air spit jolts of smoke and flame as the explosions pierced the air and volleyed with the guitars. Tiny scraps of paper packing and, yes, even some glowing embers floated down into the area we'd just been standing in. "For those about to rock . . . we salute you!" *Bang! Bang! Bang!* This was Fourth of July in December, Australian style! AC/DC had rocketed out of its life-threatening crisis with a roar and a blast of gunpowder confetti, its cannonball arc assured for many years, even decades, to come.

CHAPTER 26

U2

ROLLIN' ON THE RIVER

SS President, **New Orleans, February 11, 1982**

Listen to: "I Will Follow," "The Electric Co.," "Gloria," "New Year's Day," "Bullet Blue Sky," "I Still Haven't Found What I'm Looking For," "Desire," "When Love Comes to Town"

It seems scarcely believable now, but there was a time before the members of U2 were superstars. Of course, you could say the same about the Beatles and the Stones or any of the boldface names in the pages of rock history. So, protean stories of a band barely old enough to play in U.S. bars, balancing Big Macs and fries on orange plastic trays, sleeping on top of each other in vans or changing out of wet stage clothes in a grimy club's beer-keg storage area seem somehow fictitious. But U2 did all those things that young bands on their way up have to do, relentlessly working to have its music heard, with no guarantee of anything, really. It's a long way to the top if you want to rock and roll: climbing out of debts, squats, warm-up slots, and writer's block is the reality. But, the songs mattered to U2; they were worth suffering for. Eventually those songs were heard and then wildly appreciated, elevating the four lads based in Dublin to mythical proportions, to the point where they could skip the van and take a helicopter home instead. But it almost didn't happen because U2 nearly called it a day all the way back in 1981, even after the surprising landslide of support for its first album gained the group strong career footholds in Europe and America. It's hard to envision the eighties without *The Joshua Tree* album or 1992's over-the-top Zoo TV tour dazzling stadiums, but long before those deep impacts in our culture, U2 quite nearly became a one-hit wonder.

On February 11, 1982, U2 embarked on its fourth American tour in barely fifteen months, arriving in New Orleans as the festival fervor leading to Mardi Gras spooled up. Revelers put final touches on their multicolored costumes and assembled the fleets of parade floats that would soon take to the streets in dozens of local celebrations leading to Fat Tuesday. In a town well known for the bizarre, U2 touched down to begin its latest U.S. visit at a most unusual place, a five-decker riverboat straight out of the pages of Mark Twain. The huge paddlewheels had been removed from the SS *President* to make way for more efficient propellers, but the interior grandeur had been lavishly restored. Serving as a popular tourist destination, cruising up and down the opaque, brown Mississippi River from its downtown port, the *President* was the most spacious riverboat at the docks, featuring a ballroom that once held hundreds of waltzing couples, or now, 1,500 rock and rollers. Although only known to a limited cult of followers, U2 had made a powerful impression in this area on previous visits. While still ignored by commercial radio in New Orleans, the college stations at Tulane and LSU featured many songs off the band's 1980 album *Boy* and the very recent *October* release from (appropriately enough) October. So, the local rock audience either had witnessed the passion of these young Turks from Ireland, or had heard good things about them, enough so that the show had sold out. All aboard! Look lively! The concert hall was about to embark!

U2's early triumphs had turned into uncertainty at this point in its early career. The group's first album had lifted them into the vanguard of an early alternative-rock world, where being a big fish in a small pond had its advantages as a launching pad to greater mainstream success. *Boy* had crossed an ocean and brought the Irish group in on a high tide, its songs "I Will Follow" and "Out of Control" preparing the way for acceptance when and where the band clearly hadn't expected it. Like Led Zeppelin a generation before, U2 found much of its earliest and most generous success coming from the New World and worked hard to extend that beachhead throughout most of 1981. The sonic possibilities of the Edge's guitar matched by a solid rhythm section of Larry Mullen Jr. and Adam Clayton were offset by Bono, the lead singer, lyricist, and resident loose cannon. That recipe of musical tightness balanced by potential chaos had fueled many of rock's greatest lineups, and so it would in this case. The songs on *Boy* were taken in expanded directions when played in concert, and those treatments evolved from night to night as U2 and Bono became better at their craft, growing the courage to chase down any musical ideas that popped up, even on the fly. But the many months of touring had left only three weeks to write and rehearse material for a sophomore album. Plus, in a punishing setback, Bono's briefcase containing the lyric ideas he had been working on for the upcoming recording sessions was stolen from a Portland, Oregon, nightclub (the contents would not be discovered and retuned for twenty-three years). Nevertheless, U2 marched into the studio with high hopes, but emerged dejectedly with only three or four songs. Under extreme pressure to take what little it had and turn out a complete record in a few weeks nearly broke the band's back, but somehow U2 conjured one out of the studio jam sessions and last minute writing binges. *October* became a rather unsteady follow up to *Boy*, but its songs would grow and develop admirably in concert, becoming part of a sturdy stage show over the subsequent year.

Adding greatly to the musical uncertainty in this period was a spiritual one. Bono, the Edge, and Larry had become born-again Christians, joining a worship group named Shalom, an alternative to traditional Catholic and Protestant churches in Dublin. The nondenominational approach to a personal relationship with Jesus Christ was revolutionary in Ireland, where religions had established themselves with rigid, time-honored procedures and codes of behavior. Shalom met in regular prayer meetings and Bible studies, but soon several of its members began questioning the conflict of interest a rock group might present to worshiping God. On a worldwide scale, this point would be exhaustingly taken up in succeeding years, birthing the Christian rock movement that has flowered into thousands of bands dedicating their careers to the advancement of Jesus Christ's kingdom by playing music with spiritually oriented lyrics. But in 1981 there was no such movement; U2 found itself in a crisis. As the discussions intensified, Edge and Bono both left U2 during recording sessions and Larry abandoned Shalom. Adam, who had not been swept up in the spiritual fervor, sat bewildered on the sidelines. But, with the patience, seriousness, and fortitude to meet the crisis, qualities that would serve them well in the future, the three young Christians in U2 reasoned that it was not only possible to serve Christ and be in a rock and roll band, but in prayer believed that God had sanctioned it. Work resumed in earnest on *October*, with most of the album's lyrics reflecting the effects of Bono's biblical studies and the joy he possessed in his faith. The profound spiritual dilemma, however, came perilously close to finishing U2 only a handful of years after the group had begun.

I'd become quite a U2 fan since the beginning, so much so that I vowed to try to go to any of the band's shows within several hundred miles. This was actually possible since, as a DJ, I featured U2 music on the air frequently and soon got to know the band. Paul McGuiness, the manager, realizing my enthusiasm, was nice enough to update me with a laminate pass for each tour when it arrived in America. This blanket admission welcomed me into any of the band's concerts, so I could just show up anytime. One late night on the air in early 1982, Bonnie, a regular listener and friend, phoned to inform me that her brother in New Orleans had heard that U2 would be playing there in February. Did I want to go? The group was not scheduled to do a Boston date on this tour running through the end of March, so the idea intrigued me. That U2's performance would be on a showboat cruising the mighty Mississippi sounded quite unusual, even absurd, but after all, this was well before the band members rode horses through the snow, stared somberly into the Mojave Desert, or performed on stage in front of a 400-foot video screen with people like Bruce Springsteen or Bill Clinton "dropping in." These were early days for U2, so the occasional eccentric gig had to be expected.

"This is the first time we've ever played a venue and the venue left," Paul McGuiness joked as the sudden surge of power from the ship's engines and a lurch announced the SS *President*'s departure. I'd searched for the band members and their manager and soon found them accommodated, appropriately enough, in the captain's cabin. Hundreds of people strolled about the decks, gazing out at the muddy waters slipping by as a course was set upriver against the strong current. Soon the French Quarter and Jackson Square slipped behind as we navigated though a vast area of commercial wharfs with both brightly painted and rusty old tankers and container ships tied up at dock or anchored out in the broad waterway. As the sun dipped, RZA announced that show time had arrived, the warm-up band's pounding rhythms shuddering through the ship and over the dull throbbing of the engines to draw the crowd away from views of the increasingly rural bayou shorelines and toward the ballroom inside.

When U2 took the stage with Edge's guitar slamming out the opening salvo of "Gloria," it was instantly clear that whatever doubt and hesitation that had hampered the months leading up to the recoding of *October* had been left behind. Bono sang the new song of joyous spiritual acknowledgment with a sure, confident air, sending the crowd into hysterics. The audience bounced through that song almost violently as a ragged mosh pit opened up in the center of the floor like the eye of a hurricane forming only after its orbiting winds became turbulent and rapid enough. Slam dancers began crashing into each with delight as the band followed its opener with "Another Time Another Place," but this New Orleans U2 crowd proved to be a lot more extreme than what I was used to. Up close to the stage, I planned my retreat after taking a couple of hard knocks to the back as bodies began colliding like pool balls in a break. A wave of shouting, clawing, and kicking ensued as five zombies vied for the space I attempted to exit from. A quick side-step and I was free as U2 downshifted into the slower, bass-heavy pulse of "I Threw a Brick Through a Window" featuring some monstrous drum shots from Larry. One surprise was "A Day Without Me," the band's second Irish single, which had been dropped from the set after the first tour. Edge's guitar reached for the sky and held it high while Bono matched the furious peaks with his own focused vocal intensity.

Despite the hard-core tone of the crowd, which acted like it was at a Dead Kennedy's show, nobody directed any violence toward the band except for a few fast ice cubes loosed in the lead singer's direction. He promptly emptied a beer on the front rows in friendly retaliation. "I Fall Down" and the title track to *October*, the more relaxed selections featuring Edge on piano, were actually received well by the perspiring mass, which used those only opportunities to catch its breath. The band finished up strongly with an encore of "Fire," "11 O'Clock Tick Tock" and "The Ocean" as the riverboat, which had returned down the river along its previous course, gently touched the dock, and I headed off for a plate of red beans and rice (burp). Out on the muddy Mississippi, of all places, U2 had triumphed in merging the music from its confident first album and tentative second into one astoundingly powerful live statement. This was a model for amazing things to come, the magnificent sound of a band gaining its sea legs.

CHAPTER 27

THE J. GEILS BAND

SHOWTIME

Boston Garden, February 25, 1982

Listen to: "Whammer Jammer," "Musta Got Lost," "Give It to Me," "Ain't Nothin' but a House Party," "One Last Kiss," "Freeze Frame," "Centerfold"

The curtains surrounding three sides of the stage came tumbling down again. "Please, no more," I shouted ineffectively as the throng around me bellowed. The mighty J. Geils Band, hometown heroes on a headlining world tour, had rocked the Boston Garden and now kept pounding out the encores. After a couple of hours of dancing nonstop, my back a sweaty mess and my arms too weakened to return the 100 percent I still wanted to give, the band had won. They'd de-

feated me. I'd been beaten into an exhausted twenty-something pulp. Still, folks around me spelled each other, voices and hands rising while others like myself grabbed a quick respite. Even with so many catching their breath, there was more than enough riotous tumult to prompt the group to raise the curtain yet again. "Another encore!" Happily advanced into extra innings, the ultimate party band returned to the stage, sending life-giving rhythm to everyone's feet as a thunder of response arose and the celebration continued. The Garden curfew had been passed like a road sign at sixty, and the union stage workers were already spending their handsome overtime late fees in their heads, but it didn't look like the whirling dervish named Peter Wolf or the others behind him cared one bit about whipping out the checkbook to cover this added expense. They'd come to rock — and the job was not yet done!

That's what the original mission of the J. Geils Band, one of Boston's legendary exports to the world, had always been: get onstage and challenge the audience in a drag race of R & B, blues, and rock, punching it to the floor and seeing who ultimately came out on top. But, nobody ever lost at the end of that quarter mile; it was a match of winners. As Wolf would often say, quoting some John Lee Hooker and tossing it with his own wit, "If it's in you, it's got to come out; that's what rock and roll is all about!" He and his five bandmates employed the stagecraft of a hundred show bands from the previous decades — from the Motown stable to chitlin-circuit mainstays like Little Milton, James Brown, Bobby Bland, Jackie Wilson, and Johnny Taylor, all the way back to the primal one-chord thump of Hooker's "Boogie Chillun." Lead guitarist J. Geils rocked hard but also added excellent jazz chops, Magic Dick on the "lickin' stick" blew astonishing blues harp, rhythmists Stephen Bladd and Danny Klein provided marathon stamina, and Seth Justman brought that fat organ sound that just floored the others — they had to have him in the group. The combination scored from the very beginning, winning early fans at the Boston Tea Party before wowing Bill Graham himself, who booked them more frequently than most at his Fillmore East. He even invited the group to be in the select lineup of bands that closed that legendary hall in 1971.

Atlantic Records, home to many of R & B's greatest acts like Aretha Franklin, Wilson Pickett, Don Covay, and Ray Charles, found that these six white kids from New England shared, not only the love of the music, but the ability to churn out a tight, choreographed performance of multiple "Wait for it!" moments that always entertained and usually dazzled. The ever-restless, nonstop-dancing front-man ethic shown by Peter

Wolf dated back even further, to his early days in Cambridge, hanging around Club 47 in Harvard Square, getting to know and become friends with legends like Muddy Waters and James Cotton, studying their stage moves and divining the secrets of a hundred years of mojo. That open love of black music transcended a racial barrier erected prominently across society in the midsixties and early seventies, speaking highly of the wonderful transforming and leveling qualities of music—so let those boys boogie-woogie!

If you were in the music business in Boston, you couldn't help but get to know the band members: they were always playing in the city because break-even album sales meant that gigging paid the bills. Sure, the music was solid on all those Atlantic albums, but only a couple of them, like *Bloodshot* in '73, had managed to go gold. Meanwhile, the group would handily sell out the Boston Garden, but struggle to fill a ballroom elsewhere. My own introduction occurred when I was a kid in Pennsylvania, stuck in the mud at a quarter-million-strong rock festival at Mount Pocono. The J. Geils Band was just a young contender far back in a pack headlined by Rod Stewart and Faces and Emerson, Lake & Palmer, coming on early in the afternoon before a massive rainstorm turned the racetrack into mush. Who the heck were these guys? They got the crowd up dancing and cheering even though nobody knew who the hell they were. How cool, then, to find them alive and well in Boston half a dozen years later. A new label and a fresh album called *Sanctuary* rebooted the band's career, re-achieving gold-record status and assuming the classic "handprint" logo that would follow the group to the end. In 1980 *Love Stinks*, the album and its hit single title track (still the most requested song for this DJ on Valentine's Day) took J. Geils even higher to near-platinum territory, the R & B roots not forgotten, but the band embracing the modern synth-heavy dance beats of a new generation of eighties rock stars.

Then all hell broke loose. The band released *Freeze Frame* in September '81 and the "Centerfold" single the same day. Drolly penned by Seth Justman, the tale of a teen tryst betrayed years later by the girl's fully exposed magazine pictorial, rocketed to the top of the U.S. charts in February, dragging the album along to number 1 as well.

Freeze Frame stood proudly at the pinnacle for four whole weeks while "Centerfold" did the trick for six. Fourteen years and thirteen albums after it started, the J. Geils Band had summited the final obstacle. Now well out of debt and written into pop history, the group leapfrogged across America from arena to arena, revisiting many of the towns and cities where it had previously been received only reluctantly at some local dive. On its world-conquering yearlong tour, the J. Geils Band arrived back home for three sold-out concerts at the Garden, while its new album and single both sat firmly atop the commercial heap. Could the planets have aligned any better for these guaranteed lovefests in the venerable old barn down on Boston's Causeway Street? The event became the venue's first trio of concerts by any group to ever sell out completely in advance. A ticket for the J. Geils Band on either February 22, 23, or 25 equaled gold bullion in the weeks leading up to the shows. No doubt, a record amount of legal tender traded hands as those magical show times fast approached.

I had cheated, heading down to Providence and then out to Springfield, Massachusetts, for a pair of shows two months earlier. The usual tight sequence of songs and R & B show-band polish smartly welcomed the additions from the latest album to the set: "Just Can't Wait," "Freeze Frame," "River Blindness" and, of course, the number-1 single held back as an encore. But those shows had merely been warm-up patter compared to the steady roar of the Garden audience as the lights came up on the curtains onstage, begging to be lifted if only the noise from the crowd reached a certain threshold. Perhaps there was a device rigged backstage to measure the output of each night's house; if so, Boston hit the desired mark in seconds. Nevertheless, the stage remained cloaked, delayed until someone felt that the proper amount of impatience had been generated in the hall.

The magic moment arrived! Spotlights blazed and monster chords sounded out as the fabric ascended, revealing Wolf already in motion heading for center stage with the mic stand gripped and the group hurtling into "Jus' Can't Stop Me." The singer would barely brake all night, challenging photographers to get a clear shot as he danced incessantly on his zebra-patterned shoes, spinning on the heels, gyrating, twisting, hopping up and down and, generally, leading a gigantic fitness class. About the only time you could catch Wolf motionless was when he fell to his knees lamenting the trials and tribulations of a relationship gone bad: "Love trouble! Love trouble! Everybody's got it!" Off into the long rap introducing "Musta Got Lost," perhaps an unfamiliar song to the new fans plugged in by *Freeze Frame*, but a showstopping standard for the hooting and hollering veterans rapidly going hoarse.

Magic Dick, the highest-profile harmonica player on the planet, never failed to stun as he marched forward upon Wolf's invitation, adding a strident solo to "Sanctuary" and whooping up his obligatory centerpiece "Whammer Jammer." J. Geils kept to the rear, only advancing when the time came for a solo or to swipe out the powerful introductory riffs on "Ain't Nothin' but a House Party" or "Love Stinks." Justman swayed and crouched, fingers flying on the keys of his white grand-piano-sized keyboard (which Wolf used as a dance floor at one point), working the organ and twisting the knobs on a synthesizer added to the rack just a couple of albums back. Klein, in garishly hued, yet natty attire, throbbed on his bass, offering a solo on "River Blindness," while Stephen Bladd in the back twisted his tendons in an impossible display of endurance. In the audience I tried to keep up and did a pretty good job of it for two hours. Then, the band just screamed on ahead and I was left sweating and panting as the musicians accelerated their hot rod into the final stretch. My God! It *was* like a drag race, with smoke exploding off the tires and nobody even touching the brakes! When the echoes had finally faded and I trudged off the debris-strewn floor to head home, I resolved to get some sleep and eat my Wheaties—I was coming back tomorrow night!

The J. Geils Band remained on the road for the rest of the year, but at least the members stayed in nicer digs, not just sleeping on the tour bus or doubled up in one of those nameless roach motels as on previous tours. They returned to New England for a closing round of year-end dates, rocking Portland, Maine, on the final night of '82 and saying goodbye to *Freeze Frame* in Worcester, Massachusetts, on January 1 and 2. Now the world lay at the J. Geils Band's feet; after working so hard for so long to get this far, the group's next album masterstroke was anticipated by a worldwide audience of millions. But, amazingly, the expected follow-up never arrived. As the members basked in their top-of-the-pops afterglow, communication between Peter Wolf and the others broke down throughout 1983 over the band's musical direction. Where did the love go? In the messy divorce that followed, not only was the front man's dominant stagecraft lost to the group, but also his vital songwriting partnership with Justman. The separation proved terminal: although Wolf released a funky solo record while the J. Geils Band finished the album they'd been working on without him, both camps received only mild response for their efforts. Fifteen years would get between the two parties before they found each other again, but by that time they'd fumbled the opportunity; all their momentum had been squandered. The year 1982 became a freeze-frame of what could have been. Instead, the J. Geils Band will always be remembered as a group that fought to the top, then musta got lost.

CHAPTER 28

BLACK SABBATH AND OZZY OSBOURNE

SABBATH VS. OZZY

Boston Garden, March 4, 1982, and April 2, 1982

Listen to: Black Sabbath, "Black Sabbath," "War Pigs," "Iron Man," "Paranoid," "Children of the Grave," "Heaven and Hell"; Ozzy Osbourne, "Over the Mountain," "Crazy Train"

Ronnie James Dio regarded me from the couch, considering the question I had just asked. In that brief moment I couldn't help but be amazed that a man of his size (five feet, four inches) possessed a profound, operatic-level voice that could thrill an entire stadium audience. Considered one of the most powerful and expressive singers in hard rock, his manner in person was conversely soft-spoken and respectful, yet with a commanding presence. Two of his bandmates in the current version of Black Sabbath, original bassist Tony "Geezer" Butler and recently added drummer Vinnie Appice, skulked about, picking at an inviting room service array of breakfast pastries, juice, and coffee. It was March 1982 and I'd been sent by *Boston Rock* magazine to interview anyone in the band who wanted to talk, and, impressively, three showed up. My query was deliberately loaded: "You don't view Black Sabbath as over the hill?" Dio, though, didn't take the bait, finally responding with a grin, "Everyone hates Sabbath, but the fans sell out the shows all over the world!"

"So you're going to be out on tour for . . ."

"Forever!" Appice shot back, cracking us all up.

That Black Sabbath still sold out arenas was nothing short of remarkable, especially since the rock and roll hangman had fit his noose tightly around the band's neck at least three years earlier. As a kid, I'd discovered Sabbath on their second album, *Paranoid*, then embraced the earlier debut and snatched up each new release the moment it came out: *Masters of Reality, Vol. 4, Sabbath Bloody Sabbath*, and *Sabotage*. By 1975, however, the group's commercial peak had been realized as substance and alcohol abuse by all four members gutted their creative core while the advent of punk and a younger metal scene sidelined fans' attention. At that point, after a career that literally defined heavy metal, with headline status at colossal rock festivals and a string of million-selling albums behind them, the members of Black Sabbath somersaulted into the show-biz purgatory reserved for those who had fought their way to the top, then squandered everything away. The death-defying booze-fueled high jinks of lead singer Ozzy Osbourne outstripped that of the

others, leading to a toxic madness that dashed any efforts to return the band to fighting form.

I asked the three members of Sabbath, "What happened? It must have been incredibly messy." As the designated veteran, Geezer took a break from his coffee roll to explain. "It came to a head over a period of years. [We] were in L.A. trying to start [a new] LP. Ozzy was supposed to be with us writing the record, yunno? Then one day he crawled in the door, brainless as usual, and remained that way for about a month. We said to him that we couldn't go on like this anymore—go forth and multiply!" Equally candid in his autobiography, *I Am Ozzy*, the singer wrote, "Firing me for being fucked up was hypocritical bullshit. We were *all* fucked up. If you're stoned and I'm stoned, and you're telling me that I'm fired because I'm stoned, how can that fucking be? Because I'm *slightly* more stoned than you?" After the split, no one had given any odds for either party's survival, but here it was in 1982 and both Black Sabbath *and* Ozzy were on tour, and in fact, headlining sold-out Boston Garden shows just over a month apart.

"Ozzy has been slagging Black Sabbath left and right recently," I continued, "In *Rolling Stone*, he said you should all eat shit and die." Dio smiled; he'd heard that one before, I guessed. "I'm sure he has all sorts of great quotes; I wonder who's writing them for him," the singer replied. After the notorious divorce, Black Sabbath recovered first, adding Dio, who had recently departed Ritchie Blackmore's Rainbow. The results were nothing less than fantastic: a healing breach that restored the band's spirit and led to an extraordinary revival of Black Sabbath's fortunes. The 1980 album *Heaven and Hell* ascended to platinum success and the group toured for a year to support it. All the while, venomous rhetoric spewed from Osbourne, who decried the new Sabbath as an imitation, questioning whether his former bandmates even had the right to use the name. Two years later, the poisonous atmosphere hadn't dissipated one bit as the band released its new album *The Mob Rules* and headed back out on the road. Meanwhile, to a certain extent, Dio's assessment rang true: Osbourne's earliest efforts post-Sabbath had been braggadocio. But, confounding the doomsayers who circled ever closer, the singer recovered with a fine group of musicians and a strong batch of songs on his first solo album released just five months after Sabbath's *Heaven and Hell*. It hadn't been easy; after an uphill battle to be taken seriously in the U.K., Osbourne fought with his L.A.-based record label just to release the debut in America. It was in a contentious gathering with those executives that he had infamously bitten the head off a dove he intended to release as a symbol of peace. Now that was a memorable board meeting!

I reached over to grab a croissant and refill my coffee as Dio continued, "The band doesn't have the problem of a lead singer who can't sing anymore—I mean, he'd lose his voice after saying hello to the audience at the beginning of the show! [The band] was always doing their job, and Ozzy didn't much give a damn about doing anything. He just tried to generate publicity with his I'm-the-fool-of-the-world image . . . and he's done a good job of continuing that image, as far as I'm concerned." Dio glanced over at the others with a grin, done sticking pins in the Ozzy voodoo doll, for now. I got the signal from the attending record company rep that my time was up, so I thanked the three, stuck some grapes in my pocket and left.

That night at the Boston Garden, in front of the assembled multitude (whose flaming torches had been confiscated at the door), Dio's pride in this resuscitated version of Black Sabbath was not unfounded. The band took stage and blasted with maximum thrust into "Neon Knights," for all intents and purposes a straight rock-and-roll song with Tony Iommi's doom-laden guitar tapestries and Dio's unearthly shrieks adding the funereal elements of another Sabbath thriller. After that track from *Heaven and Hell*, the band sensibly staked out its birthright by traveling all the way back to the first album for a version of "N.I.B.," the new lead singer claiming the song as his own, pumping his hands in the devil's horns sign that he'd popularize. Tight and to the point, Black Sabbath played its biggest hits from the first two albums—"Iron Man," "War Pigs," "Black Sabbath," and "Paranoid"—ignoring anything else from the catalogue except for the two releases featuring Dio. With the crowd in sweaty hysterics by the end of the set, the rejuvenated lineup rewarded the hall with a dark jewel of an encore: "Children of the Grave" from the third album, *Masters of Reality*. By then, I'd had enough; my neck ached from trying to keep up with the beat, and my shirt hung soaked and limp. An overpowering presence of heat and body odor lifted out of the crowd, a mass of figures ideal to act as Hollywood extras piling out into the night on their way to assail Dr. Frankenstein's castle. And I guess that's what you should feel like after a tremendous Black Sabbath concert!

But, as it turned out, I hadn't seen anything yet, and it wasn't necessarily because Osbourne and his band played better than Black Sabbath, because they didn't. And it wasn't because the buzzed-out Prince of Darkness had surprisingly managed to keep pace musically on his debut *Blizzard of Oz* and a fine sophomore album entitled *Diary of a Madman*. The multiplatinum success of both releases had been largely due to a creative spark between Osbourne and his young virtuoso guitarist Randy Rhoads, whose comparison to another young player named Eddie Van Halen was not misplaced. No, the reason the manic solo singer's danse macabre at the Boston Garden matched the best his former band could offer was the sheer, all-too-real melodrama that unfolded during the four weeks in between the two shows. Osbourne's solo group had hit the road to much critical success, Rhoads lifting the grungy heavy metal affairs into a hallowed space respected by even staunch skeptics. But just over two weeks after Sabbath quit Boston, Ozzy found himself outside Orlando, awake in a terrible nightmare of pointless tragedy. His brilliant twenty-five-year-old virtuoso guitarist perished in a bizarre airplane accident, the astonishing details of which have been detailed and reviewed as one of rock's most hapless and avoidable moments. You know the story: a shady, coked-out private pilot convinced the rising star and the band's hairdresser into a small plane and proceeded to conduct low dive-bombing runs on Osbourne's tour bus parked in front of a two-story house. Asleep in the bus, Ozzy awoke to a terrific thud as one of the aircraft's wings clipped the vehicle and the plane cartwheeled into the house, exploding and killing all three aboard. Why had Randy Rhoads even gotten aboard, Osbourne asked. "He *hated* flying." Fate had intervened cruelly and lives had been irrevocably altered; the tour ground to a halt.

Within hours, though, convinced that his best recourse would be to continue as a tribute to Rhoads, the singer scurried to find a substitute. Bernie Torme stepped in temporarily, cramming for his parts in time for the tour to resume in Bethlehem, Pennsylvania, on April Fool's Day. By all reports, that show went well. But meanwhile in Boston, animal rights activists fomented more drama for Ozzy. The dove beheading from two years earlier, the famous gnawing of a very much alive bat someone had thrown onstage in Des Moines in January, and some unspecific rumors about animals being killed during his concerts led to the cancellation of the Boston Garden gig. That Ozzy had believed the unlucky bat tossed at him to be made of rubber didn't amount to much of a defense, but the other abuse allegations were easily disproved (with apologies to the dove) and the license reinstated on the very day of the show, April 2. Amazingly, the crazy train of mayhem had made it to the Garden. With all the debacles of the past month, the embattled and outrageous, substance-abused singer didn't even need to perform at a D-level to dazzle the sold-out crowd. But the metal ringmaster did, indeed, deliver beyond expectations in front of a band that musically matched Black Sabbath, even without the gigantic scope of Randy Rhoads's talent.

Osbourne front-loaded his performance with nine solo tracks before mining Black Sabbath gold on "Iron Man," "Children of the Grave," and "Paranoid." And who cared if the barrel-chested, pasty white figure ambling about almost comically onstage sometimes appeared lost; you had to love him for constantly acting as the metal cheerleader by clapping his hands, leading an army of fist pumps and shouting out his trademark, "I love you awwwwwl!" I left this show even sweatier and more disgusting then I had after the Black Sabbath concert: an accurate measure of its success. With all the chaos and confusion of this, perhaps the worst month of Osbourne's life, he couldn't have been thinking much about his former bandmates or some personal competition with Ronnie James Dio; he was thinking about survival itself. Maybe that's why the show was so good—Ozzy played it like it could have been his last. But it wasn't, so I promptly got a ticket for the gig in Providence four days later. The running verbal battle between Sabbath and Ozzy in '82 while each performed at a peak to outdo their rival became models of, and a catalyst for, an eighties metal scene about to encircle the world with ear-splitting volume. Judas Priest, Iron Maiden, Mötley Crüe, Guns N' Roses, Ratt, and a thousand others gleefully turned it up to 11, and decades later the glorious noise is still deafening millions. "I love you awwwwwwl!"

THE WHO

CHAPTER 29

WHO'S LAST...
BUT, NOT REALLY

Capitol Center, Landover, Maryland, September 21, 1982

Listen to: "My Generation," "I Can See for Miles," "Pinball Wizard,"
"Won't Get Fooled Again," "Behind Blue Eyes," "Who Are You,"
"Eminence Front"

I strolled down the long incline, following the rubber and oil spoor of a thousand tractor-trailers that had backed down this concrete slope and into the bowels of the Capitol Center. A small gaggle of hopefuls stood behind me in the early-afternoon sun, loitering lonely amid the naked expanse of 20,000 parking spaces. I'd been standing with them for an hour, collecting stories from folks who had traveled from nearby places like Washington, D.C., and Baltimore, and some others like me who had journeyed much farther. I worked at a prominent Boston radio station and was known sufficiently around that town to allow me generous latitude in "crashing back stage," but down here in Maryland, nobody had any idea who I was. I had less of a chance at getting in that door at the bottom of the ramp than Jodi from Arlington, who yearned to hand Roger Daltrey the dozen roses that she clutched protectively.

Earlier, the attractive fan had pressed forward to pass her flowers through a barely opened window on his black limousine as the face of her hero glided past. At least Jodi had been rewarded with a smile from the singer, but the car kept going, angling down with smooth Cadillac grace and disappearing into the building. Inside, Daltrey and his bandmates in the Who were in a final rehearsal before their mammoth 1982 farewell tour of North America and its first concert here tomorrow night. Like Jodi, I hoped to pass the velvet rope and witness four of rock music's greatest practitioners up close before they called it quits, but I had to admit it didn't seem likely.

Sauntering as nonchalantly as possible toward a small group of people clustered at the trailer-sized work entrance into the 19,000-seat arena, I practiced some alibis and flipped a couple of cards through my mental Rolodex for a last-ditch name-drop. The small talk went well with the five guys standing there, smoking, with no direct challenge from any of them. One mentioned he was with the film crew shooting a TV commercial with the band. A bluff occurred to me: "So, where's the security on this door?" He shrugged while dragging on his cigarette, then replied, "Not my aisle." Sensing the moment, I disengaged with a frown, sending out the best "big boss man" vibes I could, and walked inside, fully expecting to hear, "Hey you! Where are YOU going?" I knew some beefy goon would angle across my path looking for a backstage decal or a laminated tour pass, and without either I was a sitting duck. *Look like you know what you're doing,* I reminded myself, heading straight toward the back of the stage while people scurried every which way, never giving me a glance. *Are you kidding? I just walked in with that stupid line? When does that ever happen?* I continued past all the activity and out onto the floor of the Capitol Center, looking back at a couple of camera crews, a dozen roadies or sound engineers, and several officials with Schlitz Rocks America jackets milling about onstage. The beer company, as sponsor of the tour, planned to film the Who for an advertising campaign while the group worked through a short set of songs. Just as I was wondering why I couldn't find any cans of Schlitz, John Entwistle appeared in front of his amps, plucking out monstrous bass notes that echoed wildly around the nearly empty space. His appearance focused all attention toward the stage, so for the moment, I was probably safe from detection.

In 1965, the Who's visionary songwriter, guitarist, and singer Pete Townshend had perfectly captured the impatience and impetuousness of youth in his band's hit "My Generation." Featuring that fabulously famous line "I hope I die before I get old," the anthem snarled to life in the sweaty hands of four reckless English kids out to take over the world and screw anyone that didn't get the message. This was dangerous stuff by Beatles' and even Rolling Stones' standards. The now-legendary tales of equipment auto-destruction at the early gigs were not fables; for a long time the cost of replacing the obliterated guitars, amplifiers, microphones, and drums far outweighed any receipts the band earned from gigs or record sales. For Townshend, Daltrey, Entwistle, and Keith Moon, rock music became a reason to live—not mere playacting, but lifeblood that gave their mortality meaning. This commitment eventually yielded worldwide success, but the lifestyle took its toll. By 1978, after more than a decade of severe drug and alcohol abuse, Keith Moon checked out, victim of an accidental overdose. But the Who's legend had already been built, the group crafting at least three of rock's most durable works: *Tommy*, *Who's Next*, and *Quadrophenia*. Not only had those albums sold in the millions, but they were also extraordinary enough to alter the very course of popular music. The songs on 1971's *Who's Next* had become FM radio staples and would remain a sturdy chunk of classic-rock radio playlists far into the future. Director Ken Russell adapted the "rock opera" *Tommy* for the big screen, the bombastic production lifting the already famous Roger Daltrey to godlike celluloid status. By the time of Moon's death, a big-budget film version of *Quadrophenia* was in production, and some of the Who's most ardent fans had received approval to turn the band's history into a loving film documentary entitled *The Kids Are Alright*.

Now the Who had reached its toughest crossroad. While pondering how to replace an irreplaceable drummer, Townshend struggled with midlife worries of his band's relevance amid the appearance and cultural impact of punk rock. Nevertheless, the band did not waste time: in September 1978, Townshend announced in *Billboard* magazine, "We are more determined than ever to carry on, and we want the spirit of the group to which Keith contributed so much to go on." The group installed former Faces drummer Kenny Jones behind the kit, and the new Who debuted on stage at London's Rainbow Theater in May 1979. Since this represented nothing less than the rebirth of an English rock institution, media scrutiny could not have been more intense. Could this legendary group of aging musicians get back in the ring for another swing? The reviews screamed a resounding Yes! No one expected Kenny Jones to duplicate the explosiveness of Moon, but he proved to be the solid and sturdy locomotive the band needed to get back on track. Long live rock! It was the splashiest and most talked about comeback in years. That lineup of the Who created two albums, *Face Dances* and the recent *It's Hard*. Despite selling well, however, both were fairly schizophrenic affairs with moments of stratospheric brilliance blemished by some comparatively uncelestial songwriting. For most other bands, a few good songs would have been enough, but the Who's dazzling past had set the bar unattainably high, and the media savaged both efforts. The criticism had its effect: the band members announced to the world that they would be embarking on a farewell tour before turning to full-time solo careers. The sweeping goodbye to North America's arenas and stadiums would present forty shows in the fall of 1982. Some of those concerts were scheduled in the largest venues available, including two nights at New York City's legendary Shea Stadium. The band stood to make millions as fans scrambled to make sure they'd have a last encounter with one of the most important rock bands of the past two decades.

So explains the pilgrimage to witness the pair of opening shows outside D.C. When I found out about the rehearsal, I had to get into that too. *God must be a Who fan*, I reasoned, because somehow, even without a pass for protection, I'd escaped discovery. Emboldened to socialize, I approached Kenny Jones out in the sea of empty seats. The drummer looked fit and trim, amiable and talkative, but communication proved challenging with Entwistle twanging away onstage. In between the bass guitar wallops, I told the drummer that the steadier, timekeeping style of his playing, unlike Moon's explosive barrage, may better suit the dance pulse of eighties music. He was about to respond when a hand grabbed my shoulder. Busted? Fully expecting to see the gendarme who would escort me out, I turned and my dismay turned to surprise because a middle-aged man stood there smiling. "Kenny," he said, pointing, "He's got a *Face Dances* jacket on!" Jones grinned as he saw the back of my official Warner Brothers swag item, given to me by the record label for my radio station's support of the 1981 album. Suddenly, I realized that the satin garment had been my ticket into the rehearsal. With that jacket on, everyone had assumed that I worked for the Who's label. I had been wearing my backstage pass and never realized it! "Who was that?" I asked as the figure moved off.

"Glyn Johns," Jones responded, naming one of rock's greatest producers and the man who had helped craft *Who's Next* and *It's Hard*, among others.

"No shit," I muttered as someone called the drummer to the stage and he left with a spirited handshake and smile. After all, he believed I was out there promoting his new album!

Jones maneuvered inside the busy curtain of lights, cameras, and commotion to sit behind his kit as Pete Townshend materialized, black guitar hanging off his shoulder. Near forty these days, he looked fifteen years younger with a short flattop coiffure, scuffed-up jeans, striped shirt, sneakers, and a light leather jacket. He noodled around on some chords before Roger Daltrey appeared in a black T-shirt that revealed the enviable muscular build underneath. With the band members assembled, they eased into "Eminence Front," a danceable groove of a song quite unlike anything the Who had released before. Since the film crews were still figuring out angles and illumination, the band played the song and immediately repeated it. A couple of renditions of "It's Hard," "Cry If You Want," and some instrumental takes on "Athena" followed. With an atmosphere loose and devoid of tension, Daltrey launched a playful kick at two cameramen when they wandered a bit too close. He even offered a dramatic "Thank you!" a few times to acknowledge the twenty of us who were out there clapping wildly.

Since I was now an "official" Warner Brothers representative, I confidently strolled up and put my arms on the stage as the Who kicked into "Won't Get Fooled Again," Townshend's classic political kiss-off. The power soared off that stage, filling up the vast and empty coliseum. When the band stilled, leaving the prerecorded keyboard pattern in control, I hoped the Schlitz guys were still rolling those cameras because this was the moment to capture. Daltrey launched into the most famous scream in rock, then Townshend headed for home, but not before windmilling and scissor kicking his way through five or six false endings and a biblically immense pileup of frenzied distortion to end it. Sudden silence rushed in, with the pitifully inadequate response from our meager numbers sounding distantly, but there were smiles all around, even on the faces of the stage veterans, which spoke loudly enough. Those positive vibrations prevailed as the tour of 1982 began auspiciously the following night in front of a sold-out house. Some of America's most famous music writers had come to town to witness the debut and gave the shows high marks and glowing reviews.

It wouldn't last, though; despite the capacity crowds and critical support, the wear and tear on the band members began to show as the year grew longer. By the time the Who played its final concert in Toronto on December 17, the burnout was all too apparent, the band turning in an exceptionally ragged and sloppy performance. Unfortunately, that was the show filmed and recorded for posterity, a commercial video that subsequently negated much of the band's hard-won reputation as a terrific live act. Townshend appeared to have lost interest in the group, the others barely spoke, and plans for the 1983 farewell tour of Europe were scuttled. The Who had breathed its last. Of course, that's not how it would turn out. Six years later, the legendary band revitalized and reassembled, bearing the brunt of many "hope I die before I get old" jokes. Townshend and Daltrey would survive well beyond the demise of Schlitz as a company, even making it to the Who's fiftieth anniversary tour in the far-distant future. But, as much as I would enjoy the bonus of once again seeing a band I thought had checked out in '82, there would never be an episode to rival the final minute of that "final" tour rehearsal—thanks to my magic jacket, of course!

CHAPTER 30

AEROSMITH

IN A HARD PLACE

Worcester Centrum, Massachusetts, November 16, 1982

Listen to: "Dream On," "Walk this Way," "Train Kept a Rollin'," "Sweet Emotion," "Back in the Saddle," "Kings and Queens"

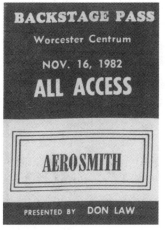

BACKSTAGE PASS
Worcester Centrum
NOV. 16, 1982
ALL ACCESS

AEROSMITH

PRESENTED BY DON LAW

It seems odd, nearly perverse, to dwell on this particular show. Aerosmith played better every other time I saw them, so why bring up this troubled period in the band's history? Joe Perry had left to form his own solo group in 1979, and Brad Whitford quit in disgust two years later as Aerosmith, crippled by drug and alcohol abuse, scuffled in the studio to finish its latest album. Two new players were slotted in as replacements and eventually that record would get done, but it would take an eternity and a king's ransom: over two years and $1.5 million to finish it. *Rock in a Hard Place*, Aerosmith's ninth release, came out in September of '82, but didn't get far, only climbing to number 32 on the album chart. There was good reason for that. Although the record sported some promising ideas and at least one great song, "Lightning Strikes," the usual Aerosmith magic had vanished in a puff of freebase.

No rabbits in the hat this time: the New York City recording sessions were invaded nightly by a parade of dealers and shady hangers-on who served only to distract the musicians. Tyler's voice mirrored the strain of too many ragged all-nighters, and the band took its stand on the weakest set of material they'd assembled to date. Listening to *Rock in a Hard Place* thirty-odd years later is a grave experience, with Aerosmith sadly revealed as a shadow of its once legendary self.

In 1982 America's premier hard rock band had a lot to celebrate. In just under a decade the Boston-based quintet had released seven platinum albums plus 1979's *Night in the Ruts*, which hadn't done as well, but still reached gold with sales of 500,000 units. Add to that a handful of songs immortalized on the Top 40 charts: "Dream On," "Sweet Emotion," "Walk This Way," and "Last Child," plus sellouts coast to coast. Aerosmith attained mythical status as a supremely visual act with a loudmouth brat lead singer, whose penchant for twirling onstage around a scarf-festooned mike stand had become a de rigueur American response to the lipstick and rouge Bowie/T-Rex–led glam rock pouring in from England. Sure, guitarist Mick Ronson added hard rock cred to Ziggy's earthly invasion, but Aerosmith had Joe Perry, who ascended to the throne of a guitar god. Worshipped by an army of blue-jeaned fans, he provided the perfect testosterone-fueled counterpoint to Tyler's more primping dalliances. Behind the Tyler-Perry tag team soon known as the Toxic Twins for their notorious chemical warfare, Aerosmith became the American standard to judge hard rock by, the only group that stood even the remotest chance of wresting away Led Zeppelin's mighty hammer. Tyler, Perry, Whitford, bassist Tom Hamilton, and drummer Joey Kramer drove to the top of the mountain, read the sacred rock-and-roll tablets and returned to preach their gospel of blues and metal to the masses. This they had accomplished with spectacular success. But the God who gave generously, could also take away, and Aerosmith was about to endure a supreme test of faith and endurance, one that would drag the band through the gates of hell itself.

Even as sales of *Rock in a Hard Place* began to plummet, Aerosmith took to the road for the first time in two years, with its new lineup of Jimmy Crespo and Rick Dufay on guitars, playing a warm-up show on

October 30 on its original New Hampshire home turf. A handful of us skeptically drove the ninety miles to Concord to witness the Capitol Theater concert. To our surprise, the show *rocked*. Aerosmith performed capably, often brilliantly, especially breathing life into some of the stillborn songs from its latest album. Jimmy Crespo proved himself worthy, deserving a gold star for replicating much of the Joe Perry style and substance while adding his own touches. Meanwhile, Dufay's playing took a back seat to an hour and a half of the wannabe's preening and posing in front of a set of imaginary MTV cameras, but even if I thought he was average, the crowd loved him. I left the theater event elated, believing Aerosmith to be a band reborn. Spreading the good news to my doubting colleagues and friends, many changed their minds and vowed to attend one of Aerosmith's two upcoming concerts, November 11 or 16, at the Centrum in Worcester. After the first show, most of them agreed that Aerosmith had hit a slam dunk: 13,000 fans screamed their heads off all night, and *Boston Globe* music critic Steve Morse had only good things to write, calling concert a "convincing thunderclap" of "barn-burning rock 'n' roll" as compared to "their sludgy, scattershot days of old." Now persuaded, and perhaps surprised, Morse urged hard-rock lovers everywhere to check out the second concert five days later.

On the sixteenth I brought my teenaged buddy George to the Centrum for his first Aerosmith show, strolling into the arena amid an excited mass of fans especially pumped after hearing how good the first concert was. As hoped, the show began impressively, galloping out of the gate with the explosive set-opener "Back in the Saddle." Jimmy Crespo ripped out the growling main riff, then added a blazing solo as Rick Dufay provided solid counterpoint while vamping rock-star moves all over the big Centrum stage, nearly running into his lead singer on a couple of occasions. It was all there—the energy, the incredible songs, Tyler bouncing around like a whirling top, Aerosmith pulling off its rebirth while George stared from his loge seat, mouth agape. The band whipped through the hits and a few songs from *Rock in a Hard Place*, arriving at "Lightning Strikes" just over an hour into the set. Weeks of radio airplay had turned the new song into a New England hit, sparking strong applause and introducing a set-closing salvo of hits designed to propel the crowd to a final ecstasy. But I noticed, with every succeeding song, that Steven Tyler had begun to struggle. His singing on "Dream On" started off strong, then wavered, and petered out in a nearly inaudible, croak. "Walk This Way" featured some of the best wisecracking lyrics in the Aerosmith catalogue, but Tyler sat out the whole first part of the song, resting up to jump in about halfway through. Fortunately for him, the group had hit the home stretch, accelerating into "Toys in the Attic," a mercurial sprint that usually left both the audience and band breathless, but on this night the singer couldn't keep up.

Like an exhausted long-distance runner weaving and bobbing toward the marathon finish line, he began to veer groggily off course, staggering away from his mic stand and back to the amplifiers where the lights were dim and less focused. Facing backward, Tyler appeared to throw up past the top of an amplifier, which seemed to do the trick because the singer strutted confidently back to his usual position front and center. However, while reaching out for the microphone, the singer's eyes suddenly widened in surprise as he rotated once before crumpling abruptly onto the plywood stage. With all the grace of a lifeless marionette released from its strings, Steven Tyler lay in a heap before an astonished full house. There he remained, motionless for a full twenty seconds or more while his bandmates continued to rage through the song around him. Whether each player was aware of the singer's plight or not, his stage crew reacted fairly quickly, waiting just long enough to make sure Tyler wasn't playing dead before two figures ran out to check on him. A quick look, a quick decision, as "Toys" continued to bang out of the speakers. The stage lights were abruptly killed, but the fading glow failed to diminish quickly enough to hide the sight of a limp and unresponsive rag doll being picked up and hauled unceremoniously around the back of the amplifiers and out of view, concluding his tragic transformation from rock god to pathetic mortal. Without a word to the audience, the band brusquely ended the song and exited in the darkness.

An unusual silence descended for a heartbeat, then tentative clapping led to scattered applause. Around me, fans were wondering if what they saw actually happened. "Did Tyler pass out? Is that the end of the show?" A few moments later when the arena houselights flared back on, the band did not reappear, only the crew returned to clear the instruments and equipment. "Maybe they're coming back?" a person close by asked hopefully. I shook my head; a roadie friend of mine had once told me that when the stagehands finally collected the microphones, it was a sure sign that the fat lady had sung. I heard some booing and my buddy George looked crestfallen, but I explained to him that at nearly seventy minutes, enough of the concert had been finished for it to be considered complete. In fact, the show came in only three songs shorter than the previous effort five days earlier and was probably as good a performance, if we ignored that crappy and infamous ending, of course!

We stuck on our backstage passes and headed downstairs. Walking around the side of the stage to the giant garage doors leading into the bowels of the Centrum, our paths were blocked by a harried band representative whom I knew well, standing with two burly security men behind him. "You don't wanna go in there tonight," he explained, as if we had a choice. "It's a mess; they're not seeing anybody." Behind him and down the hall I could hear shouted recriminations traded back and forth from a number of voices, some of them familiar. I sidled up to the gatekeeper and asked quietly, "What happened?" He looked back, replying covertly, "Joe [Perry] showed up, Brad [Whitford] too. They were talking about getting onstage to jam. But Steven and Joe did something in the dressing room, maybe snorted up something bad. Now they're all yelling at each other." He sighed, "You should just go home . . . there's nothing happening here." The words echoed as an epitaph. In three Aerosmith autobiographies (the band's, Tyler's, and Perry's), it was revealed that the singer's heroin had been the spoiler. The unusually potent mix left Perry immobile in the dressing room for much of the show, yet the band members accused him of being the culprit that had joined the Toxic Twins in a dreadful chemical reunion.

So the question remains — why dwell on a band freefalling into its pitiful career nadir? The promising second Centrum concert became a humiliating hometown defeat, widely assumed to be a knockout punch at the time. And maybe that's the moral of the story, if only for the warning it brings. Although Aerosmith would later beat all the odds to stage, perhaps, the greatest comeback in rock history, that nearly *never happens*. Once a band descends into open warfare with itself, running headlong into the warm oblivion of alcohol, drugs, or the needle, it's almost always too late. Blues players, jazz artists, rock stars — they all tell the same story: most never make it back. That Aerosmith would reclaim, then expand its fan base to succeeding generations was impossible to imagine on that night in '82. Crespo and Dufay certainly deserved a better shot, my buddy George had his teenage enthusiasm dashed, and an entire audience left the Centrum in mute shock. But maybe it was all meant to be. After all, when that version of Aerosmith blew apart at the end of the tour, the vacuum that remained eventually induced the original lineup to try it one more time, giving each the strength to wrestle with his demons and reboot a lasting career. They say you have to find the bottom before you can rise back up; on this night Aerosmith finally stopped digging and started on that long climb.

CHAPTER 31

JOAN JETT

"I LOVE ROCK 'N' ROLL"

The Metro, Boston, June 28, 1984

Listen to: "I Love Rock 'n' Roll," "Crimson and Clover," "Star Star," "Cherry Bomb"

She sounded very young on the phone, her voice shaking as she asked a question. Marina, from Brookline, had phoned the radio station to get on the air with Joan Jett, who at the moment was celebrating the night of her twenty-fifth birthday by doing an interview while sharing in the two bottles of Moët & Chandon parked happily next to the turntables. It was September 22, 1983, and Jett and her band the Blackhearts were due to warm up for ZZ Top outside of Boston in a few days, so she and her manager Kenny Laguna were out trumpeting the recent release of her third collection of songs called *Album*. I'd drawn the lucky straw to do the nighttime interview on my 6:00–10:00 show on WBCN, and at the moment we were all feeling a bit elated from the French bubbly. "What inspired you to go into rock?" the breathless, quivering voice asked.

Marina couldn't be any older than Joan Jett was when she went looking for a band at age seventeen and formed the Runaways with four other like-minded teenage girls in 1975. The L.A.-based rock-and-roll troupe managed to get signed, put out four studio albums, and became stars, at least in Japan (where they were mobbed while on tour by teenage girl fans). But they hadn't been taken very seriously in their homeland, and they should have been; I saw the Runaways play at the Rat in '77, and they rocked a whole lot better than most of the contemporary outfits of punk do-it-yourselfers starving on the club circuit. And I have to admit, as a guy, it was sexy to see an all-female group up on stage playing power chords (even if their tender ages placed them well off-limits) because that just didn't happen until the Runaways came along. Sure, there had been female-fronted rock-and-roll bands like Grace Slick with Jefferson Airplane, Janis Joplin in front of Big Brother and the Holding Company, the Wilson sisters in Heart, and Deborah Harry with Blondie, but an all-girl lineup? Later on in the eighties, the Go-Gos and the Bangles would be along to obliterate the sales charts and move millions of albums; but before all that came the Runaways. And even if America hadn't paid much notice, that rocking band of teenagers and Joan Jett as a solo artist had made quite an impact in the lives of fans like Marina, who obviously adored even the phone line that the musician spoke on.

"I just . . . wanted to do it," the rocker responded. "I didn't see anybody out there doing anything like it. Any girl that was playing a musical instrument . . . it was an acoustic guitar or a tambourine or they were just singing; there were no girls out there doing anything really active and sweaty and rowdy! That's what I wanted to do. I told my parents, 'If you're gonna get me an acoustic guitar, you might as well forget it!'"

"I think that's really great," Marina replied. The awestruck girl sounded more than a bit overwhelmed, her circuits blown, as if she had Wonder Woman herself on the phone. Joan Jett was a pioneering rock-and-roll amazon: she'd blasted onto and through the Billboard sales charts while breaking through sexist barriers at the same time. Being a hard-rockin' guitar-playing star onstage would no longer be just a man's game; a guy would have to work hard to "out-cool" her up in those lights. As we said our goodbyes and I disconnected the call, I realized that Joan Jett probably *was* Marina's Wonder Woman, a mentor with a Gibson that had shown the girl how to think for herself and take up the charge. Invigorated and emboldened, perhaps Marina was already making her next phone call, looking for a drummer.

After the demise of the Runaways, Jett had morphed into what would eventually become a successful solo career far eclipsing her former band's brief flirtation with fame. However, the early years were tough: Jett had to form her own label with Laguna and sell records, literally, out of the back of his car because no one in the music biz was interested in signing the "girl rocker." Eventually she got a shot on Boardwalk Records, then astonished everyone with the success of "I Love Rock 'n' Roll" which bulleted to number 1 in 1982 and sat rock steady on the singles chart for seven weeks. Jett released another Top 10 single, a cover of Tommy James and the Shondells' sixties anthem "Crimson and Clover," and became a major spokesperson for the whole MTV new-wave generation and the missing link between punk rock and Bruce Springsteen. Jett had truly reached rock-and-roll nirvana. However, not only had she sold a lot of records, but along with Deborah Harry, Pat Benatar, and Chrissie Hynde of the Pretenders, she'd blazed a trail for females in rock to follow, and unknowingly perhaps, been raised high on the shoulders of the entire women's rights movement. Although this would be the biggest chart success of her career, Joan Jett continued be an example for young girls to follow for decades. Eventually she'd earn music business immortality, of sorts, by being inducted into the Rock and Roll Hall of Fame in 2015. The timelessness of Jett's career was displayed in a gushing induction speech by pop star Miley Cyrus, who hadn't even been born until a decade after "I Love Rock 'n' Roll." Plus, her relevance and (bad) reputation as a rocker was shown in the previous year's Hall of Fame ceremony in which the members of Nirvana, on the occasion of their own induction, chose Jett to front their band and honor the presence of Kurt Cobain with a devastating performance of "Smells Like Teen Spirit."

After Marina's call, I asked Jett about her faithful cover of the Rolling Stones song "Star Star," which had ended up on the cassette version of *Album*. A furor had erupted when a parent heard her daughter playing the tape and the song's explicit lyrics, which included the repeated use of the F-word — over three dozen times! "That's what happened," Jett explained on the air. "I think the mother went on TV in Texas and said that 'this band must be stopped.' But, for real, we didn't put 'Star Star' [out] to make [people] angry or shock anybody. It was last minute in the mastering room and we had extra time on side one of our cassette; we had another six songs to choose from. 'Star Star' was there and I thought it was the best." The controversy threatened to squash sales, so Jett's label rereleased the tape without the offending tune, changing the color of the plastic from black to red to mark the new sanitized version. Lyrics aside, though, the Chuck Berry–style rocker made perfect rock-and-roll stew for the Blackhearts to cook up a storm with, and Jett's snarling vocals on top made it a perfect signature song. In the spirit of rock-and-roll defiance and declaring it to be the "public service" right of the people of Massachusetts to hear the track, I played it live on the air, earning bug-eyes from Jett as she gulped her Moët in surprise. Spinning the expletive-laden rocker could have resulted in an FCC fine, but somehow it all seemed so American and proper to do (the champagne certainly helped). At least, that's what I told myself as the first of the many F-bombs began lighting up the airwaves. If I was going down, though, the sight of Joan Jett shooting to her feet and leaping about made it all worthwhile. Her four minutes of Pete Townshend–style windmilling air guitar and aerial scissor kicks just made it all that much sweeter.

The spirit of the Who's guitarist and guiding light would revisit the next time I saw Jett, which was at her concert seven months later at the Metro in Boston. WBCN had hosted a local battle of the bands competition called the Rock and Roll Rumble for eight nights, and Jett, with her trusty Blackhearts in tow, were contracted to play an encore guest performance after the play-off competition between the two finalists. Timing would be critical all evening: two alternating sets from both the Schemers and Dub 7 put a lot of pressure on each stage crew to set up and break down their band's equipment twice in one night. But everything had gone as planned; now, even as the former group received its victory honors at the front of the stage, Jett's crew and the house sound personnel had begun preparations for her appearance. Time was flying, though, with last call looming less than an hour away, and the road-ies were working up a serious sweat. Through the back door onto the stage I could see them hurrying about—pulling the drum kit forward, setting the mics, and performing a cursory sound check while the au-dience milled about expectantly. The musicians waited all around me in the cramped space, fingers picking out unamplified guitar notes and the drummer rat-a-tatting on the wall to limber up.

Meanwhile, through the club's sound system, Jett's preconcert music tape blasted out of the speakers. With nearly perfect timing, the stage had been prepped and readied shortly after her final choice, the Who's "Won't Get Fooled Again," began playing. Townshend's legendary eight-minute epic filled the club as the stage manager did his last check, then leaned down in the doorway and waved a flashlight beam in my face. We're ready! Time to get the band onstage! I looked at the musi-cians, who were clearly all set, then caught Jett's eye. Ready? She shook her head side to side, then began bobbing her head to Townshend's power chords. A couple of minutes passed, the lights went down, and the stage manager returned, scowling in annoyance and waving his light more insistently. Jett paid no heed. I yelled to her, "We're kinda running low on time; are you ready?"

"No fuckin' way!" she barked back over the music. "We gotta hear the song! Wait for the scream!" She was referring, of course, to Dal-trey's blood-curdling shout near the end of "Won't Get Fooled Again." Thus, ending my intrusion, she reentered her head-bobbing personal rock-and-roll space, which I decided not to tamper with again. The stage manager reappeared, looking at the now-distant star and motion-ing me to the doorway. "Carter, what the fuck? We humped this gear all night and we're ready. Let's go!"

"Sorry, Carmine, she wants to hear 'Won't Get Fooled Again,' the whole thing."

"All of it? There's still four minutes to go!"

"All of it. Look at her: she's rocking out." He looked in at the head-banging star, eyes closed with her guitar dangling at the ready, sighed in defeat and stood to the side. He was paid to be impatient and he'd done his best.

The synthesizer section of the song, advent to the finale, pulsated nakedly as the band members began to fidget and got ready to jump; Jett's eyes were still closed, her head doing a light dance in time to the rhythm. Then Daltrey's scream! Her eyes flew open wide as she mimed a massive swipe on the unplugged Gibson, mirroring Townshend's epic chords in a foreshadowing of her own impending electric ecstasy. Just before the last note hit, we were already moving out the door, me flying to the main mic for a (real) quick intro, and Jett waving hello as the guitar tech plugged her in and she filled the room with a welcoming six-string blast, throttling up and into the first song within seconds. The band machine-gunned the audience without a break, making up some time and playing right up to last call and as far beyond as the club manager felt he could get away with. In Joan Jett's world, it was all about respect—to her rock-and-roll heroes like Townshend and to her fans in the audience, which might have included a starry-eyed Marina gazing at her Wonder Woman onstage and believing everything was possible, as long as you had the power of rock and roll in you.

CHAPTER 32

BRUCE SPRINGSTEEN AND THE E STREET BAND

TILL THE FAT LADY SINGS

Brendan Byrne (Meadowlands) Arena, East Rutherford, New Jersey, August 6, 1984

Listen to: "Rosalita," "Born to Run," "Thunder Road," "Badlands," "Prove it All Night," "Cadillac Ranch," "Hungry Heart," "The River"

They always said, "You gotta see Bruce live; then you'll understand." My friends were early birds: bigtime fans who urgently wanted to share their discovery of the rock-and-roll poet from Asbury Park. But somehow, over the years, Bruce Springsteen had been everywhere that I wasn't. I hadn't been in Cambridge in '74 when Jon Landau saw God onstage (although hundreds of people I've met over the years *insist* that they were in the Harvard Square Theater that night). I missed the tours to support Springsteen's breakthrough *Born to Run*, his fortunes soaring from the "Who cares?" category to semi-legend. I turned down an invitation to see the now-famous singer and his E Street Band in 1978, choosing instead to explore Boston's local punk-rock scene. But two years later, things changed when I heard a song called "Cadillac Ranch" on the radio. From the big-room echo on the naked drum kickoff to the cheesy sixties Farfisa organ, it yelled rock-and-roll attitude while chewing bubblegum at the same time. "That's from *The River*, Bruce Springsteen's brand new album," I heard the DJ chatter, prompting me to get my own copy of the two-record set. "The Ties That Bind," "Ramrod," and "Out in the Street" seized viscerally, while the poet pondering on "Independence Day," "Point Blank," and the title track exerted an overwhelming emotional pull. When *The River* tour reached New England in December 1980, I finally piled into a car with my Springsteen-freak friends for a road trip to Providence. Simply inexhaustible, the singer and his band set standards of endurance only rivaled by the Grateful Dead (who, albeit, took things at a more leisurely and stonier pace). During the three-hour, twenty-nine-song, basic set, then nearly forty-minutes of encore, Springsteen ruled the stage, while the E Streeters' ability to play what-ever their leader desired, whenever he wanted it, astonished me.

I witnessed a type of power onstage that I had never seen before. Over the years, countless singers had used the same old devices to cheerlead audiences: exhorting the crowd to clap, prompting sing-alongs, or even pulling individuals onstage. But one of the oldest tricks in the book was to stage a cheering competition between sections of the room. "Awl Reet! When we come around to that part in the song again, I want y'awl over here to shout as loud as you can!" My God, as much as I appreciated his stagecraft, I once witnessed Jon Bon Jovi incite not only the floor, but also the loges and four sections of the bal-cony into a competition. I excused myself, went to the bathroom, got a beer and he was still at it when I got back! But here was Bruce Spring-steen, curly hair all messed up, sweat spouting out of his pores, chest heaving—although his breathing rate had slowed somewhat because neither the singer nor his entire band were moving so much as a mus-cle. The figures remained stock still, frozen in whatever position they had been in when their leader suddenly threw up his arm and called an abrupt halt to their raging drag race. "Simon says: Stop!" Seconds passed, the audience laughed at the stunt and applauded. Now it had been a minute or two, still without movement. The crowd shrieked and the volume level peaked—perhaps that would break the spell. No dice. Moments crawled by as everyone's undivided attention focused on the stage; the band, even the roadies, remained immobile as if suspended in aspic. Then, very slowly, a smile crept onto Springsteen's face; that was all. When the throng spied it, they shouted all the louder. Then, body still immobile, his eyes glanced left. That side of the arena exploded! The smile got bigger. Then the eyes flicked to the right, erupting that quadrant. Down front: "Yayyyyy!" Left: "Yayyyyy!" Right: "Yayyyyy!" Front, left, right, front, left, right—the cheers followed, chasing the eyes around the hall a couple times. Suddenly, a signal from their leader released the band, which slammed back to life with a volcanic blast. Unbelievable! Bruce Springsteen had commanded the entire Providence Civic Center, front to back, side to side, almost 13,000 people, *with just his eyes*.

With *The River* gone multiplatinum and a long string of sold-out hockey arenas a testament to his success, Bruce Springsteen radiated the light of an ascended star perched at its zenith in the night sky. Or so we thought. After dropping back in the pocket to broaden his folk roots on the homemade *Nebraska* release in '82, Springsteen launched an atomic bomb on the country two years later with *Born in the U.S.A.*, an album that literally lifted the artist from "mere" star status to that of a cultural icon. It began in May '84 with the single "Dancing in the Dark" and its innocent, yet memorable, concert video introducing actress Courteney Cox. That song flew all the way to number 2 in America, becoming the first of *seven* Top 10 singles from *Born in the U.S.A.* that kept "the Boss," his popular nickname, on the charts until early 1986 when "My Hometown," the final vinyl seven-incher from the album, finally dropped off the survey. In the midst of that fantastic run, the title track, which went to number 9 in the winter of '84, did much more than become another hit: it became an easily misinterpreted anthem. Those who only heard the chorus assumed "Born in the U.S.A." to be a perfect flag-waving commercial, but the verses revealed a profound comment on the failure of the American "system" as seen through the eyes of an unemployed Vietnam vet. Where was he going to end up? At best he'd be on food stamps, at worst holding a gun to his head. The song was a cry of rage and anguish, certainly not the best choice to pump up a team before the big game, but that's how President Reagan used it in a speech, extracting patriotic mileage out of a song most people viewed as a worthy substitute for the "Star-Spangled Banner."

Beginning in arenas in July 1984 and ending fifteen months later in football stadiums, the tour to support *Born in the U.S.A.* grew into a mammoth globetrotting campaign as the album remained high in the charts and refused to go away. A stand of ten August '84 shows in the Brendan Byrne Arena at Meadowlands Sports Complex in East Rutherford, New Jersey, became one emotional high point of the Springsteen juggernaut. An hour's drive from Asbury Park, these were considered homecoming concerts, servicing 21,000 happy Springsteen followers at a whack. The announcement of the run prompted widespread hysteria as people rearranged their lives to find seats, which was not easy with Internet ticketing still an object of science fiction. Fans clutching sleeping bags staked out ticket windows, and people at home spent long minutes, even hours, waiting on their phones. Fortunately for me, I didn't need to do either, since Springsteen's label, Columbia Records, wanted me, a radio DJ in Boston, to witness Springsteen working on his home turf. All I needed to do was find my way to the arena somewhere in the swamps of Jersey, and I'd have a pair of tickets waiting.

I was disappointed when Springsteen only played three and a half hours this time. Jeez, what a slacker — he cut ten minutes from the show! Any music biz swagger I might have brought into the Meadowlands that night quickly vanished as the tales of chrome, factory girls, poor men, rich men, kings, desperate lovers, and tramps like us transported me out of my presumptions and into reality — romanticized certainly, but without compromise, without surrender. "Born in the U.S.A." started the set, Max Weinberg's military cadence and monstrous drum break setting the bar outrageously high right off the bat, but Springsteen controlled the flow and changed the moods at will for the rest of the night with some help from Big Bones Willie, Hazy Davy, Bad Scooter, Bobby Jean, the couple walking out on the wire, the convict in the electric chair, a town full of losers, and those two lanes that could take us any-where. By the end of his thirtieth song, a romp on the sixties hit "Twist and Shout," my arm muscles could no longer muster even a feeble re-sponse. I worried that if he came out for another encore, I might end up in the care of paramedics; fortunately the lights came up at that point. My friend and I slapped on our backstage passes and trudged wearily to the designated meeting area.

The backstage room was large, the size of a couple of tennis courts teeming with at least a hundred people with most jabbering excitedly about the show. Some folks, though, seemed unaffected by the pro-found performance. Perhaps they remained till the end to collect the bragging rights of a backstage pass and a visit beyond the velvet rope. "Rocky" came walking by and spoke in my ear, "Stick around; he'll be coming out later," and moved on to quietly inform some others. Known by this nickname to his friends, Jimmy Del Balzo would know if Bruce Springsteen planned to step into the room, since he was far up the food chain at Columbia Records. We killed time, making small talk with the few people I knew, grabbing beers before the supply disappeared, and grazing at a bowl of withered chips. The bright overhead lights cast the entire room in a stark glare, a punishing contrast to the carefully considered spectrum of Springsteen's light show, but the knowledge that "the Boss" would drop by sent a colorful glow of expectation to all corners. After an hour, any poseurs in the space had long since dis-appeared, and now there were only a couple dozen people left. Rocky mentioned that the star was doing an extended interview with MTV, but would appear as soon as he could. "Don't leave," he urged, "If he said he'd be here, he'll be here." More loitering and not a lot left to talk about slowed the clock to a tedious crawl.

At ninety minutes, there were just four of us left. The other couple began to quibble about leaving, but I had faith that the man who de-livered on his grand promises hadn't gotten there by skimping on the small ones. It turned out I was right: the door opened, our eyes shot to the entrance, and there he was, big smile and blinding white teeth lighting up the room, bulging muscles practically filling it. He looked around bemusedly at all the people who weren't there and gave us a sheepish "their loss, your gain" grin before striding over to shake hands and even hug the girls. He hung out for twenty minutes, nineteen more than I could have hoped, and there were no grand concepts explained or secrets of the universe revealed. No, the talk began with how great the show was and congratulations over *Born in the U.S.A.*, both politely received by "the Boss," but deflected into queries about our own lives. Who were we? What did we do? How were things going? Our nervousness and awe passed; this actually was an enjoyable and *relaxing* conversation. No annoyance at having to be somewhere he didn't want to be or effort to hurry things along danced in his demeanor; it seemed the impossibly fit figure standing there genuinely cared that this blip on the itinerary of his day would be a lifelong memory for us. But, then again, I'm sure Bruce (we were on a first-name basis at this point) got something out of the encounter; after all, he was a chronic people watcher. He had to be. Where else would he have discovered the parade of characters that ended up inhabiting his music, either name-checked in the lyrics or concealed in the backstreets? So, now I had a rock-and-roll fantasy of my own: perhaps I might be lurking in one of those future songs too: *the exhausted guy dressed in black hanging out backstage on night number two at the Meadowlands.* Well, then again, maybe not.

CHAPTER 33

LIVE AID

THE GLOBAL JUKEBOX

Wembley Stadium, London, England, July 13, 1985

Listen to: Boomtown Rats, "I Don't Like Mondays"; Queen, "We Are the Champions"; Elton John, "I'm Still Standing"; Dire Straits, "Money for Nothing"; U2, "Bad"

Bob Geldof was a cranky bastard, I could tell you that. The singer for the Boomtown Rats should have been in a great mood when I'd met him backstage after the band played Boston's Orpheum Theater in February 1981. After all, his group's *Mondo Bongo* album was getting played on local radio, and the concert had sold nicely. But no: I had to interview him for *Boston Rock* magazine and he fought me the whole way even though, as a fan, I lobbed him softball after softball. No one ever said that interviews are always supposed to be pleasant; rooting out a subject's inner thoughts could lead to some uncomfortably probing questions. It was obvious, though, that Geldof's gloom had been cemented in place long before I switched on the cassette recorder. The singer's mood became so sour that it amazed me when he actually allowed a photographer to step into the beat-up backstage room and snap a picture of him forcing a smile. I got the story and fulfilled my assignment, but any further desire I had to experience the Boomtown Rats vanished. The bloom was off the rose, as they say, and I'd never see the Irish band again. Well, actually I would, one more time, but not in the manner you might expect.

You see, in addition to being one of the most cynical and ornery persons I'd ever met, Bob Geldof also had one of the biggest hearts, and my interview had failed to reveal that. Maybe he didn't even know it himself at the time, but by 1984 he had had an awakening. The story of Geldof's personal transformation as he watched a BBC-TV documentary on the Ethiopian famine has been widely told. The shocking images prompted him to join with Ultravox lead singer Midge Ure to compose a Christmas song that addressed the problem and raised money for famine relief. Performed by an array of England's music elite gathered under the banner of Band-Aid, "Do They Know It's Christmas?" went on to smash sales records on both sides of the Atlantic, establishing a fund to send relief directly to the suffering African nation. By then, the Boomtown Rats were teetering on the brink of popular music irrelevancy, but the band had accomplished an unquestionable service by launching the greater role of its philanthropic, but cantankerous lead singer. Few others had the combination of uncompromising attitude and fearless constitution to browbeat a profession consumed by self-absorption and vanity to awaken to the idea of charity, and he wasn't done yet. Setting the date of July 13, 1985, for an interlinked and televised worldwide event simulcast from Wembley Stadium in London and JFK Stadium in Philadelphia, Geldof began calling on the cream of the world's talent. He wasn't afraid to ring anyone, and nobody had any good reason to refuse him.

I heard about Live Aid through the radio station I worked at, since media outlets everywhere were being contacted to carry the daylong broadcast that would begin at noon London time. In a stroke of luck, I'd already planned a vacation in Ireland for early July when my friends in U2 invited me to attend Live Aid as part of their small entourage. I'd take the shuttle from Dublin over to London and begin sending reports back to America. I wasn't getting paid, but what a fantastic opportunity to be involved with the greatest concert event in a generation. Every hotel room in London and, perhaps, the entire southeast of England had been booked solid for weeks. Fortunately, reservations had been made for me at the Mayfair Hotel, a distinguished establishment near Hyde Park. As soon as the black cab pulled up at the front entrance and a perfectly dressed, over-courteous doorman rushed out to open the car door, I realized that these stately quarters soared high over my humble pay grade. I might have been on U2's reservation list, but I was still paying my own way, so I hoped my credit could handle even the reduced "group rate." The Brits were a polite bunch, but if I couldn't pay up, would they toss me ignominiously out the front door with my bags sailing in an ungraceful arc behind me? I worried more as the porter showed me my opulent quarters, complete with a wooden writing desk probably older than America standing proudly by the windows.

I got myself organized and called Ellen Darst, who handled publicity and other details for the band. Transportation for the members of U2 with their wives, girlfriends, management, and so forth, had been arranged, but was limited. Would I mind running out to the stadium in the morning with the crew? Bono's personal onstage assistant, Greg Carroll, the New Zealand native who would tragically die on the lead singer's Harley and become the subject of U2's eulogy "One Tree Hill" a year later, drove me to Wembley at 8:00 a.m. At that early hour barely anyone loitered around the legendary stadium as we rode by its famous pair of white towers flanking the main entrance. Carroll parked in the reserved artists' area and we entered. My pass got me as far as the press and VIP viewing area, but not backstage. Since dozens of bands and musicians would be using that limited space, those passes were given out as sparingly as possible. In fact, around U2's scheduled fifteen-minute set, the band members themselves only had one hour prior to the appearance and a half-hour after to use their dressing room before giving it up to another act scheduled later.

I made my way to the VIP viewing area, passing the time by gazing over and over again at the vast interior of the stadium that would soon seat over 80,000. It was barely nine in the morning, 4:00 a.m. in Boston, and hours too early to call in a report. Boredom drove me inside to the main concourse: it would be good to scope out the facilities before they became awash in a flood of humanity. I would need to eat, so locating the nearest fish-and-chips stands became a primary goal, plus noting the positions of the telephone boxes from which I'd be delivering my actualities. Good news: lots of food stands; bad news: Wembley had been built in the twenties and the concourse was not all that wide, so congestion would be a factor, plus I found only a few payphones in the entire stadium. Although it seems unthinkable now, cell phones were still science fiction to the public, so I'd certainly be limited in the number of reports I could file when the queues for those phones grew long. Back out to my seat, I passed another slow hour watching the early birds slowly populate the vast expanse until a handful of VIP's finally arrived, and I sought some welcome conversation.

The arrival of Charles and Diana, the Prince and Princess of Wales, at noon marked the start of the concert. The enormous crowd now filling Wembley turned to face the royal box only yards away from my perch, joining in on "God Save the Queen." Just as in America when the "Star-Spangled Banner" introduced sporting events, the crowd slowly gained strength near the end, cheering wildly and obscuring the final notes. Charles and Diana sat down, but I couldn't stop staring over at them, the overly stiff prince and his beautiful wife, with her short blonde hair blown into a stylish and wavy eighties 'do, returning the looks of thousands with a warm and genuine smile. I was mesmerized by her radiance and youth; over twelve years younger than her husband, Diana's twenty-fourth birthday had only been two weeks earlier. A chap next to me noticed. "Haven't you ever seen a prince or a princess before?"

"Uh, well, actually . . . no!"

The London concert was being televised to the world, but at this early hour the American stage would not come alive until after 2:00 p.m. London time. Suitably, the initial artists were British stars largely unknown in the New World: Status Quo, Style Council, Adam Ant, Nik Kershaw, Ultravox, Spandau Ballet, and Bob Geldof's own Boomtown Rats, which took the stage at 12:44. Welcomed by an immense ovation, the singer achieved one of the greatest emotional peaks of the entire concert when the band performed its hit "I Don't Like Mondays." The song, about a school shooting, climaxed with the words, "And the lesson today is how to die!" Geldof froze, holding that image for a long suspended moment, his clenched fist high in the air. The silence stopped everyone in their tracks, even the army of roadies rushing to set up the next group's equipment. Yes, there were many stars in the house and even royalty sitting just feet away, but those words completely leveled the playing field, reminding everyone that we all had a job to do that day.

Sting and Phil Collins came on at 3:18 to do a half-hour show together. By this time, the JFK concert had begun and from now on, the sets would shuffle back and forth between London and Philadelphia. That led to some interesting segues: Sade finished her fifteen minutes of smoky, smooth-jazz-influenced hits only to be followed by the stateside reunion of Black Sabbath's classic lineup. I liked both, but that particular transition gave me whiplash!

Phil Collins departed Wembley with the announcement that he would board the Concorde and fly at Mach 2 to Philadelphia, courtesy of British Airways, which had donated the very expensive flight. With the various time zones figured in, he'd arrive onstage at nearly the same time he left London. The Concorde made a pass over the stadium, and the crowd sent a huge roar skyward that, perhaps, Collins heard even over the racket of those four great engines.

Since I was reporting at the Wembley terminus of Live Aid, I missed a lot of the Philadelphia portion being shown on a giant screen simply because I needed to wait in the queues for an open telephone. Once I got there, the process of ringing up an overseas operator and arranging for payment ate up more precious time — each visit burned up at least a half hour. How could I create a meaningful report if I couldn't see the show? On one such journey, however, I spied an open door to an office with a custodian sitting placidly at his desk. Desperate to save time, I pleaded with him: for a not-so-small compensation, could I use his office phone? The polite gent proved to be a savvy capitalist as well, and from that moment until the end of the concert my problems filing reports were over. I would leave the stadium penniless, however.

When Queen took the stage, Freddie Mercury held sway over the

80,000 as I'd never seen—nor would ever see—another performer come close to matching. He truly loved the stage as his instrument, strutting about using half of the mic stand as a baton to conduct the crowd while the enormous sound of Brian May's guitar crunched heavily into the rear decks of the huge space. This would often be cited as one of history's greatest rock-and-roll moments. Even with later sets by legends like David Bowie, the Who, Elton John, and an onstage finale including Paul McCartney, Queen's was the musical apex of a day glittering in power, emotion, and, yes, good will toward men.

I did get stuck at the stadium after the show. You know when you stay at a party too long and your ride leaves without you? U2 and crew had already cut out, so I followed the crowd into the streets. Digging for change, I remembered that my cab money had gone to that friendly janitor who could certainly afford a taxi tonight. No worries, though: I easily found a train bound for central London since most of the multitude oozed in that direction. Through the turnstiles and onto a car, I never did have to dig for the change that wasn't in my pocket; it seemed that even the civil servants from London's transportation system were in much too charitable a mood to charge.

In the end, Live Aid netted $120 million in cash and an equal amount in goods and services for the starving in Ethiopia. It was an astounding amount, Geldof admitting he thought they'd only net $10 million for all the effort. But the ever-pragmatic lead singer and activist, interviewed by *Rolling Stone* in 1990, seemed as proud of his accomplishment as embarrassed by it. He'd received a Nobel Peace Prize and was knighted by the British government, but the accolades couldn't erase the knowledge that for all the effort on that grand day in July of 1985, it was still a drop in the bucket. People remained starving in Africa at that point and millions still are. But at least Geldof tried. The cranky bastard may not admit to being a hero, but there are a lot of people out there, including myself, who think he is.

CHAPTER 34

MÖTLEY CRÜE

YOUR MASCARA IS RUNNING

Manning Bowl, Lynn, Massachusetts, August 3, 1985

Listen to: "Shout at the Devil," "Looks That Kill," "Home Sweet Home,"
"Girls, Girls, Girls"

The prevailing musical winds of the mid-eighties were scented with a peculiar mix of sweat, leather, and a lot of hairspray. "Summer Jam '84," headlined by Cheap Trick, had drawn a huge mass of spirited fans to the parched mid-July earth of Kingston Fairgrounds in New Hampshire. Although the Chicago band's star had faded somewhat with its arena-filling days behind it, the group served as an excellent dessert to an entrée of Twisted Sister and Ratt, heavy metal "hair bands" that had been unknown just a year earlier, but now burned up the sales charts. This new wave of hard-rock aggressors took their cue from a decade earlier, when Kiss and Sweet had pioneered glam metal and spent as much time in front of the makeup mirror as they did onstage. With lips pursed in endless photo sessions and pounds of rouge and lipstick applied under piles of teased locks wafting toward the heavens, the hair bands had taken the high ground. This was their day!

The hard bluesy rock of seventies bands like the Who, Aerosmith, Bad Company, Foghat, and ZZ Top was accompanied by its darker and heftier cousin named heavy metal, with Black Sabbath and Deep Purple leading the way. Those styles would inspire new generations to take up their axes and stride onstage hammering monstrous power chords that punished the biggest and baddest amplifiers and speaker cabinets ever forged in the devil's workshop. Kiss, Cheap Trick, and Van Halen begat Mötley Crüe, Guns N' Roses, Quiet Riot, Iron Maiden, Def Leppard, and a solo Ozzy Osbourne, all of whom carried the requisite level of overdriven decibels into a new decade. Soon the metal monsters began racking up impressive sales figures, so much so that a thousand more groups appeared on the scene, many of them emulating the look of their predecessors—even if their songwriting and musical chops didn't come close. High-pitched vocals and overpowering volume were essential, as were the tight black jeans and leather accoutrements of the earlier metal bands that had developed into a mandatory eighties uniform.

One defining feature was the hair: flowing locks and billowing manes, frozen fashionably into place and plunging past the shoulders, became vogue essential; and band members now devoted serious preshow prep time at the makeup mirror applying creams and colors from heavy-duty, giant-sized jars of cosmetics. With the arrival of revolutionary MTV in 1981, the armies of pure style rolled back the retreating forces of substance, and planted their flags in the makeup department rather than the guitar shop; on the video set, rather than the music studio. The term *hair band* was born. Even though many of these acts moved a treasure trove of platinum and gold, as the years flew by, the metal would become ever thinner and the bands increasingly brittle (Cinderella, Poison, Warrant, White Lion, Britny Fox . . . ad nauseam).

In 1981 Mötley Crüe led the charge out of L.A., releasing an independent album, scoring a major-label deal with Elektra Records soon after, and discovering success on MTV's heavy metal haven. Groups that rocked too hard for conservative radio programmers found a new star-making machine, the video channel feeding hungrily on the visually outrageous; the more extreme a band was, the better, and Mötley Crüe played its brazen cards to the max. The camera loved the members' head-to-toe leather (jackets, thigh boots, codpieces, even jock straps), polished pyramid belts and gleaming chains, maximum hair length *and* elevation, with layers of colorful mascara and lipstick tying it all together. An illusion of shrewdly calculated biker-warrior disarray tailored this fashion statement, with the final fabrication assigning a mostly black theme to the three instrumentalists while the singer, Vince Neil, with his bouncy blonde curls, contrasted in light-colored leather highlights. It was heavy metal showbiz from the Sunset Strip, glued together with gallons of extra-hold hairspray and mega-decibels of punishing volume. 1985 became Mötley Crüe's breakthrough year, a gateway the bandmates drove their motorcycles through to reach true stardom, selling over twenty-five million albums in the United States and leading the hair band pack all the way to the early nineties.

Theatre of Pain, Mötley Crüe's third album, came out in June '85; and with the band on the road and a remake of the seventies teen anthem "Smokin' in the Boys Room" riding the charts, it went gold by August and reached one million copies sold before the end of September. With the group's previous album, *Shout at the Devil*, also certified platinum, this was the Crüe's summer. What made these achievements somewhat surprising is that Neil had survived the fallout from a December 1984 DUI sports car crash that killed his passenger, Hanoi Rocks drummer Razzle (Nicholas Dingley), and left two others with permanent brain damage. A thirty-day jail sentence, five-year probation, some community service, and 2.7 million dollars in restitution cleared the way for the front man to continue his career. But, would America forgive the singer? Could the promise of the Crüe's first two records be fulfilled in the new release or would popular disdain crush the group's burgeoning career? As perceived outlaws, usurping the "bad boy" standard that Aerosmith had championed a decade earlier, Mötley Crüe crossed the nation on its *Theatre of Pain* tour. When succeeding concerts continued to draw larger numbers and album sales spiked ever higher, it was clear that both the band and its singer had been pardoned.

Mark Hildonen, former professional drag racer turned concert promoter, had created a successful franchise of hard rock festivals in the "Summer Jam" series at Kingston Fairgrounds. His proposed Mötley Crüe show the following August, though, ran into snags. To cover the expenses of this, the biggest concert Hildonen had ever promoted, he needed to sell more than the 14,000-ticket limit imposed by town officials. A series of legal battles played out, chewing up the summer of '85 as tickets were put on sale anyway. With just a week till show time, all had been purchased, but a superior court decision supported Kingston's right to cap the ticket sales at 14,000. Faced with losing money on a sellout show, the desperate promoter cast his net for an alternate venue and found a willing suitor in the city of Lynn, Massachusetts, a stone's throw north of Boston, with its Manning Bowl football stadium. The only other rock concert of note held at the stadium had been a Rolling Stones show in June 1966, which ended in a riot subdued by police using tear gas. For nineteen years rock events at the venue had been banned (except for an inoffensive Beach Boys show in '84), but Lynn's urgent need for funds to maintain the Bowl softened the city council's attitude. Working on a fast track, they granted a license for a 20,000-ticket concert with Mötley Crüe. With mere days to shift production to an unfamiliar venue while redoubling efforts to sell more tickets, Mark Hildonen and his company flew into panic mode. Opponents cited worries of their own: With the Manning Bowl located in the middle of a residential neighborhood, would there be a repeat of the 1966 debacle? City officials addressed this concern with a 7 p.m. curfew.

August 3 dawned and before midday I headed up to the stadium, assigned by my radio station to host part of the event. I always enjoyed arriving at concerts super early; even if you didn't have a parking pass, you could always find a space nearby. I left my car fifty feet from the backstage gate and talked my way to the production trailer to claim an all-access pass. This was another great reason to show up early; the lack of foot traffic and individuals securing the perimeter meant that any plausible explanation, even my Catch-22 situation ("I have to get in first to get my pass to get in") was generally accepted. As more people arrived, though, the bullshit factor would soar through the roof and nobody's story would be believed. I strolled around the stadium, surprised at the absence of equipment onstage; the PA speaker stacks had not yet been erected, and no stage lights mounted above. None of the bands had arrived, so I sacked out under the stage, catnapping away the effects of a late night while the hellishly tardy crew madly assembled equipment above me.

Eventually I headed back to the production trailer to receive my instructions and found that Mötley Crüe had its own stage introduction planned, so I was off the hook unless some mischief occurred. While loitering around I looked out a small window and witnessed one of the weirdest sights I'd ever see at a rock-and-roll show: A fantastic mix of odd bedfellows including members of the Crüe, bikers wearing jean jackets emblazoned with the unmistakable Hell's Angels logo, local and state police standing at ease among them, and, at the center of it all, a jewel in white named Heather Locklear. Ladies have always loved outlaws, and Crüe drummer Tommy Lee had become the latest rocker to attract the attention of a famous Hollywood starlet. Wrapped in chiffon, Locklear stood out as a beauty amid the rank and file in their blue, gray, and black, bringing to mind a medieval scene in which a virginal maiden transfixed a king's court filled with noblemen, knights, and servants.

Showtime arrived and the small-screen goddess floated to the side of the stage where her beau was soon pounding out an insanely amplified beat that thundered through the stadium and deep into the neighborhood beyond while Nikki Sixx smacked his booming bass and Mick Mars assailed the city limits with ridiculously loud guitar. Vince Neil's vocals were completely lost within the primal scream of the band's sheer volume, but he looked good moving about, working the crowd. Mötley Crüe would never earn much praise from the media; on that tour *Billboard* magazine's Ethlie Ann Vare wrote, "They don't play very well, haven't an original move among them, write terrible songs and have filthy mouths." So, okay, all of that was true—but who cared? The Crüe rocked the Manning Bowl in a seventeen-song set that left all its fans deliriously elated and totally exhausted while Heather *friggin'* Locklear danced on the side of the stage! Now, how often did that happen in little ol' Lynn, Massachusetts?

CHAPTER 35

STEVIE RAY VAUGHAN

LIVE ... AND ALIVE

The Metro, Boston, February 24, 1987

**Listen to: "Pride and Joy," "Cold Shot," "Voodoo Chile (Slight Return),"
"Change It," "Life by the Drop," "Leave My Girl Alone," "Riviera
Paradise," "Little Wing"**

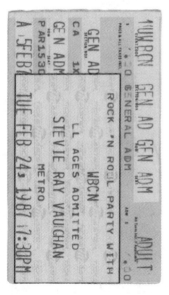

Stevie Ray Vaughan had a reputation —not only as one of the finest guitarists on the planet, but also for being a complete asshole. People I talked to mentioned how he was always messed up and difficult to deal with. I heard stories of wild drinking and snorting, marathons of sleeplessness during which he'd blister through a couple of gigs then crash for a day. In a cocaine trail of "eight balls" and a highway littered by Crown Royal bottles, the Vaughan tours went around and around the world, usually racking up over two hundred shows a year, and he'd throttle you if you got in the way. Now, there he was onstage behind the curtain, just twenty or thirty feet away, fiddling around on his guitar and obviously enjoying some solitude. But, I had drawn the short straw, my assignment to interview either the legend or a beast—I didn't know which one—but folks around me seemed to think I'd probably get both. Maybe after he'd torn my head off, he'd allow me enough of his words on tape that my boss would be happy and Boston could chew on a couple of new insights about Stevie Ray on the radio. Silently, I rehearsed a line and moved closer to that figure with the Mexican hat and the guitar.

The all-too familiar story of rock-and-roll excess had begun innocently enough (they always did) at home in Dallas and then later in the bars of Austin, the wide-eyed teenager watching his older brother Jimmie rip it up onstage and salivating over the blues greats who passed through clubs like Antones: Muddy Waters, the three Kings (Albert, B. B. and Freddie, but especially Albert), Otis Rush, Willie Dixon, Howlin' Wolf, Buddy Guy and Junior Wells. Then the ascent began as session work with David Bowie, a deal with Epic Records, and the 1983 debut album *Texas Flood* saw the twenty-nine-year-old Vaughan and his two-man backing unit Double Trouble wrestle blues back into a mainstream that was busily mainlining MTV. The onrush of success didn't come easily or cheap: the world wasn't just going to embrace this old-school guitar player from Texas no matter how fast his fingers flew nor how authentically they searched the depths of pain. The tour bus became the chariot, the clubs across America the fields of battle, and the young champion took the fight to the people. Believers arose at every nightspot, the songs beckoned from the radio, the album sold—went gold—got some awards and swiftly spread the news.

On a second album, the young upstart had the audacity to take on Jimi Hendrix! He covered the untouchable "Voodoo Chile (Slight Return)," which had been placed on holy ground after 1968 and never meant to be disturbed. Man, did he disturb it! The crackerjack nailed the *Electric Ladyland* track and even wound it out for a couple of minutes longer than Jimi's original just to savor the moment(s). The song ate up rock radio, along with his version of a song kicking around Austin called "Cold Shot," and that second album, *Couldn't Stand the Weather*, outsold its predecessor. Even though he said it was a tough record to make, 1985's *Soul to Soul* also sold well, maintaining Vaughan's upward trajectory. But, now there were too many arms reaching in the tour bus window, too many backstage passes handed out, and too many people that the record label wanted him to meet. He didn't help by insisting on answering all his fan mail and autographing every item handed him. Easily, the Devil exploited the opportunity, encouraging an attitude within Vaughan that it was actually possible to keep up with the accelerating ride. And so, the drugs maintained the pace and the drink mellowed out the worry as the interest charges on SRV's psyche and body steadily mounted.

And that's where the story had been left when I entered it. Stevie Ray Vaughan and Double Trouble had released *Live Alive* in November '86; now they were out promoting the double in-concert album with its lead single of "Willie the Wimp," an inspired tale of a Chicago gangster's late son presented at his viewing in a coffin customized to look like a Cadillac with working headlights, fins, and a glass windshield. Epic Records brokered a deal with my radio station, WBCN-FM in Boston, to sponsor a club show at the Metro in February and give all 1,300-odd tickets away on the air. Since Vaughan had performed two nights at the downtown Orpheum Theater just three months previously and sold over 5,000 seats in the process, a Metro ticket became a high-demand item that required listeners to tune in the radio station for long periods of time to win—that was the idea! The difficulty in obtaining each precious admission ducat meant that everybody in that place would be a tried-and-true fan; this should be a cake assignment for the guitarist no matter how far down the bottle he had sunk. And now it was nearly show time. I hadn't run into many artists who liked to talk just before they went onstage, but that was the arrangement this time around; so with the sound of the crowd only a few feet away on the other side of the curtain, I angled my way over toward the solitary figure sitting on a big road case.

"Uh . . . Stevie?" The eyes flickered up from the pick guard and frets of Number One, his wonderfully beat-up, but meticulously maintained Stratocaster, and searched for the source of the voice. Instantly I felt devastated for interrupting him. Suppose he was working out the melody to a new song or changing the usual course of one of his solos? *You idiot! You interrupted a genius!*

"Yeah, man?" he replied in a soft voice after his eyes had found me, friendly eyes without any edge of anger in them. Perhaps I'd found him in a good moment? He wasn't going to eat me alive? I smiled and introduced myself, hiding the wireless microphone in my back pocket almost in embarrassment. "The record label said you might want to do a quick interview for the radio station, maybe an ID for the radio?"

"Sure, man. No problem." His smile was warm and welcoming. *He isn't having a problem with this?* I didn't have time to wonder about that or consider how fortunate I was, so I revealed the evil mic feeding its signal back to the station where tape was already rolling. I lobbed some softballs like "How far along are you on the tour? You've been on the road quite a while with this album."

"Seems like we've been the road forever," he laughed. "We get a break here before too long!" Then he continued with a hint of some dissatisfaction with the recent live album: "We're gonna start writing for the next record; we're gonna go and take our time on this one and do it right!" Then he happily obliged with a station identification plug for BCN before we tried to out-thank-you each other. It was all smiles as I left, then he went back to picking on Number One, complacent and seemingly content just moments away from curtain time.

The Metro was stuffed with the rapturous, so there was little Stevie Ray Vaughan could do — short of a face-plant — that would disappoint this crowd. He came out swinging, transformed utterly from the mellow individual I'd just encountered, "Scuttle Buttin'" his way through the club like a knife through butter. Double Trouble, fleshed out to a trio now that Reese Wynans had been added on keyboards, hung on that man like glue: there was nothing he could do (as great and slippery on the guitar as he was) to shake 'em. The fire in those fingers astonished the audience on the fast scorchers, the faces in the audience amazed with more than one mouth caught hanging open. His slow blues licks were cries of love, notes lingering on in perfect duration and tone before succumbing reluctantly to the next. I felt a tap on my shoulder and turned to see Epic's label rep, who asked if I'd gotten to talk with the guitarist. "Yeah, and he was really nice; I didn't expect that." The rep clued me in and told me the whole story that most people didn't know at this point. Vaughan had obviously gone on too fast and too hard for way too long. He'd hit the wall during the European tour that previous summer, collapsing and coughing up blood from a stomach riddled with holes and a body hovering perilously near death. He was an alcoholic and a drug addict, no more than that, and if he didn't stop the abuse — well, all the gold and platinum in the world certainly wouldn't help him. The rest of the tour had been canceled; Vaughan sought help in London at the same clinic where Eric Clapton had been freed from his heroin demon and then came back to Atlanta for a permanent (he hoped) cure. Now a steadfast devotee of Alcoholics Anonymous, he grabbed the lifeline to pull himself successfully through the Twelve Step program. For the first time in years, Vaughan was absolutely drug free and sober, playing onstage completely straight. Not only that, but his longtime Double Trouble bass player and friend, Tommy Shannon, had gone through the treatment as well and stood by his side.

I listened to the record guy in amazement. Years later, in the present, rehab stints seem to be discovered and exposed even before a star has the chance to sign-in at the clinic's reception desk, then amplified mercilessly by an endless blizzard of social media. Sometimes a trip to the hospital has less to do with a star's health and more about revamping a bad image or reversing a spate of unsavory and destructive public relations incidents. But in 1987, matters like this could often be kept quiet, and so had been Stevie Ray Vaughan's tangle with addiction. It is to the credit of his talent that he was able to hide the debilitating effects to his playing for so long. The label rep even admitted that Vaughan hated *Live Alive* and thought his playing had been shit, plus the guitarist had suffered great uncertainty as to whether or not he could even perform without the drink or drugs. "Well, he seems to be doing pretty damn well without them!" I added, looking over at a remarkable player onstage who seemed to be trying to make up for lost time with his slow blues workout on "Ain't Gone 'n' Give Up on Love." The crowd hooted and hollered, sometimes in the right spots, as the player cranked new energy and precision into the track from *Soul to Soul*. Mr. Hyde had left the building — this was a new era for Stevie Ray Vaughan. I felt somewhat ashamed for being presumptuous of the man's character, but mostly just happy for him, sincerely hoping that his cure would stick.

Ultimately, it would. The guitarist remained clean on the road with all of its attendant temptations and long periods of restless downtime between shows. He channeled his efforts into mending fences with former friends and furiously writing new music. What he said about wanting to get it right next time around proved to be prophetic: *In Step*, the first record he ever recorded straight, would be the finest album he'd do with Double Trouble. Some of the new songs, like "Wall of Denial," were openly confessional, but Stevie had nothing to hide at this point. Even the title of the album reflected his battle back to clarity as revealed by the Twelve Steps. Everyone around him was inspired at just how remarkably changed and loving he became from the end of '86 onward. Vaughan's was a classic story of a soul's passage out of the darkness and into the welcoming arms of a world still getting to know him. That successful journey shines much brighter than anything else we can ever say of him.

CHAPTER 36

ROGER WATERS AND PINK FLOYD

WHICH ONE IS PINK?

Providence Civic Center, August 13 and October 16, 1987

Listen to: Pink Floyd, "One of These Days," "Time," "Wish You Were Here," "Shine On You Crazy Diamond," "Comfortably Numb," "Learning to Fly"; Roger Waters, "Radio Waves"

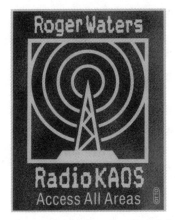

Roger Waters stepped into the small control room dressed in a black, loose-fitting sport coat with matching pants, dark shirt, and black hair flecked with distinguishing gray. The narrow face framed by a pair of mirrored sunglasses returned no smile, only a polite, but perfunctory acknowledgment. As he seated himself, two workers buzzed about, hastily fitting the star with a microphone. The lighting in the room was dim: would the iconic singer-songwriter-bassist of the legendary Pink Floyd remove his shades? Absolutely not. They remained, perched on his nose as immobile and resolute orbs of reflection. I found myself wondering if they ever came off.

Thirty seconds away from talking live on the air across a satellite to over one hundred radio stations, I pondered with dismay that there would be no chance to develop any connection with the guest. In fact, a definite frost hung in the air of the studio as we sized each other up. Rather than a fireside chat between musical compatriots, this felt more like dancing inside the ropes at a championship boxing match.

Roger Waters had distinguished himself for nearly twenty years as the one who conceived and wrote the majority of Pink Floyd's greatest known works, but it did not begin that way. The group took form within London's sixties underground scene as envisioned by its brilliant singer and guitarist Syd Barrett, who wrote, then recorded, the band's first album before rolling LSD dice and coming up snake eyes. After Barrett essentially lost his mind in '68, the remaining unit of Waters, Rick Wright on keyboards, and drummer Nick Mason added guitarist-singer David Gilmour to forge on and create several innovative and artistically challenging works. This phase culminated in the 1973 release of *Dark Side of the Moon*, which exploded in popularity, selling somewhere north of forty million copies around the word and permanently erasing the group's status as an underground curio. Subsequently, Roger Waters's album concepts and writing efforts far surpassed that of his companions: by the time of *The Wall* in 1979, the musician completely dominated this aspect of the band.

Tensions pried the group apart during the recording of its next album, *The Final Cut*, in which Waters dealt acridly with the politics of warfare and the emotional and physical costs of conflict. It was daunting stuff, and his iron grip over the entire project alienated his bandmates so completely that the 1983 release of the album found Pink Floyd dead in the water as a functioning unit. Its members quickly scattered to separate studios with solo projects in mind and very different visions of the band's status and future. Waters interpreted this split to mean the end of Pink Floyd, while the others reasoned that, as traumatic as it was, the period represented a necessary sabbatical. Three years later, the situation exploded in the press and the courtroom as recording sessions for a new Floyd album were convened without the involvement of Waters. Gilmour and Mason maintained that their former partner had announced his intent to leave the band in a December 1985 letter to the record label, so they embarked on the project without him. Waters countered that Pink Floyd had become "a spent force creatively" and filed suit in London's High Court to have the partnership officially dissolved. As both parties lobbed legal hand grenades, they somehow found the time and concentration necessary to continue working. The reconstituted Pink Floyd, represented by three-fourths of the classic lineup, labored on a worthy addition to its catalogue while Waters hammered out a complex solo album of music and dialogue entitled *Radio K.A.O.S.* By the summer of 1987, both camps had their respective projects prepared for release.

Roger Waters jumped off the starting block first. I received an invitation from Columbia Records to interview the reclusive musician along with the affable Ray White, a DJ from WNEW-FM in New York City, as cohost. The conversation would be broadcast live to America from Abbey Road Studios in London, where Pink Floyd had created much of its music. But after journeying to England, fighting off jet lag, and spending hours in preparation, where was Roger Waters? White and I waited uneasily in our chairs in the cramped control room, feeling like astronauts perched high in their capsule moments away from a fiery Cape Canaveral launch. With only two minutes to go, when it seemed likely that we'd be punching the "abort" button, the mysterious and lanky guest finally shuffled into the room. Had he loitered just outside the door, to the last possible second, to avoid this unpleasant, but necessary duty? Understandably, our conversation began stiffly, but warmed considerably as Waters became comfortable, even excited, in describing his latest album concept. The end of the interview, though, brought out the harder questions. I asked, "Roger, why did Pink Floyd disintegrate during the recording of *The Final Cut?*"

"We'd all grown in different ways and by that time we'd been working together for fifteen or sixteen years. I just think it was time for it to finish. It reached the natural end of its life."

"Does it distress you that Pink Floyd is, indeed, recording an album and will go on tour without you?"

"Uhmmm . . . yes," he replied guardedly. "It distresses me less than it did six months ago, and hopefully in six [more] months it will distress me [even] less . . ."

"They will be performing some of your songs." The mirrored orbs dipped for a moment, then fixed me in a hypnotizing grip before the voice cackled dryly, "Yes, I suspect they will. Isn't that flattering?"

Back in America nine days later on August 13, Columbia Records hosted a gathering of radio programmers and personalities at the Providence Civic Center for a full dress rehearsal of the *Radio K.A.O.S.* tour, which would begin officially the following night in the same place. The label had flown in the industry heavyweights with hopes that seeing Waters's solo production would ignite enthusiasm to support the project. I surveyed the thousands of vacant seats before being advised to join everyone in the back of the hall at the main bar directly opposite the stage. The place could only be reached at the top of a long set of steep concrete steps, a challenging climb that left anyone who attempted the summit gasping and barely able to place their drink order. Everyone managed it, though, because Columbia was running an open tab. Jim Ladd, legendary Los Angeles DJ who played a part in the show, came upstairs to chat. As soon as he'd stopped huffing and puffing from his own ascent, he pointed across the gulf to the two-story stage and identified the mockup of a radio control room he'd occupy during the concert. There was also a phone booth placed halfway back on the Civic Center floor, and Ladd explained that members of the audience would be able to direct questions to the band members from that location. Both queries and answers would be amplified through the PA system for all to hear. "The whole show," he continued, "is based on the idea that it's actually going out [on the air] as if it's a live radio broadcast."

For over two hours the multimedia romp unfolded onstage as the guests sat scattered about the arena like random ants munching on a picnic. Ladd began the show in character as a DJ taking calls from his listeners; he picked up the phone, and the Bleeding Heart Band launched into the opening "Radio Waves." Roger Waters, those perpetual shades reflecting the stage lights, stood near stage center cradling his bass; he'd miss nothing during this concert run-through, noting any infinitesimal error for later review. A circular screen flickered to life from behind, showing an animated metallic dinosaur approaching across an imaginary wasteland as the band slipped into the Pink Floyd warhorse "Welcome to the Machine." Waters unveiled more classic footage with shots of the band's famous inflatable swine floating in all its pink glory over Battersea Power Station and also flashed back to Floyd's earliest days with a rare 1967 black-and-white promotional video for "Arnold Lane." Dramatic new films were also introduced — one of them swiftly transporting the audience, as if on the end of a pencil, into a massive set of computer-generated stage and arena blueprints.

Waters had rearranged his latest musical adventure so that the new songs alternated with proven Pink Floyd standards. The production built to a shattering crescendo simulating the world on the brink of thermonuclear destruction. At the zero mark, a tremendous white pyrotechnic display accompanied by total whiteout on the movie screen engulfed the arena as the sound reached a climax before abruptly ceasing. All the lights switched off, plunging the Civic Center into utter blackness. In Waters's tale, this terrifying taste of Armageddon was actually a computer simulation intended to teach the world a harsh lesson. When Jim Ladd lit a match in his booth a couple of moments later, a solitary light in the profound darkness, he was supposed to have been scared to death. The emotional impact of Waters's show depended on whether or not those in the audience had felt some of that fear too. Although the size of our group was ridiculously tiny in the cavernous space, I heard wild applause erupt throughout the arena. While the stage lights came up slowly, I couldn't stop applauding as well — the full-on rehearsal had been no less than stunning. We reached a consensus afterward that even if the public didn't understand all the concepts Waters tried to get across, they'd still get one hell of a ride!

Coincidentally, within days of Waters's practice run, the reconstituted Pink Floyd released its album *A Momentary Lapse of Reason*. This was the record that "we will stand or fall by," Gilmour had stated in January of 1987, "If the fans like it, nothing else will matter." Whether one lauded the band's return or sided with *Rolling Stone* critic Mark Coleman who wrote, "Waters' absence reduces Pink Floyd to an FM rock oldies act (at best) or a lumbering self-parody (at worst),"

A Momentary Lapse of Reason became an immediate and massive sales success. The album shot to number 3 on the U.S. sales chart and went on to move over five million copies, while *Radio K.A.O.S.* never reached beyond a comparatively paltry number 50. Although Waters struggled to fill any arena he played, Pink Floyd easily sold out three nights in advance at the 15,000-seat Montreal Forum and would regularly fill stadiums three times that size. Extended, then extended again, the globetrotting road trip continued until July 1989 and became one of the highest-grossing tours in history.

Playing leapfrog with Waters's own traveling circus, the Pink juggernaut reached the Providence Civic Center two months after the band's former partner had rehearsed there. I journeyed south for the spectacle and noticed many younger fans in the audience who couldn't have been in kindergarten when *Dark Side of the Moon* came out. Fourteen years of steady radio airplay and no extensive tour since 1977 had made Floyd's return a highly prized event for all ages. Showtime arrived with an ominous cloud of dry-ice vapor rising up and sliding off the front of the stage as the Civic Center's bright interior abdicated to an eerie purple glow shining down into the fog. I sat close enough on the floor to feel the chilling mist as the dry ice evaporated and noticed David Gilmour's smile as the stocky forty-two-year-old walked into the dim light holding his Stratocaster. Eschewing a flashy opening salvo, Pink Floyd eased gently into a dreamy fifteen-minute version of "Echoes," the centerpiece to 1971's *Meddle* album. An essential part of the catalogue ignored in concert since the *Wish You Were Here* era, its performance incited a standing ovation. During the ensuing three-hour set, Floyd included nearly all the music from its latest album and unleashed a huge replica of its inflatable swine from '77 to lurch about clumsily during "One of These Days." Then, even more outrageously, the band ignited an oversized metal bed in the rafters and released it to hurtle down a cable trailing flames all the way and crashing into the stage during the synthesizer-driven "On the Run."

Pink Floyd's production assault completely overwhelmed the senses, adding mightily to its career-long legacy as a cutting edge innovator in concert. Along with the many selections played from its latest release, the band concentrated on the classic albums that featured balance between Roger Waters's lyrical ambition and the other band members' musical contributions—completely avoiding any music from the Waters-dominated *Animals* or *The Final Cut* albums. Later, as the Providence Civic Center slowly emptied, I questioned my loyalties: whose side was I on? Not unlike David taking on a modern-day Goliath armed with deep pockets and two-decade-old brand name, Roger Waters wielded a slingshot against his archrival's sword. But would he get in a lucky shot? Both champions appeared sincere and willing to go to enormous lengths in time, effort, and money to carry on their separate visions. But, I concluded, why choose to follow only one of them? Rather than analyzing the merits of the bitter Floydian feud, perhaps it was better to just sit back and enjoy the sudden surplus of interstellar sounds from both.

Roger Waters returned to New England in November '87 to finish up his North American tour at the Centrum in Worcester, Massachusetts. After a spectacular performance, the capacity crowd gave it all they had for this last stateside rendition of *Radio K.A.O.S.* The awkward moment came later when I met Waters backstage to congratulate him on what had been a truly mesmerizing concert. Smiling and dressed in a black turtleneck with charcoal slacks *and no sunglasses*, the upbeat and still-adrenalized musician chatted breezily for a few moments, then asked me pointedly if I'd seen the "other" show yet.

"Yes," I replied, "it came through Providence a month ago."

"Did you like it?" the figure demanded.

"Yes, it was very impressive," I answered, more than a bit uneasily as he scowled back.

"It's all smoke and mirrors," he answered in a whisper. Then his thin withering smile returned. "I'm sure they'll make millions." With that, the man in black waved goodbye, spun on his heels and disappeared out the doorway.

CHAPTER 37

GUNS N' ROSES

MEANWHILE, BACK IN THE JUNGLE...

Paradise Theater, Boston, October 27, 1987

Listen to: "Welcome to the Jungle," "Sweet Child O' Mine," "Paradise City," "November Rain"

The whole "hair band" ride through the eighties had been a hoot. Gathering at metal hotspots in Boston like the Channel and Narcissus, the scene makers had met nightly amid the perfumed stink of L'Oréal and Paul Mitchell. The fabulous bouffants bobbed and banged to the hard-rock cheese churned out by an endless succession of pop-metal groups. The problem was, as the decade wore on, the names changed weekly, but the song remained the same: the music, the stage moves, the faux attitude, the makeup, and the f@#!in' use of the F-word every time a lead singer couldn't f@#!in' think of something to say—which happened all the f@#!in' time! Somewhere in '86, I'd had enough: the band was Europe, and "The Final Countdown" pushed me over the edge. Our radio station received a platinum album for the group's debut, but everyone was too embarrassed by the award to hang it up on the wall. Years later when we were rearranging the office, I actually found the plaque jammed between two desks, caked with layers of dust and the distant echoes of an outdated era. Yet, like a horror-film slasher that refused to die no matter how many bullets raked his chest, the lurch of mascara rock from bands like Cinderella, Faster Pussycat, Britny Fox, Warrant, the Bulletboys, Slaughter, and FireHouse would survive on into the nineties. So, when *Appetite for Destruction* from Guns N' Roses arrived in the summer of '87, the album appeared as just another unwanted guest from a tired genre invading your house, drinking your booze, and overstaying the welcome it never got. Of course, I'd soon realize that was not the case at all; *Appetite* sat patiently on my desk like a ticking time bomb.

Rob Tannenbaum writing in *Rolling Stone* in 1988 summed up Guns N' Roses best when he called the band a "musical sawed-off shotgun." Not only did the members come packing a dangerous piece, they wielded it with a reckless and malicious mind. Rather than scrutinizing the gutter-life world of sex and drugs teeming along the back alleys around Sunset Strip and writing about it, they actually walked that walk (or crawled that crawl). The booze and the needles, blackouts and ODs mentioned in the lyrics were lifted from experience. With all of that personal horror going on for Guns N' Roses, it was easy to assume that image alone captained this ship and the band couldn't play worth a damn. After all, most of its hair-band predecessors never managed a decent lick, but still sold millions dipping pop clichés into a vat of sugary hard rock with zero nutritional value. And if a group couldn't play for crap, there was always the age-old soundboard solution: turn it up to the painful threshold of a 747 screaming down the runway on takeoff roll. At that volume, small problems like a singer who couldn't sing or a guitarist still struggling to master a riff as traumatically challenging as "Smoke on the Water" could all magically disappear in the obscuring waves of white noise. At first, it was easy, even typical to lump Guns N' Roses in with all this pabulum.

But as time went on, the signs indicated otherwise. "Welcome to the Jungle," a violently thrashing single, broke through on MTV and FM radio with a relentless attack that had more in common with punk rock, Aerosmith, and the Rolling Stones on crack. It was a messy, treacherous and uncompromising view of hell on earth: if it wasn't experienced by Axl Rose, the lead singer, than he sure sounded convincing. The cover of the album with its cartoon depiction of a robotic rape scene appalled retailers. A pushback from some of the big chains resulted, so the group agreed to change the cover, all the while gaining significant notoriety and scads of press. Guns N' Roses hit the road in a tour that would continue on and on as the album slowly built momentum and charged ahead, keeping the group out on the road to support its rapidly catalyzing career for a full sixteen months. Early in that endless road trip and three months after the release of *Appetite for Destruction*, Guns N' Roses visited Boston's Paradise Theater. Little known aside from some scattered airplay at the time, the group's name appeared in miniscule font on the club's schedule: Would this show become one of the blots of red on the Paradise balance sheet for the year? For a little while, that seemed to be the case before the ascent of "Welcome to the Jungle" precipitated a tsunami rush for tickets that soon swallowed every available square foot in the place. My friends at Geffen Records insisted that I come; if they hadn't held a few tickets for some people in the media, I'd never have witnessed Guns N' Roses in its first and last visit to a club in Boston.

I arrived with skepticism, still scarred by my overdose on Europe and a hair-band scene that had become dead to me. Plus, further ambivalence resulted from being blinded by other brilliant lights released at the same time—particularly *The Joshua Tree* from U2, John Mellencamp's *The Lonesome Jubilee*, reactivation of Pink Floyd on *A Momentary Lapse of Reason*, and the *Radio K.A.O.S.* solo rebuttal from Roger Waters. But, the palpable buzz flying around the sold-out room couldn't be ignored as the record label folks bought a round of drinks, and the time bomb counted down the final seconds before stage time. Small talk centered on the success of the Whitesnake album that Geffen had released in the spring, finally pushing that longtime U.K. group over the top. At one point there was hope that this Guns N' Roses club tour might morph into a support slot for Whitesnake in November, but that prospect had fallen through. With Geffen already experiencing some significant traction for Aerosmith's *Permanent Vacation* album earlier in the fall, perhaps that would be a great bill, someone suggested. The words hung in the air for a second before being extinguished by the roar of voices as the houselights died and Guns N' Roses bolted on-stage. The hour or so of metallic mayhem began instantly with "It's So Easy," Duff McKagan's bass announcing a relentless rhythm matched on top by dual guitar ferocity from Slash and Izzy Stradlin. The former, stripped to his waist and banging on a Les Paul, maintained what would become his classic pose with an eternal cigarette dangling out of the black corkscrews of hair that blotted away any clear view of his face. If I didn't know all of the music on *Appetite for Destruction* yet, clearly I was in the minority as everyone else in the house joined Rose in shouting out the signature "Fuck off!" in the middle of the first song. It would be the first expletive of a multitude.

Guns began at supersonic speed and kept the pace up for the entire show, persistent and unapologetic, driven by a reckless abandon fueled by the boundless energy of youth (both Slash and drummer Steven Adler were only twenty-two, Duff twenty-three, and Axl and Izzy a relatively ancient twenty-five). This was a hell-bent sprint to the finish; a fifty-yard dash employing maximum effort that featured nearly all of the debut album, the highlights being a magnificent "Paradise Theater" that sent the crowd into a club-wide fit of hyperventilation and the one cursory nod to a power ballad entitled "Sweet Child of Mine." At this point, that type of slow and dreamy, female-targeted song style had been a godsend to many a hair band and metal outfit, including Night Ranger with its massive "Sister Christian" and the Scorpions "Still Loving You." Like a musical baked Alaska, the hard, electric power chords on the outside protected a soft and vulnerable interior, a blend of hot and cold that successfully won over the sales charts time and time again. That would happen with "Sweet Child of Mine," but the march to number 1 for this single was still over six months in the future. At the Paradise, the song revealed itself as a fleeting sign of tenderness, but Guns N' Roses didn't sugarcoat the love letter as Slash pummeled the track with a blistering monument of a solo. Onward to the end with a Hiroshima-level blast on "Welcome to the Jungle," followed by the surprising cover of "Knocking on Heaven's Door."

Off for a quick towel or two and a smoke and then back in the lights for a breathless encore. The band's debt to Aerosmith in the layout of the lineup and powerful guitar-heavy approach couldn't be concealed, but Guns acknowledged it in full by finishing up with a delirious run-through of "Mama Kin." To anyone who had seen the band rise from its beginnings on the Sunset Strip, this cover choice brought no surprise since the group played it nearly every night, but to a virginal Boston audience, Guns' heartfelt tribute to the hometown heroes blew the ceiling off the place. No more encores were forthcoming, but the end aroused no disappointment to me since topping that final moment seemed fairly impossible. My mind was blown! Everyone else seemed dazed as well, breathlessly reviewing in their skulls what had just happened as the sudden glare of the houselights snapped on, screaming, "Go home!"

My friends at the record label smiled with knowing glances. This had been a true rock-and-roll experience; this bunch of L.A. mutts had more in common with the Stones, Aerosmith, Sex Pistols, or the Clash than with any glam metal band currently applying makeup backstage. I felt as if I needed to share this knowledge, and so would everyone else—enough so that when the group returned in May '88, it graduated to the far-larger Orpheum Theater and then again as a warm-up to Aerosmith playing three nights for over 50,000 at nearby Great Woods Amphitheater in August. This one tour took Guns N' Roses from the clubs to the stadiums, a dizzying road trip that spiraled into a success so wildly overwhelming and sudden that it would shatter all of the band members' lives, at least for a little while.

Overcoming all the drugs and the booze, seeing past the madness of an entire world knocking on the backstage door and struggling to calm the party down long enough to write and record new material became the main concerns in Guns N' Roses' future. The group did no less than bludgeon the metal scene back from the pop-music abyss that had nearly consumed it, returning the music to its essential and daring rock-and-roll core. It was a dangerous band doing everything that came naturally, saving rock even as the members ravaged themselves to near death. This *authentic* version of Guns N' Roses would blow apart in '93, Rose then taking a surrogate lineup into the new millennium; but it was okay, by then the band's mission had already been accomplished. On this particular night, though, all the calamity and destruction lay ahead. The Paradise concert would be an unencumbered and naked snapshot of a bunch of misfits welded together and driven on by their insatiable hunger for rock and roll. And that was enough, as far as I was concerned: you could take the rest of the drama and shove it.

CHAPTER 38

ROGER WATERS

"TEAR DOWN THE WALL!"

Potsdamer Platz, Berlin, Germany, July 21, 1990

Listen to: Pink Floyd, *The Wall* album

From my vantage point on the stainless steel bleachers set up against this section of the Berlin Wall, I could see a block of ugly apartments bordering the site on the eastern side. For almost forty years these yellowing structures and their anxious inhabitants had witnessed the beats of a thousand sentries patrolling slowly past, the sound of guard dogs suddenly barking or even the dismaying bursts of gunfire. More than a generation had been spent cowering behind those drawn window shades with anxiety and fear accepted as basic facts of life. But all semblance of that past had been shed as hundreds of partygoers shouted and danced on those rows of apartment balconies. Dozens of East German military trucks and armored personnel carriers had pulled up alongside the Wall so soldiers in khaki could stand on top of the vehicles for a better view. Along with the quarter million spectators standing in the festival site in front of them, they could never have imagined the fantastic scene as Pink Floyd's Roger Waters staged his band's 1979 masterpiece *The Wall* on ground zero of Europe's terrible past and a hopeful future. It appeared as if Joni Mitchell's utopian vision expressed in her song "Woodstock" had truly blossomed thirty years later and nearly four thousand miles away. Could the death bombers really be turning into butterflies?

Roger Waters, who wrote most of Pink Floyd's iconic tale of alienation and division, staged his celebration and charity event at the actual Berlin Wall after rapid social, economic, and political transformation had crumbled the East German government and crippled its once-powerful patron, the USSR. By the autumn of 1989, residents of a city long divided in two by the hated twenty-eight-mile concrete, steel, and barbed wire wall had begun knocking small holes in it. When Soviet guards failed to intervene, whole sections of the graffiti-covered barrier were toppled before East Germany threw in the towel and officially removed restrictions to travel through its borders in November 1989. For the first time since the Wall was erected in 1961, East and West Berliners could pass unhampered to the other side of their city. Waters's performance would take place on July 21, 1990, in Potsdamer Platz, a huge area of no-man's land located inside the still-standing Wall near Berlin's landmark Brandenburg Gate. This was an infamous place. Forces from each side had eyeballed the other across its desolate ground during the Cold War, and many brave souls had been gunned down in their attempts to escape to the West. Years before that, Adolf Hitler had directed the final days of his Third Reich from a command bunker here as Allied forces closed in to end World War II. Now transformed into a sanctuary for peace, this historic killing field would accommodate the thousands who traveled there while millions more in thirty countries watched on television.

Soon after receiving word that my presence was requested as part of the press pool going to Berlin to cover Waters's latest grand vision, I sat on an airliner winging across East Germany through one of the narrow air corridors the Soviets had designated years before to allow safe passage to the divided capital. When I arrived the day before the concert, a citywide carnival appeared to be going on. With the hot July sun blaring down invitingly, the populace had taken to the streets, strolling through the city, spilling off the sidewalks, and constantly blocking traffic. There were knots of people talking excitedly everywhere: tearful reunions and happy conversations, emotions overflowing all around in Berlin's "summer of love." I joined a small group of American correspondents who stuffed themselves into a pair of Volkswagen minivans and headed to Checkpoint Charlie. This had been Berlin's primary Cold War junction, where NATO tanks and troops once stood only yards away from the cream of Russia's armored force, one bullet away from a potential world conflict. Now, hundreds of citizens crowded this once treacherous stretch of road, strolling freely back and forth. Chunks of the Berlin Wall, colorfully spray-painted over the years on the western side and dull gray or sandy-colored on the eastern half, were available for a hefty sum. Or, for a couple of coins, you could rent a hammer and chisel from one of the kids sitting on the curb and chip out a piece of your own. That wouldn't last; in a few weeks the remaining sections of the Wall would either be hammered away completely by tourists or removed in large sections by the united government for museums and monuments around the world. Checkpoint Charlie disappeared behind us as we gawked at the tired and colorless facades of East Berlin's buildings, staring inertly back at us like the black-and-white photos of a bygone era.

By the morning of Saturday, July 21, Berlin had swelled like a bloated bratwurst as hundreds of thousands had arrived. Most Europeans had entered the city by train, filling the Berliner Hauptbahnhof with record crowds, while others simply accepted the pros and cons of hitchhiking and stuck out a thumb to arrive via autobahn. Roger Waters's crew had spent months designing and assembling a show, which included 2,500 white Styrofoam blocks to be methodically assembled during the performance into an obstructing wall across a stage two football fields wide and over sixty feet high. The show incorporated many guest-star appearances along with an East German symphony orchestra and choir, the one-hundred-piece Red Army Marching Band, as well as hundreds more extras from the armed forces of both East and West. During the brilliantly sunlit afternoon, a lineup of warm-up bands entertained the gathering mass: the Band, flautist James Galway, the Chieftains, and the Hooters.

Now as twilight descended, the impossibly wide stage waited impassively, construction cranes and Brandenburg Gate looming behind. As I climbed up to my bleacher perch a sudden commotion in front of the stage quieted the crowd. A white limousine drove through the large area between the stage and front row, slamming to a stop in a cloud of dust. Out clambered the five members of West Germany's most popular rock band, the Scorpions, to run onstage and perform the overture "In the Flesh." Wild applause greeted the opening, but even as the overture's final guitar blast echoed into the rear of the great expanse, Waters's massive production hit its first snag. The monitoring system that allowed each musician to hear his or her performance failed. "The Thin Ice," began, halted briefly, began again, then stopped. The performers looked about helplessly. Roger Waters and German chanteuse Ute Lemper were unable to proceed since they couldn't possibly hear each other's voices from across the huge stage. Awkward moments passed, with the crowd bewildered, but polite. Waters stepped forward, shrugged his shoulders and sheepishly did a brief tap dance while technicians sweated out the problem.

By the time the musicians reached "The Happiest Days of Our Lives," things had fallen back in sync. A helicopter from the U.S. Seventh Airborne appeared right on cue, buzzing the audience as an oversized, spindly schoolteacher puppet inflated over the stage, staring out with cold spotlights as eyes. Even those not very familiar with the album must have known what came next: Floyd's monster hit single "Another Brick in the Wall, Part 2." The song began as singer Cyndi Lauper with her multicolored riot of hair strutted across the big stage. The crowd erupted as soon as her unmistakable voice piped in the first words, "We don't need no . . . educaaaaashun!" Following that slice of high camp, Irish singer Sinead O'Connor, who arguably possessed one of the world's finest and most acclaimed voices, walked out to the microphone to sing "Mother" with members of the Band. One source later claimed that upon witnessing the assembled multitude, the diminutive singer suffered from a severe attack of nerves, while another insisted that she hadn't rehearsed adequately. Whatever the reason, Sinead O'Connor fumbled her performance: not only were the Irish singer's vocals nearly inaudible, but she seemed distracted and forgot many of the words. With dozens of cameras and tape machines capturing the event, mistakes in the live production had to be expected, but this moment was simply too embarrassing to remain. Waters would have to reshoot the song onstage with O'Connor as soon as the concert finished. That would be the last major snafu in the rest of the concert, though, which got back on track when Joni Mitchell impeccably sang "Goodbye Blue Sky" to erase the blemish of O'Connor's bumpy attempt.

During the show, stagehands had been dutifully positioning Styrofoam bricks onstage and assembling a wall to either side of the musicians. Now, as Waters sang "Goodbye Cruel World," the workers closed the gap. Brick after brick snapped into position until only one space remained in the massive white expanse. Cameras pointing into the hole projected Waters's lone form to the entire crowd as he croaked out his final and bleak, " . . . goodbye." With that word, invisible stagehands popped the last cube into place and the music ended. The East Berliners in their apartments waved towels and shirts while the soldiers stomped on the roofs of their trucks and blasted air horns, the ovation continuing unabated for minutes until the lights came up for the short intermission. I high-fived everyone in reach, mostly members of the American media pool clustered together because of our common tongue. But, people of many languages and nationalities were perched on the bleachers all around us. I exchanged pleasantries with an English chap one moment, then bluffed my way in broken German through a conversation with an attractive female radio announcer from Hamburg the next. The pageant of international color was stirring: a rock-and-roll version of the UN General Assembly united by the auspicious winds of change in Berlin. Intermission became one gigantic international bear hug as people from all across the globe shared conversations, wine, joints, and goodwill. As the huge stage came alive once again, Roger Waters had already managed to accomplish what perhaps only one other person in history had done. Like Bob Geldof at Live Aid, he had used technology and electronic media to unite Europe and the entire world, if only for a handful of hours.

Far from being an annoying obstruction to all the onstage action,

the imposing expanse of interlocked white bricks was now cleverly uti-
lized as a massive movie screen with projected images flashing across
its long expanse. An actual ambulance drove onstage, slamming to a
halt and disgorging several doctors in surgical masks who grabbed
Waters and clothed him in a white lab coat. Assuming the role of a
physician, he reached for an oversized syringe and plunged it into the
Styrofoam, injecting the wall before dueting with Van Morrison on
"Comfortably Numb." During "Run Like Hell," an immense inflated
swine with beady red lights as eyes suddenly loomed high above the
wall. The familiar Pink Floyd prop soared dramatically out over the
stage but didn't lift quite high enough, striking the top of the wall and
sending a few white blocks tumbling down from the heights. Unlike
Sinead O'Connor's gaffe from earlier, however, this mistake actually
dramatized the effect even more effectively.

The final quarter of the show was a bit harder to follow—just as it
had been on the original album. Roger Waters, who played the main
character and had placed himself behind a wall of emotional isolation,
put himself on trial. The litigation that occurred inside his head and out
on the stage for all to see resulted in the judge declaring that he must remove his barrier and reintegrate himself into the world. Once this happened, the physical wall of bricks on stage would be removed as well.
Pure Broadway took over as actors read their lines onstage while images
of the same scene from *The Wall* movie flashed on the white bricks behind. With verdict delivered, the show headed for its climax. The music
reached a crescendo with the words, "Tear down the wall . . . tear down
the wall," the crowd picking up the phrase and chanting it over and
over again. Soon, the immense shout of over a quarter million voices
boomed into the Berlin night—"Tear down the wall!" Roger Waters's
rock opera about exorcising inner demons of paranoia and alienation
had morphed into a historically charged moment of release never imagined by its creator. For those in Potsdamer Platz, it was an apology to
the millions who had died in wars here, a shout to the governments that
allowed it to happen, and a eulogy to the many who perished trying to
cross over a bloody barrier of iron and concrete. It became a mighty
effort not to weep from all the emotion, but why stop it? Tears streamed
openly down the faces of people everywhere.

Bright white lights on the huge stage switched on to reveal a fantastic scene as the six-hundred-foot wall began to disintegrate. Bricks fell steadily from the top rows, some cascading out into the pit in front of the audience, others tumbling into the scaffolding on the wings. Block after block plummeted to earth as the applause grew and grew. By the time the final brick had rolled to a halt, the crowd directed an earth-shaking roar toward the now-silent pile of Styrofoam rubble and the musicians who must be standing somewhere beyond it. The clamor continued for minutes until band and cast members, now assembled on a section of staging attached to the truss above, were hauled up and into view over the remains of the wall. The wild ovation deepened, then fell silent as the musicians encored with "The Tide Is Turning," a song Waters was inspired to write after Live Aid. After the many waves of thanks from the stage and a dessert of fireworks, the satiated and enlightened crowd slowly exited the dusty place. The sea of excited faces left the glow of the lights behind, fanning out through the streets of the united Berlin and a future that now seemed a whole lot brighter.

CHAPTER 39

PAUL McCARTNEY

GETTING BACK

Foxboro Stadium, Massachusetts, July 24 and 26, 1990

Listen to: "Got to Get You into My Life," "Get Back," "Hey Jude," "Let It Be," "Band on the Run," "Jet," "Live and Let Die," "My Brave Face"

The laser beams split off from behind the drum kit, brilliant light sabers waving starkly in the billowing smoke onstage, then invisible higher in the air before dancing in crazy lime-green patterns on the clouds hanging over the stadium. I had looked straight up from my floor seat to witness that magical mystery sight, tearing away, only briefly, from watching Paul McCartney and his superb backing band, including his wife Linda, time-travel along memory after memory. It was a good thirty-song set, a long time to be standing up, craning the neck to catch all the words, every note, and each move of the most famous musician in the world. After all, who was more famous in 1990? Madonna? Guns N' Roses? Please. Perhaps Michael Jackson could qualify for the title, but, simply put, he wasn't a Beatle. He hadn't been a member of the most influential and successful band in pop-music history, a group that had split acrimoniously in 1970, but not before leading culture on a chase from black-and-white innocence to full Technicolor innovation. The shamans had walked off in four separate directions, often producing brilliance on their own and claiming gold and platinum rewards through the decades, but the fans' fondest wish—that the individual wanderers would reunite in their mythical alliance—never materialized.

Ten years after the Beatles' final tour of the United States, Paul McCartney brought Wings, his new band, back across the Atlantic during a bicentennial summer. By then, McCartney had amassed a formidable solo dowry and wooed crowd after sold-out crowd with his own hits, then sent them into hysterics with a generous portion of Liverpudlian memories. *Wings over America*, the consequent triple-record live set, became McCartney's sixth number-1 album in America, certainly cementing his performance capabilities and paving the way for more visits. But that didn't happen—for a long time. He toured the world, but folded his Wings and spent the eighties shielded in the studio working on a series of solo releases. *Flowers in the Dirt*, the last of the lot and a fine return to form, finally brought McCartney out of hiding: he assembled his best group since the Beatles and hit the road in September 1989, moving out across Europe and subsequently logging over 100,000 miles in 102 concerts for 2,742,000 people. Fourteen years since his previous tour of America, Paul McCartney's first official "solo" jaunt arrived. Triumphant with a world's worth of victories won over nine long months, the massive stadium-sized operation wound down to its final quartet of concerts. After a pair of shows on July 24 and 26 in Foxboro Stadium outside of Boston, the tour would hit Soldier's Field in Chicago for another pair, before McCartney and the dozens of musicians, technicians, and support personnel called it a tour and scattered.

McCartney's incredible solo success ensured that a large audience would always be waiting wherever he chose to perform. But, it was the lingering, evergreen presence of his Beatles years that supercharged the size of those crowds to the stadium level. In the summer of 1990, it had been twenty years since the final album *Let It Be*, yet the hunger for the Beatles' music remained incredibly strong. Without the band being active, you'd expect some attrition of excitement among the original fans as the years passed, but amazingly, the passion for the world-shaking group had now spread to subsequent generations. A spate of rereleases and compilations since the breakup had fueled this response, but clearly, the reaction from fans who hadn't even been born when McCartney announced his intention to leave the Beatles was completely unexpected. The sight of teenagers in the audience at all of the solo star's gigs would become a common sight on this tour and in the years to come. Indeed, when the Beatles' *1* album hit stores in 2000, the compilation of sixties hits already released many times over sold an astounding 20 million copies around the globe. That simply wouldn't happen unless a new audience was also out there buying it.

Backstage before the first Foxboro show, the upbeat mood of the English crew was noticeable. This had been a long trip, crossing back and forth from Europe to America three times and once across the Pacific. The logistics of moving a complex stadium-filling production around the world could only be entrusted to a team of experts accustomed to this kind of work, but even McCartney's team of grizzled veterans now pined for home. The operation had long ago fallen into a groove of impeccable English efficiency: if something was set up on the phone in advance, it was all set to go at the stadium. That may sound elemental, but having organized dozens of remote broadcasts and interviews for my radio station in Boston by this point, I was dismayed at how often our carefully laid plans would be met with dumbfounded stares at the venue on the day of the show. Our radio crew included engineers who maintained the broadcast link from the stadium to the station, DJs to report live before showtime, and a special ops team set to interview Paul McCartney himself. Intent on promoting *Flowers in the Dirt* and propping up an image tarnished by recent business sparring with his former Beatle mates and John Lennon's widow, Yoko Ono, even prompting his boycott of the band's Rock and Roll Hall of Fame induction, the star had granted rare access to our radio station.

Four of us were included in the special meeting set up in one of the many rented trailers parked behind the massive stage and at least two lines of security. I didn't know it for sure, but I suspected that there had to be some undercover muscle always close to McCartney in the wake of Lennon's murder ten years earlier. That requirement would certainly unsettle me, but the star showed no such uneasiness when he appeared suddenly at the door and waded in, all handshakes and smiles with his boyish good looks belying a recent forty-eighth birthday. Making his way easily around the room, giving each of us an instant of thrilling personal interaction, I thought that McCartney could have made an excellent politician. Thank goodness a career in civil service hadn't come calling: I couldn't imagine a life without "Yesterday," "Get Back," "Hey Jude," "Let It Be," or "Band on the Run." The entertainer, though, had entered the political arena somewhat as an environmental advocate, inviting members of Friends of the Earth along on the tour to present their chilling outlooks on global warming, rainforest destruction, and other ecological concerns. The worldwide organization had received generous space in McCartney's lavish ninety-eight-page tour booklet given to concertgoers as they entered the stadium as well as a special block of prime tickets offered to the public with an added premium earmarked to help fund the Friends of the Earth operation.

As part of my jobs as DJ and music director, I conducted a lot of interviews, but I was only a spectator on this one, having relegated the task to the two resident McCartney experts at our station, Tom Sandman and Larry "Chachi" Loprete. I enjoyed the lack of pressure in my role of observer as the three got on famously and without tension of any kind. Some musicians seemed to dwell on the discomfort they could instill in their examiners, sharing whatever neurosis they might harbor by steering the interview experience through one confrontation after another. But none of that with McCartney: he spoke enthusiastically of the tour, the environmental aspect, the latest album, and even the Beatles with upbeat transparency and eagerness. Afterward, the star remained in front of the trailer for a couple of group photos and parting handshakes before an assistant took charge and spirited him away.

While Tom and Chachi floated off euphorically, a lieutenant on McCartney's production staff stepped in and asked if we could help him with a problem. Hey, maybe he needed someone to emcee the show! It wasn't that, but it turned out to be almost as good. The representative told us that each night, a certain number of tickets were held aside for the special Friends of the Earth donation. With the show beginning within a half hour, several of those seats had not been sold, and the ticket office didn't expect they would since most of the crowd had already arrived. Would we do McCartney's staff the favor of giving away the extra tickets to fans who didn't have the cash? This seemed like an unusual gesture; the typical process would be to hold onto their tickets and sell whatever was possible even as the show began. But, if that's how they wanted to do it, we were delighted to help. Tasked with our peach of an assignment, my engineer John Mullaney and I hurried out of the backstage area heading for the front entrance, both of us holding ten pairs of tickets, or "miracles" as the Grateful Dead fans would certainly call them.

As the last arrivals streamed through the front gates, we made a bee-line past them and out to the parking lot. We'd have to choose care-fully; it just wouldn't be right to give a free pair of tickets to someone who'd turn around and sell them to a desperate latecomer. As it turned out, it was easy to spot the ideal candidates, betrayed by their downcast eyes, fixed frowns, and subdued conversations among each other. We approached a young couple smoking between two cars.

"Are you going in?"

"Nah. We can't afford tickets," the girl answered, dismissing me as a scalper.

"Well then, here!" I thrust a pair toward her. The eyes did not become excited, but suspicious. She asked warily, "How much?"

"Nothing."

"Really?"

"Really." I handed them over. "Go ahead. It's a pair of tickets from Friends of the Earth." That scenario repeated so many times made John and me feel like Santa Claus might, even though he'd have long ago stripped off his red suit and thermal underwear on this hot July night. To a person, the lucky recipients thought we were conniving ticket mer-chants running out of time and trying to force a deal. They all ended up in happy amazement, not believing their good fortune. "Hurry up; the show's about to start!"

"John, I think we should take a pair too," I mentioned. We had McCartney VIP passes, but they only provided access to a limited view and poor sound from behind the speakers. Often, bands set up an area at their sound and light control boards in the middle of the stadium for their guests, but I hadn't checked to see if that was the case. He nodded, "Why not? They're decent seats near the front, on the floor." What the hell: we'd worked down in Foxboro for the radio station all day, so why not enjoy the most famous musician in the world from a good spot? Using the tickets to get back in the stadium, we hurried to our designated seats, a mere twenty-five rows back from where Paul McCartney would stroll out and pick up that famous Hofner bass.

Suddenly, the girl next to me squealed, "Hi there! Thank you so much for these tickets. They're so awesome!"

"Hey, it's the dudes!" someone else chimed in from the other direction. From the row in front, two guys whirled around and gave us thumbs up. "These seats are unbelievable!" one of them gasped. From behind, I felt enthusiastic backslapping. I'd completely overlooked that we'd be sur-rounded by the people we'd handed tickets to. The guests were, indeed, all around us and absolutely pumped! "Here, drink this!" "Want some smoke?" How about pizza?" Just as it seemed we were about to be hoisted up on their shoulders and paraded around the stadium in tribute, the lights finally went down and the real star of the night arrived!

CHAPTER 40

THE BLACK CROWES

EXILE ON MONROE DRIVE

Dupree's, Atlanta, Georgia, May 2, 1992

Listen to: "Hard to Handle," "She Talks to Angels," "Jealous Again," "Remedy"

Skunk and Doyle, Chris Robinson's two British bulldogs, eagerly competed to draw the attention of their master, bursting through the door and hovering close by, sniveling and snorting wetly on the porch as I sat with the Black Crowes' singer. A cassette recorder rested on the table between us, taping a conversation that I planned to return to Boston and use a few days later on my radio show. I'd been driven to Robinson's home in the forested and affluent Buckhead section of Atlanta, where the cherry-red Cadillac convertible in the driveway betrayed the only clue that a rock star actually lived in the surprisingly modest wood-shingled house. During the gorgeous spring day, the singer planned to hold court with a few writers and media types, but things were running late. "I'm one whole interview behind schedule," he apologized while shaking my hand in the living room, which looked like a sixties hippie crash pad or my college dorm room a decade later. "Can I get you something to drink . . . or smoke?" A beer would be fine. The singer returned with a Red Stripe, "Make yourself at home."

Little Feat's first album played on the stereo and a picture of Robinson and a couple of other Crowes with John Lee Hooker caught my eye. I had a half hour (and two beers) to riffle through his record collection, and as you might expect, considering the group's inspired cover of Otis Redding's "Hard to Handle," there were quite a few albums from the legendary R & B singer to be found. I could see Robinson loved Humble Pie and, of course, the Rolling Stones, plus the album he told me he'd grab on the way out if the house was burning down: Dylan's *Highway 61 Revisited*. I noticed a dog-eared Rod Stewart record just as the Crowes' road manager beckoned me to follow him into the backyard where Robinson and a dozen guests lounged about in various states of lucidity by a small pond stocked with large and lazy goldfish. *Tonight's the Night* from Neil Young boomed out of some hidden speakers. As it seemed to interrupt the good time going on, my interview began awkwardly at first, but soon amped up into a friendly chat about the Crowes' whirlwind career and brand-new album *The Southern Harmony and Musical Companion*, due out in ten days.

The Black Crowes had burst onto the national scene hawking their love of blues-based classic rock and wrought-iron soul. This flew in the face of the two major types of rock currently vying for control: the hairband hangover from the eighties and a new fuzz-based firebrand called grunge, which had emerged from the basements of Seattle behind Nirvana, Alice in Chains, and Pearl Jam, among others. As the latter was inspired by a true rock-and-roll grit rather than manipulative heavy metal pop, the Crowes actually had more in common with the grunge movement, even though the band digressed significantly by drawing inspiration from traditional American roots music. The approach struck a nerve: the Black Crowes' 1990 debut sold three million copies. Two years later, the follow-up was already on a fast track to reach platinum as rock radio embraced its advance single "Remedy." But Def American, the band's record company, decided not to take chances, inviting a short list of key radio programmers from around the country to a May 2 listening party in Atlanta, with each one flown in, met by limousine, and then feted with five-star deference at the downtown Ritz-Carlton. Personally, I already loved the Crowes and didn't need to be convinced, but who would say no to any offer like that? To an FCC skeptic, the junket might have hinted at payola, so technically, I was being flown to Georgia to tape a conversation with Chris Robinson for my radio station, and, by the way, there was all this other fun stuff going on that I could take advantage of, especially the complimentary room service!

"The Black Crowes and Def American Recordings invite you to enjoy an evening of debauchery, raucousness and southern hospitality," read the printed invitation in the packet of documents sent to me. We'd all be bussed to the Variety Playhouse Theater on Euclid Avenue to listen to a playback of the new album while videos scrolled on the big screen, then retire to Dupree's, a pool hall on Monroe Drive, where drinks would flow and the band planned to perform. I wondered how Robinson could recharge himself after a long day of interviews to focus on delivering a set strong enough to impress a roomful of judgmental music-business reptiles. He didn't seem overly concerned about it, though; in fact, he didn't appear worried about much of anything. As his home faded in the rearview mirror, I wondered how much usable material I really had, since a lot of our talk had been downright silly and somewhat random. I guess I should have expected that since the guy who interviewed Robinson before me wrote for *High Times*.

My duty fulfilled, I was driven back to the Ritz-Carlton, grateful to be rid of the heavy tape deck and happy to spread out in the air-conditioned opulence that Def American had paid for—no doubt charged against the Black Crowes' account. Out of the blue and into the black, I mused as I looked around the beautifully appointed room. This new album had better sell when it came out, or the group might not survive its own press party! Downstairs in the lobby at 7:30 p.m., the chatting gaggle of industry insiders was herded out the doors and into a few luxury coaches for the ride to the theater, the racket of conversation never letting up for a second, which makes sense when you consider this was a gathering of radio representatives who, by nature, dreaded the absence of sound. On the job, silence meant there was nothing on the air and you better do something quick! At the Variety Playhouse, the libations loosened everyone's tongues even more, so much so that after an attentive beginning, the film promoting and playing *The Southern Harmony and Musical Companion* soon faded to background noise against the humdrum of industry voices and clink of glasses.

What I managed to hear impressed me: the taut mélange of blues, R & B, and sixties and seventies Brit-rock on the debut album had transformed into a "live in the studio" openness. It was if the engineers had merely turned on the tape machines and let the Black Crowes wing their entire sophomore album from start to finish. "Sting Me" opened the session with brother Rich Robinson and Marc Ford's ferocious guitars blasting out a path accented by Eddie Harsch's electric piano and Chris wailing away like a young Rod Stewart working on his own legend in front of the Faces back in 1972. "Thorn in My Pride" also stood out proudly through the din in the theater, a slow and loping blues that picked up speed and transformed into an epic. "Hotel Illness" caught a groove that Keith Richards would have been proud to have on *Exile on Main Street*, even though that Stones milestone had assuredly helped the Atlanta band from diapers to their guitars years earlier. At 10:00 p.m., word circulated to hit the busses again; we were off to Dupree's for a late-night meal and some friendly wagering on the pool tables there. The pièce de résistance, of course, would be the band's performance. Last time I'd seen the Crowes, they warmed up for ZZ Top at the arena in Providence, Rhode Island; this occasion would be immeasurably more intimate.

Most of the radio pundits grabbed a pool cue and racked up right away or headed outside to sit at one of many tables bathed in the midtown Atlanta streetlights and a comfortable spring night. With no stage to work from, the dining tables in the main room were pulled aside and the band's gear set up in the middle. The words Black Crowes stenciled in white letters on most of the road-beaten equipment cases spoke loudly of being manhandled across state lines on dozens of far-flung tour dates, yet this scene appeared more like local-band night in some high school cafeteria (albeit with a full bar to one side). When the members meandered to their appointed places, I stood four or five feet away with my friend Karen from the record label, an avowed Crowes fanatic who would not be denied this moment. The first notes hit and sent shock waves through the room, overwhelming my senses and driving the rhythms deep. After months of rehearsing and recording tracks, the members were in relaxed form and in easy reach of their best effort. Chris Robinson had shed any vestige of an afternoon cannabis hangover as he primped, preened, and strutted about, channeling Rod, Mick, and Otis — they were all in there. We responded by dancing directly in his face, digging the privilege as some others joined in next to us.

A London club goer in '64 might have felt like this as he or she grooved to a young and barely known Rolling Stones or Yardbirds at the Marquee; this moment seemed like a similar discovery. But at one point when I glanced around to check the crowd behind me, I saw — hardly anyone there! This was shocking; while the Black Crowes destroyed a local pool hall (of all places), most of the record company and radio pros in attendance showed little interest, instead remaining stuck in their conversations or intent on chalking cue sticks. The appalling lack of attention disheartened, even embarrassed, me. I wanted to run through the entire place grabbing shirt collars and yelling, "Can't you hear what's going on here? This *is* the real deal!" But most of these music-biz mavens, who clearly made a good living selling rock and roll, revealed a disturbing lack of passion for the music itself. In this environment I couldn't escape the feeling that the Black Crowes — and, indeed, all fledgling bands fighting to be noticed — had been reduced to just another commodity. I could have easily been at a General Motors or Starbucks sales conference. The big execs of American rock radio had forgotten how to dance. As the band members finished up their short and brilliant set, I wandered off, dripping in sweat, to the bar and chased my empty feelings with a beer and some fine southern bourbon.

But, at least I came back with a one-on-one interview with Chris

Robinson *at his house*. How cool was that? It would sound great on the air and justify the entire trip. But as I listened to the playback, my excitement faded with each passing second. I couldn't use any of it! Through the entire conversation with my completely laid-back subject, our words were dominated, sometimes even obscured, by the slurping, wheezing, and farting chorus from Chris Robinson's two biggest fans — Skunk and Doyle!

THE ALLMAN BROTHERS BAND

A WYLDE NIGHT

Great Woods, Mansfield, Massachusetts, August 1, 1993

Listen to: "Dreams," "Trouble No More," "Statesboro Blues," "Stormy Monday," "Whipping Post," "Southbound," "Jessica"

The look was priceless—the best inside glance I'd ever seen anybody give on-stage. I was lucky to catch it too since I sat halfway up the hill only a few feet from the mixing console; a great location for sound, but certainly not close enough to see the whites of the players' eyes. But, after someone handed over a pair of binoculars, I dialed in tightly for a piece of the action and arrived in focus just at the moment. Once again, the Allman Brothers Band had returned to Great Woods, the summertime concert shed south of Boston that the group first visited on its twentieth-anniversary reunion tour of 1989. Now four years later, that temporary remarriage of the archetypal classic southern rock band had become a permanent endeavor, with the revitalized group releasing two solid studio albums,

Seven Turns and *Shades of Two Worlds*, plus the more recent live release *An Evening with the Allman Brothers: First Set*. Fans in the Boston area always welcomed the group, from its earliest days at the city's hippie ballroom the Boston Tea Party to tonight with over 12,000 jamming the venue, a collection of old-time fans and their kids as well as a whole new generation of college-age disciples. Along with the Grateful Dead, the "Brothers" had become the granddaddies of the nineties jam-band revival, powered by young groups like Blues Traveler, Phish, and Widespread Panic.

The Allman Brothers band paved the way for southern rock, becoming stars in the process and enduring well-documented tragedy with the early career deaths of its founder Duane Allman and bassist Berry Oakley. Drug and alcohol abuse would nearly kill some of the others too as success took the band for a wild ride through the top of the charts in the midseventies. Like English rock royalty Led Zeppelin, the Allman Brothers Band flew from gig to gig in the Starship, a converted United Airlines Boeing 720 infamous for its opulence and the extravagant expense it took to operate. As the band's fame grew, principal writers Gregg Allman and Dickey Betts clashed regularly over personal and professional matters, the former abdicating much of his power as drug dependency took hold. In 1982, the Allman Brothers Band split apart as a parade of MTV-fueled "skinny-tie bands" kicked southern rock out of the arenas and back into those sweaty bars with chicken wire stretched in front of the stage. The music had died and the Brothers broke up permanently: roll the credits.

But, by 1989 the rise of classic rock as a prosperous radio format fueled a renewed interest in the group's music. *Dreams*, the Allman Brothers Band's retrospective box set, kept selling out in the stores, and the label was hard-pressed to keep up with orders. The reunion tour went off splendidly owing to the reformed attitudes of Allman and Betts who, although not necessarily free of their dependencies, remained sober enough to act civilly and perform near the top of their abilities. Strong support from guitar wunderkind Warren Haynes, a member of Betts's solo band, reestablished the classic twin-guitar interplay that had typified the early group. The band's other trademark, double drummers, remained constant as original players Butch Trucks and Jaimoe eagerly returned. From coast to coast, the vibes were great and the audiences loved the shows.

But, old habits die hard: by 1993 tempers had flared again behind the scenes as Dickey Betts's drinking habit got the better of him. Just one day before the Great Woods gig, the guitarist ran into trouble with the law in Saratoga Springs, New York, striking two policemen at a hotel after his wife called in a complaint accusing the intoxicated musician of abuse. The group headed off to its next show scheduled that night in nearby Stowe, Vermont, while Betts was sprung from jail, but the guitarist inexplicably flew home to Florida rather than join his bandmates. Slated in as part of the traveling jam-band tour known as the H.O.R.D.E. Festival, the Brothers were fortunate to have Jimmy Herring from Colonel Bruce Hampton and the Aquarian Rescue Unit on hand to fill Betts's shoes. But after that, Herring's itinerary took him in one direction while the Allman Brothers Band headed for another, into Massachusetts for the Great Woods show that it could surely not afford to cancel.

Another substitute needed to be found — fast. The band members, manager Bert Holman, and booking agent Jonny Podell began furiously working the phones. They contacted Jack Pearson, a red-hot slide guitarist out of Nashville, but he had tour commitments going on. David Grissom, gigging as part of John Mellencamp's backing group, was considered, but he didn't get the phone call until too late. Deprived of those two aces, Podell, who booked both the Allman Brothers Band and Ozzy Osbourne, threw out his next best face card: what about Zakk Wylde? He knew that Ozzy's guitarist, although known as a heavy metal player, loved southern rock and even moonlighted in an L.A. cover band named Lynyrd Skynhead performing the Allmans' and Skynyrd's hits. With nothing left in the deck to play, Podell got the nod to call Wylde. The twenty-six-year-old immediately expressed his excitement to help out, hopping a red-eye from the left coast and bound for what would be, perhaps, the most unusual gig the Allman Brothers Band ever performed.

Once again, Warren Haynes demonstrated that he was the hardest-working artist in show business, not only fulfilling his role as one of the Brothers' guitarists, but also bringing a solo band along on this tour and warming up with a set of his own material. My wife and I loved his album *Tales of Ordinary Madness*, so we got there early enough to see him open. Most people were partying it up in the parking lot or stuck in the dreadful traffic nightmare that always accompanied getting into this place, so they missed some real value for their money as Haynes displayed the brilliance that many would become accustomed to later in his career. As he left the stage, idle talk about the night's main attraction took over. "Ozzy's guitarist is supposed to play in the band tonight," I mentioned to my friends standing in the beer line, receiving only skeptical looks in return. "Yeah, right!" and "What are you smoking?" The rumors ran rampant, though, with some insisting Betts was in the house while most agreed that some substitute would sit in, although certainly not a person as disparate to the Allmans' legacy as a twenty-something heavy metal guy! Still others believed that Haynes would perform as the only guitarist: after all, the Allman Brothers Band worked in that format for years after Duane Allman died in 1971.

The answer arrived as soon as the lights welled up and the group opened with the crowd-pleasing boogie thump of "Statesboro Blues." Haynes's slide offered the signature guitar part and Gregg Allman growled the vocals from behind his stately wooden Hammond B-3. But wait! Who was that other figure rushing up to the lip of the stage to grab his first guitar solo of the night? It didn't take long to figure out because no one else in the business owned an ax like that white Les Paul with its distinctive concentric bull's-eye painted in black. The rumors about Zakk Wylde were true! Last time I'd seen the guitarist, he'd pasted us up against our seats in a searing wall of power chords and an endless rippling of notes as Ozzy's latest metal-guitar master. How could this work? Was the good-time, laid-back atmosphere of an Allman Brothers Band concert compatible with Wylde's typical Thor-like display of intemperate passion and brazen power chords? I was not optimistic; in the same moment I recognized the "target" Gibson and the player behind it, I also had a vision of two locomotives powering firmly and unerringly down the same tracks directly at one another. He hadn't even played a note yet, but I was convinced of an impending collision. We were going to catch some shrapnel tonight!

Overeager and excited, Wylde rushed the first solo, perched on the stage edge in a posture of pure metal imperiousness, yanking out his notes with great flourish while thrusting his guitar (and crotch) at the sky. That was just an introduction. "Dreams," the gorgeous anthem from the band's first album, which had originally provided Duane Allman with a vehicle for some of his most melodic and beautiful slide playing on record, passed the torch to Warren Haynes who emblazoned Duane's fire in a worthy pinnacle night after night. The song had also allowed generous opportunity for answering solos from Dickey Betts, and tonight the performance ran on to three times its original seven-minute length as Wylde crashed his Sunset Strip attitude into the sacred space like a bull in a Georgia china shop. A blaring solo wasn't quite enough; he continued by playing the guitar behind his head and then yanked it forward to pick the strings with his teeth. Warren Haynes leaned in, hoping to catch the guitarist's eye and communicate the song's proper pace and transitions, but the frenetic substitute remained oblivious in his excitement.

The band retained its usual "unplugged" segment of the concert, but without Betts to sing his own songs, this portion was whittled down to just two songs: "Midnight Rider" and "Melissa." Since Gregg Allman also played acoustic guitar on these, things settled down a bit. The break did allow for a huddle, in which the members no doubt read their guest the riot act, but as soon as the electrics went back on, the bombastic contradiction returned in full force. Wylde pulled out a Les Paul emblazoned with a Confederate flag and studded by beer-bottle caps, then channeled "War Pigs" into his next few solos while chugging brew and spitting it high in the air as he raced about the stage.

A typical show on that tour with Dickey Betts in good health had been twenty or twenty-one songs. Tonight, the set list had been slashed to fifteen selections with more jamming to fill the time. We hit bottom on "Whipping Post," normally a long vehicle held for the climax of most concerts, but tonight the track extended on and on until it became a half-hour brute. I lost it when I realized that both drummers and even percussionist Mark Quinones were all taking their own lengthy solos. Off I went for a walk, hitting the bathrooms, which were unusually busy for what was typically the emotional peak of an Allman Brothers Band show. I strolled down the concourse looking at the juice bars, beer stops, and veggie-wrap stands before returning to my seat to find Quinones still into his solo, banging on assorted clanging surfaces and third-world wooden blocks. By the time the other musicians returned to their places and eased their bass-heavy melody back in, this version of "Whipping Post" had certainly reached the band's record book as one of the longest, dwarfing even the definitive twenty-three-minute version found on *At Fillmore East*.

While he was nice enough to help the Allman Brothers Band, Wylde's contribution would be limited to this single night: he simply couldn't contain himself as his guitar screamed in consort with the metallic blizzard shrieking along in his head. Then there was that precious look. Through the binoculars I focused on Gregg Allman as he bent over his keyboard, deftly dashing out seasoned blues licks as Betts's replacement stood tiptoe on his monitor cabinet burying Allman's soulful effort in a carpet-bombing run of notes lifted from "Crazy Train." The grizzled veteran glanced over at Haynes, raising an eyebrow to the sky, then grinning widely as if to say, "Really?" But Allman just followed that with a knowing smile and a chuckle, returning his attention to the keyboard. This might be one of the weirdest gigs he'd seen along an endless, rolling highway of shows, but he left Wylde alone. After all, a Brother was family, even if he was only going to be a Brother for one night.

CHAPTER 42

NIRVANA

"THIS GUITAR IS BRAND NEW, AND I DECIDED I DON'T LIKE IT"

Wallace Civic Center, Fitchburg, Massachusetts, November 12, 1993

Listen to: "Smells Like Teen Spirit," "Come as You Are," "Heart-Shaped Box," "All Apologies," "The Man Who Sold the World"

Kurt Cobain wasn't really an important part of my world. But, as an unwitting and unwilling talisman for his own generation, he connected with the disaffected just as rock and roll's heroes had succored followers in the past. If you thought that you were a loser, well, then maybe you had a chaperone to show you that, perhaps, you were in good company. You'd head out to a club to see that guiding light perform, and damn if there weren't a whole bunch of others there that felt just the same as you. Those feelings of low esteem could vanish in the pit, the energy expelling the emptiness, at least for a little while. So, amid the power chords, feedback, and Cobain's stark-naked words, Nirvana was certainly a band worth respect, even if its leader never applied for, nor desired, the job of "head spokesman." By '92, after the *Nevermind* album had become the biggest album on the planet and fame plowed into Nirvana like an express train, I could look at the accident scene and admit that I'd seen this sort of thing before: new boss—same as the old boss. Here was great talent out of the blue and into the black, a supreme promise to deliver rock music itself, but ultimately, the responsibility would prove to be too much. Personally, I didn't consider Nirvana more than a tremendous rock-and-roll band with an enlightened writer who just happened to be the flavor of the moment. I failed to deify the group or even attach to it any of the larger sociological implications it seemed to raise. Some would say I missed that boat, but somehow I think it's the way Kurt Cobain would have preferred it.

I'd told someone once that the Wallace Civic Center must be a pretty close approximation of hell. The comment got into print and the venue sent a card thanking me for the promotion. Fitchburg State University and local high schools played hockey in the place, so for a concert they'd put a wooden cover over the ice and open the floor to the audience. As the concerts got started, the body heat and exhalations ascending toward the roof would condense on the steel beams above, dripping as "rain" back into the space below. Since this arena, for a time, became Boston's designated hitter for grunge and alternative hard-rock concerts, the energy unleashed by these aggressive bands could lead to some lively rainstorms. At a Soundgarden show in '94, I stood next to the soundboard and watched water droplets splatter on the black metal desk of glowing meters, knobs, and sliders, then roll unavoidably down into the delicate electronics underneath. Although that band's sound man seemed prepared to take one for the team, I was not so inclined toward electrocution, getting the hell out of that spot as fast as possible! Crammed tightly into the crush on that general-admission floor, even expanding one's lungs could be a challenge, but if you stood your ground, the sound drilling forth from the speakers onstage could actually be quite good.

Nirvana had played Boston a few times before, but this would be the group's first trip to the area since "Smells Like Teen Spirit" had meteorically shot the suburban Seattle punk band to the top of the sales charts. It had been way too fast an adjustment for Cobain, who struggled with the sudden onrush of fame, sometimes not too well with his medications and subsequent addictions. *Nevermind* was a defining statement that helped remake the entire rock culture, heralding the rise of Seattle's grunge scene and the rebirth of punk, then pushing most of the heavy metal hair bands then in vogue out of the arenas of America and back into the clubs. The sudden fame had its upside, like financial rewards, but the success also bred internal conflict: How did an underground punk band rationalize its mainstream acceptance? Cobain and Nirvana solved that, in part, by creating a follow-up album that rejected much of the polish and hard-rock gloss found on its predecessor, instead restoring the primal energy and attitude that fueled the band's beginnings. *In Utero*, released in September 1993, challenged Nirvana's new audience to return with the band to its punk roots; even so, the album featured two very playable singles, "Heart-Shaped Box" and "All Apologies," which kept the band solidly on the radio. For all the angst in his attitude, Cobain couldn't help but be an expert tunesmith churning out appealing melodies amid the squeals of punishing feedback.

Now the trio headed out for a fall/winter tour of the United States augmented by ex-Germs guitarist Pat Smear and cellist Lori Golston. As ridiculous as the latter's presence might have seemed initially to some, Nirvana had always made dynamic use of balancing extreme volume with breaths of restraint, so Goldston added a great deal to the band's less-chaotic moments onstage. Six days after the Wallace concert, the band would record an unplugged performance for MTV in New York, soon to be Nirvana's very famous and final album release while it was together, fully revealing that often hidden "softer" aspect of the group.

I decided to go to the show because I'd never seen Nirvana, as a few of my friends had. One commented to me: "You remember what you felt when you saw the Clash? You'll feel that from this band." Perhaps that was enough, but I also had an acute curiosity to explore what all the hysteria was about. Like most skeptics, though, instead of hungering to prove the band's genius, I approached the performance with doubts that I wanted to confirm. Rather than searching for the positive, I preferred to endorse my disbelief. How could that band be so good? It had to be hype. Others certainly felt that way; maybe that's why I couldn't find anyone to take my extra ticket. I ended up driving the sixty miles from Boston through the wilderness out to Fitchburg by myself and handed my plus-one to the first person in the parking lot who was looking. Since the show had been sold out for weeks, there were a lot of them too: kids shuffling around and loitering near the entranceway to the building. The concrete interior — unremarkable, utilitarian, and certainly more suited to collegiate sports — nevertheless had decent sightlines down to the stage even if all the smokers in the hall had already created a respectable preconcert smog. After the Breeders had played, the haze had only grown thicker, now punctured occasionally by those little droplets of water that pooled and then dribbled gently off the girders above. I walked around the arena, looking for familiar faces and musing about how well mushrooms could grow in this environment, which resembled Seattle's climate, appropriately enough.

Nirvana came on, and Cobain laid down a squalling welcome of feedback to start the show on "Radio Friendly Unit Shifter," a winking howl of rock and roll that was anything but a spotless and comfortable hit single. The music sounded surprisingly clear in the room while the expected shit-storm of thrashing on the floor remained remarkably controlled, making it simple for me to sidle nearly all the way up to the stage. As chaotic an image that the "Smells Like Teen Spirit" video may have prepared me for, there was more respect than anarchy in this audience. People gave Nirvana their undivided attention, focusing on a set that would have felt right at home in a tiny dive, devoid of any rock-star conceit or posturing typical at big rock shows. Adorned with two angel statues and some wooden treelike props that cast huge finger-puppet shadows on the back wall from an assortment of simple and colorful lights hanging above, the stage was devoid of anything fancy, like strobes or lasers, but still more than I expected. On the softer songs like "Polly" and "Dumb," the cello was easily heard, an armistice in the action before the war of noise resumed on "In Bloom" and "Milk It." Applause greeted the beginning of "Come as You Are," a tease before

Cobain complained: "This guitar is brand new, and I decided I don't like it." The expected fit of ax destruction didn't ensue, however, and the band restarted the single, a song I thought they'd surely drop from the set considering how negative Cobain had been in interviews concerning his stardom. I mean, if he rejected that, then why play a hit single? But I was glad they did; it was a damn good song.

Even if Nirvana played "Come as You Are," I thought that surely the band would eliminate "Teen Spirit" from the set; after all, it had been that song that started all the trouble. At his most cynical, and if bored or angry with an audience, Cobain would refrain from playing it just to spite them, but in Fitchburg he delivered the anthem faithfully and without sarcasm, demonstrating how powerful a song it truly was. The audience zombied out in abandon with fits of head banging and areas of slam dancing driving the show to an emotional nirvana, if you will. The band followed with the confessional "All Apologies," perhaps the only selection that could stand up to the monster before it, to end the set. An anticlimactic encore of five songs added to a concert surprising in its generosity of time and detail. The show absolutely drained me of energy, yet renewed my spirit completely. Sheepishly, I realized my cynicism had been unfounded: Nirvana was the real deal. The group that had experienced so much frenzied change in the past two years had managed to live up to the impossible image thrust upon it by so many.

The majesty of that hour and a half concert would always trouble me once Cobain's inner turmoil got the upper hand just a few months later. In a career born of tearing down the old and noisily announcing its replacement, why couldn't he take pleasure in knowing that 3,200 people in a tired old mill town off the beaten track in Massachusetts had been absolutely lit on fire because of his band? Maybe he had; but sadly, it would never be enough.

CHAPTER 43

PEARL JAM

DIGGING IN
THE GARDEN

Boston Garden, April 11, 1994

Listen to: "Alive," "Even Flow," "Yellow Ledbetter," "Jeremy," "Daughter," "Dissident"

In 1991, a rain-lashed, force-10 squall of dense rhythm and electric energy rolled in from the northwest, its howling guitar distortion overwhelming the fashionable fragments of an eighties rock scene still preening in front of the mirror. Rarely do cataclysmic cultural forces change the landscape in an instant, but this was one of those: the final "perfect storm" of the twentieth century. Within mere weeks, the hair bands that had clogged MTV and filled "sheds" on the summer tour circuit could barely compete with the regulars vamping it up at local karaoke bars coast to coast. After the flashpoint of Nirvana's "Smells Like Teen Spirit," the revival of rock and roll supplanted lipstick faux as popular taste crowd-surfed back to its roots. The Seattle bands in on the gestation of this amplified takeover advanced into the gap: Soundgarden, Alice in Chains, Screaming Trees, and Pearl Jam rapidly assumed positions of importance in the new order. The latter received an unexpected kick in the ass when its debut album *Ten* bulleted into the heavens strapped on the back of a missile entitled "Alive," the single storming radio-airplay charts in January '92 and opening a can of brilliant songs for all to hear. By May, *Ten* had gone platinum, heading past thirteen million in sales and gilding the names Mike McCready, Stone Gossard, Jeff Ament, and lead singer Eddie Vedder.

Of course, that sort of sudden fame always creates problems, and the history of rock is littered with accounts of those broken by it, with Kurt Cobain only recently added to that sad list. Like Nirvana's doomed lead singer, the members of Pearl Jam tangled in a love-hate relationship with fame, cursed because they actually cared about their music while resisting the sudden allures of rock-star arrogance and extravagance. After all, perhaps the easiest way to deal with celebrity was to give into it: believing all the hype while racing out of the blue and into the black, taking limos to the grocery store, and wallowing in glittering distrac-tion till all the fame ran out. But, Pearl Jam, with its twin-guitar buzz saw and an explosive poet of a lead singer, hung on to its music like a thrown life raft, managing to navigate through the most serious perils of startling success and survive its initial storm of acclaim.

A rock-solid sophomore album, *Vs.*, appeared in '93, satisfying both the media, which continued to illuminate the band in a white-hot spot-light, and an exploding fan base that marched out and bought nearly one million copies of the new album in a single week. During the final days of October, *Vs.* debuted at number 1 on the *Billboard* album-sales chart, and the group graced the cover of *Rolling Stone*. Certainly the best-selling rock band in the world at this point and perhaps the big-gest group of any genre, Pearl Jam returned to the road squarely in the driver's seat, able to call the shots, playing whatever and wherever it wanted. However, the news of Kurt Cobain's death on April 8, 1994, clarified how deadly the "game" could be. Two days later, his specter hung conspicuously over Pearl Jam and its audience when the group arrived in New England for a pair of shows at the Boston Garden fol-lowed by a concert at the smaller Orpheum Theater.

Pearl Jam's members hunkered down and played through their emotions the first night. I swore to myself that on this occasion they'd never do "Jeremy," the graphic story of school suicide, but seven songs in, there it was. It revealed a group unafraid to confront the issues or situations it encountered, not taking the easier way around for comfort's sake. "I've got to admit, we've got a lot on our minds," Vedder spoke from stage. "It is tough to play." Later on, the set climaxed with "Alive," the singer reasoning, "As long as you're alive, be glad you're alive!" Backstage afterward, no one in the group seemed much in the mood to socialize, but maybe I wasn't either as the general tone remained subdued. Kelly Curtis, Pearl Jam's manager, urged me to come back the following night. I'd known Curtis for over ten years as the manager for Heart, and I valued his opinion: if he thought I should return for night number two, I would. But it wasn't like I really needed to be convinced.

I'd seen Pearl Jam destroy the Axis nightclub right across the street from Fenway Park in April '92, open for U2 in Europe a year later, and also play Springfield, Massachusetts, on its current *Vs.* tour at the Civic Center. Those three shows were completely different from each other, responding to the moods of the five musicians and whatever provocations happened along: an asshole in the crowd, some request from a crew member, the band's fatigue — whatever. The key was spontaneity — things could veer off in a new direction at any moment. Like the Grateful Dead, a vastly different band musically, Pearl Jam gave value and importance to the immediacy of performing, following the moment wherever it took them. Then there was Eddie Vedder, the loosest cannon in the bunch. He dangled from the low-hanging pipes at Axis, dove off U2's giant stage onto knots of supportive Italians, and duct-taped ragged shorts to his torso so they wouldn't be ripped off during his many forays into the crowd. Going to the second night at the Garden guaranteed a different experience, and maybe that's why it would always be difficult to get a ticket to a Pearl Jam show: all the fans wanted to go to all the nights!

Curtis wanted a few of us from the radio station I worked at to come backstage early while fellow Seattle group Mudhoney opened the show. No one from Pearl Jam was in view, which was not surprising since most every performer I'd ever met needed some space before a concert to get their head in the game, usually in the off-limits intimacy of their dressing room. The manager showed us around everywhere else though, introducing us to some of his staff and the production people behind the scenes. After the stage crew retreated to light a forest of candles on the backline of amps and assembled for a brief prayer circle, showtime was imminent. Curtis took us off the stage and to the side as the lights went down and the crowd detonated in a thunderclap of welcome. The members of Pearl Jam filed past us, took the stairs up to the stage and slipped into the slow-burning "Release" under a barely-brightened lighting rig. After that subdued intro, all hell broke loose for a six-song drag race beginning with "Rearview Mirror," the audience responding as a turbulent, heaving mass that threw off a wave of body heat that could actually be felt from our position. "Do you want to watch on the stage?" Curtis shouted. A moment later we were up there, twenty feet off to the side. With Pearl Jam working on an uncluttered space with scarcely more than monitor cabinets, drum set, and amp line ringing them in, I felt horribly exposed on the expanse. But, no one cared about our little group clustered there; with all the action happening at stage center, our presence didn't even register.

Pearl Jam's show was already unlike the previous night's, when its typically passionate performance had been restrained, emerging essentially as the band's twenty-one-gun salute for a mentor and a friend. Tonight the body had been buried and the eulogy spoken: the band shrugged off Cobain's burial shroud and leapt out of the hole. Instead of a short set and two multiple-song encores as in the first night, the members were focused so cathartically that they blew right through their general ending time and on into one long and blistering two-dozen-song set. I figured that the massive quartet from *Ten*—"Jeremy," "Even Flow," "Black," and "Alive"—delivered one after the other like an artillery barrage, would be the impossibly high emotional climax to an unbelievable night. I was wrong; they kept on going—for another forty spellbinding minutes. Covering Henry Rollins's "Tearing" and bulleting into "Porch" and "Rats" kept the pace alive before the band dropped down into "Immortality" and "Corduroy," two songs that would not appear until the *Vitalogy* album seven months later. Kelly Curtis disappeared for a while, but returned as the group punished the Boston Garden audience with "Leash." His eyebrows went up, "Still going?" Then a knowing smile—he'd seen everything. But, as we'd see, perhaps not.

Pearl Jam had been playing Neil Young's anthem "Rocking in the Free World" since its early days, and once rather famously in 1993 in a duet with the "Godfather of Grunge" at the MTV Video Music Awards. Now the group selected the song as a suitable climax to its frenzied nonstop set. Vedder had been hefting the mike stand as he sang, as if to gauge its weight and balance, when suddenly he whirled it violently over his head and buried the heavy base into the plywood stage, sending splinters and fragments flying. As the rock-and-roll battle hymn raged on with monstrous salvos of guitar and pounding drums, the singer continued to smash the stand into the floor over and over again. With remarkable intensity, Vedder concentrated on his task, steadily chopping wood; what seemed like a simple move at first had elevated into obsession as his metal club repeatedly crunched into the stage. With heads down, hair in their eyes, the musicians noticed little of this, lost as they were in the careening momentum of the song. From my incredible vantage point, I watched as the singer's efforts actually began to tear open a hole in the plywood, the initial crater giving way to ragged edges of wood framed by the darkness below. The people up above in the balcony and the nearby loges could see the hole widening too, offering hoarse yells of encouragement barely heard in the tumult. The lucky ones standing in front just shook their heads in amazement and cheered him on. Vedder kept swinging his "ax," sometimes driving the base right through the wood and yanking it out with difficulty as he stubbornly enlarged the cavity. Then, in a moment that couldn't possibly have been timed (because who rehearsed something like *this*?), the singer tossed the mike stand like a discarded cigarette butt and sat down, legs dangling into the hole. As Pearl Jam pounded out the con-cluding notes of Neil Young's epic in a howling finale of heroic racket, Vedder dropped down into his aperture, holding himself in place with his elbows and looking at the figures jammed up against the stage only a few feet away. Then, on the last drum crash, he simply pulled in his elbows and disappeared from sight.

CHAPTER 44

BUSH, GOO GOO DOLLS, AND NO DOUBT

THE OCEAN

Providence Civic Center, April 10, 1996

Listen to: Bush, "Glycerine," "Everything Zen"; Goo Goo Dolls, "Name," "Iris"; No Doubt, "Don't Speak," "Just a Girl"

The final decade of the century ticked away and a young twenty-year-old kid jammed in the front row at a Rolling Stones show in 1975 had reached forty. Many of his fellow travelers were now married with children and absorbed in lifelong careers. They'd disappeared into their homes and their commutes, standing at school-bus stops and shuttling kids in minivans. Serving the day, they steadily lost their nocturnal rock-and-roll instincts until the old way of life had vanished. But, as the veterans rotated out, fresh replacements arrived at the front every night, yearning to experience the latest and the greatest shows on earth. Twenty years on, the audience was still out there, an "ocean," as Led Zeppelin once described it, that continued to crash, wave after wave, on the shores of concert halls every night. Not much had changed in the process of star making either. A parade of young faces drawn in curiosity to the art of songwriting continued to shuffle past and then assemble nervously onstage to work out their kinks in microchip-sized nightclubs. At those rock-and-roll boot camps, experiences piled up into experience, and chosen ones ascended to the next rank. Thrust into the spotlights and anointed with fame, they stood on the beach, gazing out on that restless surface, amazed that the ocean could roll and foam from their music, responding to their very presence.

For concert veterans no longer fascinated by the nightly pursuit of the new, the groups on the poster stapled on the telephone pole in Providence probably wouldn't have exerted much pull: Bush, the Goo Goo Dolls, and No Doubt were names assigned to a new generation. All three, though, were massively on the move. London-born Bush had gotten off the mark in '94 with *Sixteen Stone*, a surprisingly retro collection of hard rock in the mold of Black Sabbath with an inciting jolt of much more recent Nirvana. Buffalo's Goo Goo Dolls used less rock and more roll than Bush and had a string of albums out since the late eighties that Cheap Trick would have been proud to have released. The California newcomers No Doubt, together since '87, placed hope in the quirky reggae and pop found on *Tragic Kingdom*, the band's second disc, just starting to get hot on the radio. Built around Bush, which had sold three million copies of its album by early '96, the tour benefited greatly from the presence of the Goo Goo Dolls with its platinum-selling *A Boy Named Goo* offering strong support in markets where Bush hadn't penetrated. No Doubt, already building a recognizable name and an interest in the stunning lead vocalist Gwen Stefani, could offer a memorable nightly opening.

I was delighted when my wife mentioned that she'd like to go, surprised that her interest hadn't been motivated by Gavin Rossdale's celebrated looks. Splashed initially over the pages of the entertainment magazines as *Sixteen Stone* ascended the charts, the mug of Bush's lead singer was soon featured in full-color gossip-magazine glory as female America rushed to embrace his heroically chiseled features. The girls also found John Rzeznik from the Goo Goos easy on the eyes, fawning mightily over his Jon Bon Jovi–like visage. I didn't think Carrie had jumped in the lake of estrogen being splashed around in that pair's honor, but even if she did, I still had my Gwen to admire, so it kind of balanced out.

The seats were perfect: right in the middle, twenty rows back on the floor. We had to find them ourselves, though, when the ushers directed us to the edge of the floor and no farther. *That's an easy job*, I thought. It might as well have been a general-admission concert for all the effort they were putting in. A fleeting and minor observation at the time, it would soon prove prophetic. No Doubt hit the stage on time, not wasting a moment of its opportunity. Stefani seemed born for the role she played, working the entire expanse side to side and projecting her energy and larger-than-life glamour into the entire arena. The successful groove of No Doubt's set was confirmed, uh, no doubt, by the sight of people in the front row standing up, grabbing their plastic seats and passing them back or off to the sides to create a dance floor for themselves. The area widened considerably as the set continued and others surged forward. Soon the benign dance floor had mutated into a ragged mosh pit as the aggressive dancers dove in, abutters fleeing their chairs in panic rather than be caught in the fracas of hurtling bodies. The folks who wanted to stand joined the dancers' ranks by handing over their seats, but others resisted and remained in their chairs. Eventually, though, they'd have no choice, as their positions were isolated into pockets as the rows behind them vanished. They'd hold on for a while, but finally give in after one or two burly moshers whizzed past within inches of knocking out a few teeth.

After the set change for the Goo Goo Dolls, the lights blacked out as the band took stage and the girls snapped to attention and took special notice. The Buffalo trio's set was anything but flashy and ornate like the previous act's, its songs performed with a minimum of frills or effects. The screams from the excited women that burst out every time Rzeznik tossed his blond locks about seemed to embarrass the players, but they also didn't blanch when several well-endowed females pulled up their shirts to advertise. The audience reserved its greatest applause for the Goo Goo Dolls' breakthrough hit "Name," a song which everyone in the arena appeared to know, even if they hadn't reacted strongly to the band up to that point. As the set continued, the cavity in the floor seats continued to expand. I'd seen plenty of mosh pits spontaneously open up in clubs, the participants careening into the sudden space in the crowd, doing their moves and quickly exiting before being bashed by the next incoming stunt pilot. I hadn't even entertained the possibility that the brawl would ever reach our row, but as the Goo Goos finished up the last couple of songs, the rumble of distant artillery fire had finally arrived at our home front. Five rows away, then four . . . three . . . two . . . one! Now we were front-row spectators on the very edge of an open field, observers with the best possible view of a pulsating mob of figures jumping and running, colliding and falling—having a great time, I had to admit. As everyone in front of us had, would we also lose our seats and be forced to stand or even retreat to the rear?

The answer was delayed when the music ended and motion ceased. We sat on the outside of a space that claimed over a third of the arena's floor section, neatly devoid of chairs as figures gathered in clumps, chatting animatedly and killing time. "Are we going to have to move?" my wife asked, "I love these seats." Me too, but I didn't see an alternative. Once Bush got onstage, it was guaranteed to get even crazier. Sure enough, the blast of hard rock from the headliners sent frenzied shock waves rippling through the crowd. Stubbornly, we remained in our chairs as the dancing boiled backward toward us and we lost sight of the stage. Defenders on both sides surrendered without a fight, giving up their chairs and disappearing somewhere as the chaos absorbed these fresh areas. Then . . . no! The people behind us abandoned their positions as well! Suddenly we were cut off, besieged on every side as Bush rocked solidly on the songs from its only album. Since half of the material had been featured prominently on the radio, the band never strayed too far from playing a hit. As such, the momentum carried strongly from beginning to end, aided in no small part by the girls who screamed for Rossdale's booty every time a song ended. For his part, he looked disaffected and bored at all the fuss, but didn't shrink a bit on his singing or playing. Meanwhile, Carrie and I considered abandoning ship as we became more and more isolated. When a giant slab of beef impacted my seat, sending me sprawling onto the floor, we decided to bail.

Retreating to the edge of the pit, where loose chairs haphazardly framed the organized rows of seats behind, I suddenly had an idea. "Carrie, stack your chair on one of those others. Keep doing it!" I grabbed seats and piled them on top of each other, the frames fitting neatly into each other, not stopping until I had at least ten high. With the top chair now elevated several feet off the floor, I helped my wife up onto her tower before climbing onto mine. We could either sit normally up there or stand on a back rung and lean forward onto the seat back. Either way, we were high off the dance floor and out of danger—our view of the band also improving considerably. When others saw our example, they began assembling their own stacks. Soon there were plastic-chair towers all around us, tenaciously fixed on the edge of the raging dance floor or, in our case, surrounded completely by the storm below. It appeared as if a tempest drove a pitching and angry sea onto a jagged shoreline, the salty spray blasting high into the air as the dark rumblings of impact shuddered our artificial reef. In fact, one of those slam-dancing breakers smashed full speed into the base of Carrie's perch, pitching her backwards and off the precipice. With disaster, or at least a nasty bruise looming, a pair of strong arms suddenly reached out from a tower of chairs behind, preventing the fall and steadying her safely.

At one point, a female bodysurfer clambered up to us, the cute teen-aged blonde asking politely "Can you launch me?"

"Uh, yeah," I responded before helping my wife position the girl at the edge of the seats, then tossing her down into the squall, like a life-boat jettisoned overboard and sent boiling away in the spray. I certainly wouldn't have done that. But I had an excuse: at her age, she'd only bend a bit leaping down onto that boiling mass, but I'd surely break from the effort and end up as a loser on a stretcher heading to Roger Williams Medical. Even so, that's not the way I danced twenty years earlier. Different times, different customs, I guess.

But aside from variations in how we observed and enjoyed rock and roll, the ritual remained constant—stars were born nightly, and these three nineties bands confirmed it. Within a year, Bush's debut would become a six-times-platinum monster. *A Boy Named Goo* would move two million for the Goo Goo Dolls, but even greater success arrived in

'98 with their single "Iris." Ironically, the baby band of the night, No Doubt, would become the most famous by far. With hit singles to spare and videos prominently displaying Stefani's natural allure on camera, *Tragic Kingdom* sold an astonishing ten million copies by early 1999 and lifted the lead singer into a meteoric solo career. Looking back, it's hard to believe all that platinum tonnage overflowed one space on April 10, 1996, a concert I was lucky to witness, even if it was from the rocks of my own "private island" perched precipitously in the middle of a dark and stormy sea.

CHAPTER 45

PHISH

CLIFF NOTES FROM UPSTATE

The Clifford Ball, Plattsburgh, New York, August 16 and 17, 1996

Listen to: "You Enjoy Myself," "Stash (Live)," "Wilson," "Free," "Character Zero"

"Forget it, man. Rock festivals are nothing but a pain in the ass."

"Not this one," David interrupted. "This will be mellow, plus you know the band and you can get us backstage. Maybe we can even camp back there!" My friend and I were talking about the upcoming Phish concert in upstate New York, the Vermont band's first full-blown, self-produced music festival. We both loved the four quirky but exceptionally gifted musicians whose versatility seemed to know no bounds, able to carve out a progressive jazz piece or funk groove one moment and then harmonize in a barbershop-quartet mode the next. Trey Anastasio, Page McConnell, Mike Gordon, and Jon Fishman constantly challenged themselves onstage, leaping from rehearsed melodies into long expanses of fearless improvisation. A lot of folks loved them for trying it too: Phish had advanced to the point of selling out hockey arenas at will. Many other bands could claim that, but did they have another three or four thousand people milling around outside around the venue still trying to score a "miracle" to get in? The same sort of love that had inspired a huge nomadic following for the Grateful Dead during the two previous decades had now grown to crave the similarly unpredictable vibes of each Phish concert, so its audience hung like a comet trail to every tour. The group clearly loved the audience back too: the attention and creativity they showered on not only the music, but production details like gigantic overhead balloon deluges or individual trampolines to bounce on while performing showed almost limitless creativity and a childlike will to use it.

Phish was as organic a band as you could hope for, coming together at the University of Vermont in the early eighties and gelling first as a solid friendship and then a band. The members' musical gifts were evident even at this early stage, and they could usually count on a packed club or bar whenever they performed local dates around the Burlington area. In just a few years the band had released its first official album *Junta*, the 1989 double-disc collection containing eleven songs filled with instrumental explorations. But, while the fledgling group enjoyed ever-growing support for its efforts from a loyal base of die-hard fans, its artistic direction was perceived as obsolete or off base by the music industry. The members of Phish ignored the snubs and followed their own path, which eventually began selling out urban clubs, even some in Boston. Elektra Records took note and started releasing the band's music; although it would take years before Phish broke gold and then platinum territory, its albums were sturdy sellers for the label.

All the while, Phish was the band the industry chose to overlook, but its following continued to increase dramatically, a nation on the move selling out any venue the band saw fit to book. In the early nineties as the group moved into the sports arenas of the Northeast, even the skeptics had to revise their opinions. They might not have liked Phish, but they certainly had to respect a band that sold out a 12,000-seater performing original songs filled with extended jams inspired by the examples of musicians like the Grateful Dead, Frank Zappa, and Miles Davis (three disparate, yet similarly open artists noted for the unpredictability of their work). And it didn't stop there: the jam band's influence grew in leaps and bounds as it grabbed the baton of free-form music born in the sixties and ran it clear through into the nineties, an essential link inspiring an entire movement of similarly motivated groups taking the attitude into a new millennium.

Dubbed the Clifford Ball, Phish's two-day festival would be at Plattsburgh Air Force Base, a massive installation with two-mile runways that had staged B-52 bombers and F-111 fighters until being decommissioned a year earlier. Now, not unlike the famous sixties antiwar photo of a young pacifist inserting flowers into the gun barrels of opposing National Guardsmen, a tide of 70,000 per day would descend on the rural, barbed-wire-enclosed area seeking nirvana through music, art, and like-minded Phish-heads. My reluctance to go, though, persisted. With each music festival I'd experienced, my willingness to plunge back into a creeping twenty-mile caterpillar of cars heading toward some distant, rustic concert site had diminished. "The show is practically in Canada," I protested. My sparring partner calmly neutralized the objection like an expert lawyer countering a first-year legal student. "Easy drive, all interstates, plus we can go up the night before and get in there before anybody! Phish is doing three sets a day; we can't miss this!" I didn't realize I was nodding at that until I saw him smiling—he knew he'd put enough points on the board. "I'll make some calls," I relented. Since I'd gotten to know the band's management quite well through my radio station interaction with them, they were not surprised to hear from me. The friendly response was disarming: *This is going to be special; you don't want to miss it; please come.*

Now I-89 northwest through New Hampshire and Vermont and a ferry ride across Lake Champlain lay behind as we finally turned the last corner onto the base in my SUV. The idea of arriving on Thursday night had delivered us from the following day's inevitable traffic nightmare. Picking up a package of colorful passes, wristbands, and instructions, we snaked along the VIP access road leading past the parking and camping areas toward the stage, passing through two checkpoints of friendly security staffers as we paralleled an enormous and never-ending runway. The final gate blocked the stage area itself, but after consulting on his walkie-talkie, the last guardian smiled and pointed to a large meadow of knee-high grass behind him. "VIP camping is straight around the back of the stage there; keep your parking pass on the dash." How cool was this? Tomorrow, we'd be able to roll out of our sleeping bags at noon, make brunch on the gas stove and check out Phish's first set from our campsite. It was dusk by the time we broke out the tent. David had finagled his girlfriend along, and between us we managed to fight the jumble of fabric and poles into a reasonable dwelling. On the other side of the security fence, early arrivals were also setting up in their campgrounds, shafts of light bouncing crazily as they aimed their flashes against the night that descended with cool suddenness. Twilight passed to complete darkness in moments, the Milky Way clearly visible above as we rested for the first time all day.

Then, a pulsing bass note with drums joining in penetrated the surrounding wilderness. It sounded at first like a tape playing in a sound system—a big one. Actually, it was the biggest one around. We poked our heads out and looked over at the stage, now blazing with lights, and picked out the guys from Phish plugged in and staking out a filthy James Brown–inspired rhythm. It stood to reason that there would be an elaborate sound check to insure a good listening experience for everyone on the vast concert field, so perhaps we'd get lucky and have a mini-concert. Few spectators were present as we freely walked the grass in front of the stage while the funky and nameless improvisation snaked along. Some instruments would be silenced for a moment or blare out in sudden volume as the soundman adjusted his levels. After a half hour, with no interference from anyone, I noticed a security detail heading directly for us. I suspected we'd be asked to leave. However, the lead figure merely yelled in my ear, "This is cool, isn't it? We've got a private concert!" I nodded emphatically, realizing they were just looking for a better spot to watch. Truly, I wasn't used to this level of "un-uptightness" at a concert.

This same model of openness, fairness, and freedom had been tried before, with success at certain times and places, especially that midsixties counterculture scene in San Francisco. There, in an unlikely scenario in the midst of capitalist America, a hippie community had shared equally, and, in effect, governed themselves peacefully with enough justice for all. But at some point, as more arrived to climb aboard the free bus, the whole idyllic scene had collapsed as resources were stretched thin and community sharing succumbed to individual grabbing. That was the major challenge at the Clifford Ball: to police a vast gathering of free spirits and protect the good vibes of the event. Fortunately, the Phish-heads were mostly an enlightened lot, valuing their community and realizing that discord threatened the entire blueprint, so they shared in the goal of a peaceful experience. But, the organizers also knew it was critical to provide ample services and resources, so 950 portable toilets, dozens of food kiosks and low-priced offerings, free water supplies, a fully equipped field hospital, telephone network, police and fire departments, post office, and trash pickup were all on site. In effect, an entire city had been erected on the runways and fields complete with a town center, dubbed Ball Square, containing a general store, barber, small church, and artists' display area. Phish had even applied to the FCC for a temporary low-power radio license, with Clifford Ball Radio broadcasting music, interviews, and all the live onstage action at 88.9 FM.

Friday dawned like the first day of summer vacation. A generous and cloudless sky greeted us as we stepped out into the dewy grass, fired up the stove, and made breakfast. Several tents had closed in tightly around us during the night, odd since there was such a large field available. I joked that the occupants must be from New York City and couldn't stand to be out of sight of their neighbors. We had an entire day free until Phish began the first of its sets at 6:30 p.m. Strolling around, we marveled at the organization of it all, wandering into Ball Square and through the campgrounds as a steady line of cars arrived. Returning to our tent, a long-haired security honcho in cargo shorts apologized for asking us to move our campsite: "Phish is shooting fireworks after the encore; you're downrange!" he laughed. We relocated onto the edge of a huge concrete turnout, where jet bombers had once awaited their place on the runway for a mile-long takeoff roll. It was a perfect camping spot, the only downside being that we missed the band's unannounced 4:00 a.m. performance as it was driven through the now-distant campground on a flatbed truck complete with instruments, amplifiers, and flaming tiki torches.

Just over 135,000 people attended the two days of the festival, Phish performing six exemplary, and, at times, groundbreaking sets. The band spared no expense in additional delights: after the first set on Friday, the Plattsburgh Symphony Orchestra took stage while we watched a glider accompany the music in a lilting aerial ballet. Stunt planes flew high above spelling out crazy phrases in smoke, while crop dusters loitered by trailing banners and fighter jets screamed from horizon to horizon in an instant. At different points while Phish played, a female trapeze artist performed high over the band, an acrobatic team cavorted onstage, and the other Vermont superstars Ben & Jerry joined in on vocals. Between sets, we roamed the grounds, observing sculptors a-sculpting, painters a-painting, and glass blowers, uh, a-blowing. It seemed like every person I squeezed by in the vast moving throng was genuinely happy, even exhilarated. Had Phish managed to create a temporary Utopia in this place, raising our eyes off a weary worldview and into the presence of beauty? It certainly seemed so. But even if the band had missed that mark, its creativity, exacting detail and obvious sparing of no expense spoke clearly of a grand ambition to try.

CHAPTER 46

JOE PERRY WITH CHEAP TRICK

A CHEAP GOLDEN JUBILEE

Mount Blue, Norwell, Massachusetts, September 24, 2000

Listen to: "I Want You to Want Me (Live)," "Ain't That a Shame," "Dream Police," "Surrender," "The Flame"

Long before his fiftieth birthday, Joe Perry had come to terms with the drugs and the downward spiral; he'd turned away toward the light of his wife, Billie, his family, and making great music. Perry had survived many storms, and he had a lot to be thankful for, so his fiftieth would be no trifling commemoration. If you were Joe Perry, you'd merit a birthday party to wow even yourself. Why not ask your favorite band to play, and who would say no to that request? Why not throw the bash in your own restaurant south of Boston—heck, you already paid the taxes on the joint, so why not use it? Then, perhaps you could invite a couple of hundred friends to the shindig, a small enough gathering so you could recognize everyone there, and hip enough to create an event destined to spark local hysteria. Billie, with the help of some Aerosmith staffers, got to work organizing the whole affair. Once contacted, the members of Joe's beloved Cheap Trick elatedly agreed to perform, then extended the guest of honor the privilege of handpicking their set list. A night was set aside at Mount Blue, the establishment in Norwell that Joe and Steven Tyler were part owners of, and some street performers and side-show eccentrics were hired to delight the guests as they arrived. Then Joe's wife got to the most difficult part: assembling the guest list.

I'd gotten to know the members of Aerosmith just before their leap into the abyss of the early eighties, a place from which I had sadly thought they'd never return. How wonderful, then, to receive an invitation to such a celebration of, not only Joe's life, but the survival of the entire band and the organization that thrived around it. Having grown up listening to Aerosmith, my wife was ecstatic at the prospect of going, but as a lovely reincarnation of one of those screaming Japanese girls in Cheap Trick's Budokan audience, much of her enthusiasm gushed from an immoderate love of the evening's house band. Robin Zander became her fantasy date for the night; but with the understanding that comes only from years of a happy marriage, I realized my place and took no offense. I duly noted the date, put it in my calendar, and went about my daily business while Carrie obsessed for weeks about what to wear.

We knew we'd arrived after we turned the last corner and stared down the road at the crowd of Aerosmith fans flanking the entrance to Mount Blue. The club itself was fronted by a huge tent, a kids' bounce house, portable rock-climbing wall, and even amusement park rides. The buffet area, dining tables, and a bar were located under the outdoor canvas, resupplied regularly by a collection of BBQ grills and smokers, one of the pits slow-roasting an entire pig. An Elvis imperson-ator strolled by in his satin suit studded with bright rhinestones, and an Austin Powers look-alike investigated everyone, awarding some a loud, "Groovy, baby!" Done up in his English frock, he was pretty good, even if his teeth were far too even for the character. I heard Marilyn Monroe dropped by too, but I must have missed her. Magicians dazzled the young ones, keeping them preoccupied with disappearing scarfs and lightning bursts of flash paper as their parents gawked at the huge floral display spelling out Joe Perry's name and a mountain of gifts that grew steadily on the table nearby. The celebrity witch from Salem, Massachusetts, Laurie Cabot, whose ancestors survived the infamous witch trials in the 1690s, held court off to the right for those who wanted their fortunes told, along with astrologers reading charts and palm readers for those so inclined. We checked in and signed the guest register, obtained adult beverages, and were well on our way to polishing them off when my wife realized she'd forgotten her camera. She insisted on going to the car to get it and on the way back noticed someone walk by with a commemorative birthday T-shirt in hand. "Where'd you get that?" He pointed to a table outside where every guest had a goodie-bag with shirt, collectibles, and a pass waiting for them, so she slipped in line to get ours.

With amazement, Carrie noticed her dream date Robin Zander standing to the side, completely undefended and smoking a cigarette as he watched his seven-year-old son maneuvering on the climbing wall. This was a golden opportunity! When the singer looked over and noticed her, she waved and he actually joined her. The two sparked up a friendly conversation, Zander mentioning that he and Joe were good friends and the band was truly honored to be doing this show for him. In a moment they reached the table where a young girl checked names off a list and handed over the bags. Zander insisted that Carrie go first, and in a moment she was all set. Then the Cheap Trick front man gave his own name, joking, "It would be at the end of the list." The girl, who hadn't retracted a welcoming smile all evening, began to look troubled as she scanned the pages of names back and forth several times. She'd probably been minus-three when *Dream Police* came out, so the twenty-something hadn't automatically recognized the singer with his distinctive long and straight blond hair. "I'm sorry," the girl said, "I don't see your name on any of my lists." Carrie stepped in, "This would be Robin Zander of Cheap Trick . . . please put him at the *top* of your list!" The girl's eyes went wide as she squirmed for a second, but recovered nicely. "I'm so sorry, sir. You can go right in." Zander smiled at the gatekeeper's reddened face, thanking her and my wife, who flushed for different reasons, then vanished inside. Carrie beamed: as far as she was concerned, her reason for existence had been justified.

After that earthshaking event, I held on to Carrie like a balloon floating on a string. The room was prepped for a rock-and-roll show, the small stage groaning under the weight of speakers and equipment, the dance floor ringed by chairs waiting to accept a gallery of Boston's rock elite. At the inside bar, local guitar ace Johnny A and his wife Beth greeted us while sipping martinis and next to them stood singer Mach Bell with various other members of the three Joe Perry Project lineups over the years. When James Montgomery, possessor of the fastest harmonica in New England, strolled over and kissed Carrie's hand, it seemed that all the usual suspects were in attendance. But, even with a tight guest list of just two hundred close friends of the family, when the guys in Aerosmith stepped out of their limos, the atmosphere began crackling with electricity. All five of them showed up: Steven Tyler, of course, dazzling the most in his striped corduroy suit, while Joe Perry opted for his usual preferred black pants and jacket. The socializing ratcheted up a dozen notches, the buzz-buzz of conversation overwhelming the canned rock-and-roll tunes pumping loudly through the place. Sexy waitresses glided by, constantly replenishing drinks, as Tyler worked the entire restaurant while the usually reserved birthday boy also made sure to get around to just about everybody. Some horn players appeared out of nowhere, blowing a fanfare to announce the arrival of a humongous cake shaped like a guitar before accompanying a rousing "Happy Birthday" sing-along. After another hour or so, as the children started falling asleep, the first segment of the party drew to a close. The parents and their slumbering charges were excused and the amplifiers were switched on!

Cheap Trick took stage in front of, undoubtedly, its smallest audience since the earliest days of the band, but the musicians tore into their first set with the same fury and passion they'd delivered at the Boston Garden in front of thousands. Clearly they were inspired to bring their A game to Joe Perry, a guitarist who, in no small part, had informed the group's very existence. While people scrambled to stake out prime viewing spots, Carrie and I were amazed that few chose to stand on the dance floor itself. We parked ourselves right in front of the band with Mach Bell and his wife, Julia, as people broke from their spells and filed in behind us. The band tore into "On Top of the World" with "Clock Strikes Ten," "Southern Girls," and "Dream Police" framing a thunderous set. Guitarist Rick Nielsen, his long beard wound weirdly into a pony tail with price tags taped to the end (a true cheap trick), called Joe to the stage and handed him gifts including a book of guitar lessons and a cheap (trick) guitar, both signed by all the band members. Joe's selected song list wasn't all Chuck Berry–style rock and roll: some of the selections included the slower "Voices" and the band's number-1 hit "The Flame." His voice always tested on the latter song, Zander pulled off the high notes impeccably. Meanwhile, the rhythm squad of Tom Petersson on bass and drummer Bun E. Carlos, the insurance salesman look-alike, just beamed and delivered their backing wallop with delight. Cheap Trick had never done a show quietly and didn't begin on this night either, so when the final booming note of the set ended, the echoes continued pounding around in my skull for a few seconds. I saw Mach Bell talking to me, but I sure couldn't hear what he was saying.

The band took a break, during which the question of whether or not Joe would sit in with Cheap Trick was answered as an additional stack of amps and a Les Paul on a stand appeared. The guitarist had decided to enjoy his birthday gift to the fullest by playing the entire second set, which began with guns blazing on "Hello There." The song that had opened many a Cheap Trick show led into the thumping "Big Eyes," with Joe Perry cracking a rare smile as wide as the room itself. Steven Tyler appeared at the main mike with Zander and Nielsen to the side for a smoking version of the Beatles' tribute to Little Richard, "I'm Down." Tyler jumped on and off for subsequent songs, Joe's son Adrian played some guitar and even Aerosmith's Joey Kramer sat in on the drums. Aside from the partially planned musical chairs going on, Joe had anticipated most everything happening onstage so far, but he never suspected what was coming. After another sweaty Beatles track, "Day Tripper," a guitar tech walked out and placed an additional instrument onstage. Years earlier, when the guitarist had been going through hard times, desperate for cash, he'd sold off a prized Les Paul '59 tobacco-burst Gibson that had sounded out the immortal riffs on *Rocks* and *Draw the Line*. He'd wanted to buy that guitar back for years, finally tracing it through a few owners to Slash from Guns N' Roses, an un-abashed Joe Perry freak who wasn't about to part with one of his he-ro's own original axes, even for many thousands of dollars. But there it was. The real McCoy rested on its stand next to him like the prodigal son returned to father. There was no price tag: this was a gift from Slash . . . the *perfect* gift. Joe Perry was a pretty guarded, Cool Hand Luke–kind of guy—the Fonz had nothing on him. But you never saw any eyes grow bigger than on the guitarist at that moment. Years in the making, the surprise was absolute. Perhaps even a tear started to form on that legend's face, but we'd never know as the pair were reunited in Joe's hands and they honeymooned off together into the old Stones hit, "It's All Over Now." That song choice seemed quite appropriate: Joe's past fifty years were done, and the quest for that guitar had ended. And, by the way, at last check, both guitar and player were living hap-pily ever after.

CHAPTER 47

U2

U2 RECLAIMS ITS MOJO (OR) FIGHTING THE BONO MONO

Fleet Center, Boston, June 6, 2001

Listen to: "Until the End of the World," "Beautiful Day," "Elevation," "Kite"

From the pit looking forward at the stage, I could see Adam Clayton on his bass measuring out the stout, booming chords that wrapped like a boa constrictor around an unshakably steady thump from drummer Larry Mullen Jr. But the main event was occurring behind me and to the left, out on the catwalk that completely encircled the hundreds of fans bouncing up and down to one of U2's loudest and most powerful rockers. "Until the End of the World," the twisted tale of Judas rationalizing his betrayal of Jesus, raged from the dozens of speakers in Boston's Fleet Center as Bono and the Edge battled on the narrow walkway with microphone parrying against lead guitar, each darting forward and back like duelists searching to inflict the decisive wound. The howling metallic coda raged on and on, the guitarist filling the arena with deafening chords as his vocalist created fake devil's horns with his fingers and advanced, leaping to thrust his mic past the thundering Les Paul. The Edge, ostensibly the God figure in this struggle, would (thankfully) not retreat, pressing his attack to force Bono onto his back.

As the final crashing notes were struck, the Devil lashed out from the ground, flailing and kicking at the guitar, jabbing out in a desperate attempt to land a vital blow. Not so, until a final lunge landed the microphone solidly on the guitar strings, the two locking together to spark an explosion of wailing electronic feedback that soared divinely out of the power chords and assailed the crowd. Like a mosquito caught in a megawatt bug zapper, the two sizzled together for a long instant before the Devil fell exhausted in defeat. A bit of theater to illustrate the eternal battle of good versus evil? The members of U2 had never been strangers to the ambitious, and Bono's utter belief in the presence of Jesus Christ made this demonstration as real as the band's tribute to Martin Luther King Jr. To the singer (and at least the members of U2 who were Christians), this wasn't so much a passion play as real passion; to the healthy share of atheists, agnostics, and those of other religious beliefs in the crowd, it was still a stirring and overwhelming moment from U2's Elevation Tour of 2001.

I've read dissertations on the Internet (where everything is correct, you know) that cite justifications for why Bono had to be the Antichrist prophesized in the New Testament. One of those reasons listed was the dramatic episode just described: rather than an illustration of true faith and belief, detractors considered this an authentic rant from the Devil's agent himself. But, if that were true, then the Antichrist would never have allowed his band to release *Pop*. Now, far be it from me to dismiss an entire U2 album—I haven't the journalistic gall to do so. Although the band's 1997 collection of dance beats and club culture was panned in every review and lambasted even by ardent fans, it did feature the tightest playing yet by the group's rhythm section and an astonishing range of sounds conjured up by the Edge. Greater sins lay ahead when U2 hit the road with Popmart, its gigantic summer tour playing stadiums beneath a towering yellow arch I referred to as Big Mac. From the furious dance collage of "Mojo" that opened each show to the forty-foot mirror-ball "lemon" with flashing strobes out of which the band members would emerge for each encore, the satirical comments of Popmart slid right past audiences who thought they were witnessing a glorified Village People lip sync. When it finally wrapped up, the tour—which cost $250,000 a *day* to operate—had hemorrhaged millions, but U2 lost an even greater amount in the currency of credibility.

A band as adventurous as U2 could be expected to make a strategic blunder here and there; and as they forged ahead, the band crafted a new album heavily weighted on the strength of songs, not style. *All That You Can't Leave Behind* emerged in 2000 and was instantly hailed: *Rolling Stone* calling it the band's "third masterpiece" after *The Joshua Tree* and *Achtung! Baby*. U2 doubled up with the hit single "Beautiful Day," which garnered three Grammy Awards and decisively took the group off America's shit list. Bono cheekily told the audience at the awards ceremony that U2 was reapplying for the job of best band in the world; it launched a scaled back tour in 2001 playing 20,000-seaters and not the football stadiums of its previous misstep. Massively restorative, the Elevation Tour reconnected the band with its audience and led to some terrific in-your-face performances in every city. Near the end of the first leg, U2 reached Boston to play four nights in the Fleet Center, a new building constructed next to the venerable and demolished Boston Garden where the band had performed several legendary gigs. The band decided to record the first two shows there for a live DVD. One of U2's three initial areas of support in America (along with New York City and L.A.), Boston had always been special to the band, so much so that Bono often called the city's audience a "hometown crowd." This would be an ideal location to capture "Elevation," and more importantly, a re-centered U2 with an album of terrific new songs.

In the true fashion of many U2 loyalists, I resolved to go to all four shows. The band's penchant for playing different material from night to night and responding uniquely to a fresh audience always lent each concert its own personality. As I walked into the Fleet Center the first night, I noticed the dominant feature of the stage set, its long catwalk in the shape of a heart extending out onto the floor. In fact, Bono would refer to this area during the show as exactly that: "the heart." The prop revealed the theme for the entire album/tour experience: the only thing one couldn't (or shouldn't) leave behind was love. Although all the reviews positively glowed for that first show, Bono's voice had sounded a bit rough and his performance seemed subdued, perhaps influenced by the daunting sight of wall-to-wall movie cameras pointing in his direction.

The second evening, I brought my wife, Carrie, and we arrived early for a taste of PJ Harvey, who was warming up each concert. The rock-and-roll chanteuse mingled sexiness with alternative pop, smartly setting the stage for the headliner, but we only made it halfway through her set before being summoned backstage by an assistant of U2's manager Paul McGuiness. Inside the cement-block maze of the arena, we met the man whom I'd known for years as the business genius who had guided the band through the pitfalls of the industry since the beginning. After greeting us pleasantly, the usually beaming McGuiness quickly turned serious. "You might know that we are recording a DVD." I nodded. "Well, last night we definitely did not get the performance we needed. Bono is ill; he's had a rough time." That admission confirmed why the show had been good, but not great by U2's high standards. It also implied that there was a lot riding on tonight's performance since a two-day shoot meant that all the cameras were set up and their operators ready, but they'd be going home tomorrow. I shuddered to think of how much money was on the line. "Bono wants to talk to you." Huh? I didn't have time to speculate. McGuinness politely apologized to my wife, directing her into the cozy backstage bar, then led me down another corridor.

Shown into the lead singer's dressing room, I saw a huddled figure bundled up in a white Turkish spa robe, face down in the healing mist of a vaporizer. Glancing back, Bono noticed me and got up to offer a hug. But with his eyes red and a sickly look hardly concealed by a smile, I realized why the usually unflappable McGuiness was so worried. I'd known Bono since 1980, and after we quickly caught up, he got right to the point. The singer was far from 100 percent and acutely worried about the success of that evening's goal: to capture U2 in an ideal live situation inspired by one of the best audiences it had ever played to. He felt that many in the crowd, some of them infants when the group first played the tiny Paradise Theater on its initial visit, were not aware of U2's special bond with the city. He believed that most of the people didn't realize that the band was shooting a movie and wanted to apologize for the presence of the extra equipment and viewing obstructions during the show. Bono also felt that a pep talk was necessary to pump up the crowd before U2 came out. Would I do that?

An hour later my wife and I walked along the fluorescent duct-tape-lined path that stretched from the dressing rooms around the back of stage and up a steep stairway onto the platform itself. Emceeing a U2 concert was insanely easy, as the fans were always enthusiastic and supportive. They reacted warmly when I spoke, almost neutralizing the self-consciousness I felt as a film crew followed me onstage and nearly jammed their camera down my throat!

Ten minutes later, with the houselights still blazing, U2 stepped onstage performing the song "Elevation." Catching much of the audience by surprise, people were frozen in mid sentence or on the way to their seats as they realized the show had just begun. A second later, thousands of arms in the air and a tremendous shout had been raised in greeting. Bono in his leather jacket and a perpetual pair of sunglasses gamboled about, exhorting more response and singing strongly. I was quite stunned, not believing it possible after witnessing the miserable condition he had been in just an hour or so previously. With voice happily restored as the band swung into "Beautiful Day," Bono's dramatic stage presence also returned throughout the famous duel between God and the Devil from *Achtung! Baby*. With evil vanquished (for the moment), the band moved confidently into some new songs plus "Gone," a tougher hard-rock reboot of the only surviving track from *Pop*. Bono seemed to slap the hands of each person squashed against the sides of the catwalk as he headed out to a smaller stage area located at the very bottom of the heart. Edge came down the other side and joined him on the light and airy "In a Little While," introduced as one of Joey Ramone's favorite songs before he had died from cancer seven weeks earlier. The entire band assembled in the small area to perform a stripped-down "Desire" and then the emotional "Bad," during which the singer's voice cracked for the first time, but it could have easily been the emotion of the song carrying those notes away. After forty more minutes to the final chords of the set-closing "Walk On," the house-lights came up once again and the members of U2 gazed out with gratitude plus more than a bit of relief in their eyes. "Elevation" had been captured; that it had been done under such difficult conditions made the victory so much sweeter and the concert unforgettable.

Of course, Bono hadn't gotten out of the woods yet; he was still sick. That didn't stop him from having a drink or two at U2's small cele-bratory party at the hotel afterwards. Everyone knew that the group had come through with a special performance recorded under great duress. Bono ambled up, placed a sodden kiss on my cheek and laughed as we raised our glasses high. The remaining two concerts at the Fleet Center were both exceptional, and as U2's tour headed off to Philadel-phia, it seemed like everything in Boston had gone off splendidly and everyone had gotten their wish. Maybe not in my case, though. A few days later I'd come down with a case of the dreaded "Bono mono" that the singer had brought into town from some far-flung land. That bug was tough! It rendered me useless in bed for a week. And even if I could sing, I'd have been a puddle on the floor the night Bono pulled it off. Maybe that's just an example of a normal Irish constitution, but I credit it to something bigger—that thing "that you can't leave behind."

CHAPTER 48

ROBERT PLANT AND ALISON KRAUSS

SIDE BY SIDE, THEY WALK THE NIGHT

Bank of America Pavilion, Boston, June 5, 2008

Listen to: "Rich Woman," "Fortune Teller," "Gone Gone Gone," "Please Read the Letter"

He could be her father, I thought as I watched Robert Plant, a couple of months shy of sixty, standing alongside the stunning Alison Krauss, twenty-three years his junior. Maybe he was! Had the formidably voiced superstar kept track of the oats he sowed back in the wild days of his youth when the mighty Zeppelin scoured the earth? *Perish the thought*, I scolded myself. Krauss came from an upright Illinois background far removed from the bluesman born in Bromley, England. However, Zeppelin was playing throughout the United States in 1970 when such a tryst could have occurred, so . . . I scrutinized the pair onstage at Boston's Bank of America Pavilion, the latest name for a venue that was actually a semipermanent tent seating around 5,000. No, there wasn't even the remotest resemblance: their genes were at different ends of the pool, and so was the music that brought them together. And that was the beauty of it: Robert Plant and Alison Krauss had become the most inspired and brilliant musical mash-up of the year. Their collaborative album *Raising Sand* had charted higher than any studio album by either of them, gone platinum three months earlier, and would win five Grammy Awards including Album of the Year in February '09. The tour featured an ace band assembled by guitarist, singer, producer, and songwriter T-Bone Burnett, an American roots musician who became a star after his success with the *O Brother, Where Art Thou* and *Walk the Line* movie soundtracks. Burnett had been the key to this collaboration, picking the songs and gluing together Krauss's breathtaking bluegrass background with one of the icons of rock.

In 1985, a couple of months after Live Aid, Plant had a solo album in trouble: the abstruse *Shaken 'n' Stirred*, a follow-up to his first two platinum-selling solo releases. This one didn't have the obvious hit single on it, so someone prevailed on the singer to promote the album on several radio stations, also thanking the DJs and encouraging them to continue their support. On my particular Boston station, I drew the straw to interview Plant. Unquestionably an honor to talk to the legend, I wasn't nervous in the least. Why? Because no one involved in setting up the interview had remembered to tell me about it! When the hotline rang and a cultured English voice informed me that I'd have Robert calling me back in five minutes, I had to ask, "Robert who?" The maître d' of the interview paused, thinking it must be a joke, then replied with a chuckle, "Robert Plant, of course." At least I knew—I might have prepared myself for a chat with Robert Palmer! After I panicked briefly, Plant called back, but he was polite, unpretentious, and easy to talk to. Near the end of the chat, he brought up the Boston music scene and name-checked the Del Fuegos and Tarbox Ramblers as his favorites, bands that had barely scratched success at the time even within city limits. Eighteen years later Plant and I talked again on the air, and this time I was better prepared because I had been the one who set up the interview. Our conversation centered on both American blues and his exploration of African music styles, which had prompted him to recently visit Mali and play a music festival near Timbuktu, jamming with the local musicians there. Clearly, the singer was an informed and questing musicologist!

That hunger led Robert Plant through some interesting twists and turns over a long career, but playing onstage with Alison Krauss at a 2004 Rock and Roll Hall of Fame tribute to legendary American tunesmith Leadbelly sparked an idea for the pair to work together in the future. Krauss, the American bluegrass and country-music star matched Plant as a vocal powerhouse, plus her mastery of the violin had given her more Grammies than any female artist, period. But, even as highly decorated as she was, I still didn't know much about her music, my world centering squarely in Robert Plant's wheelhouse. *Raising Sand*, though, had been stunning, mixing all sorts of traditional and contemporary Americana with the rural blues and R & B tradition. The odds of it ever working out were stacked against it, but it did! Now I counted along, tapping my toes to the strumming banjo, bouncing along to happy fiddlin' and sobbing in my beer (not really) during the mournful laments. Putting his gifts in service to the songs from *Raising Sand*, Plant had left his ego at home, caressing the music rather than lording about onstage wielding the hammer and playing God on a sacred canon of classic rock scripture. I'd gotten the impression from my interviews and reading others that he'd gotten pretty tired of being "that guy" in Led Zeppelin anyway.

The audience didn't know exactly what to expect. Many had an open mind, but more than a few wished that Plant would just break out the Zeppelin catalogue and get on with it. While he'd have the difficult task of denying the audience most of the music that had made him an icon, his collaborator would have an equally difficult job of winning over a crowd largely unfamiliar with her considerable résumé of a dozen albums. The band came onstage, herded into the lights by Burnett, who picked up his guitar and led the musicians into the thumping instrumental introduction to "Rich Woman," the smoky and enigmatic track that had opened *Raising Sand*. Plant and Krauss walked out together, tremendous applause greeting them before they began singing. The two blended magically: accustomed to being the lead voice and a solo one at that, Plant had obviously learned a great deal from Krauss, who grew up harmonizing daily on those old Appalachian mountain songs. The second selection brought the first of many changes of pace, brightening into square-dance mode with fiddle, mandolin, and pickin' guitar. Then a mystical tone returned on the huge hit rendered virtually unrecognizable at first in its altered state. A guy behind me suddenly blurted out, "No shit, it's 'Black Dog!'" This was not unprecedented: Plant had mutated much of the Zeppelin catalogue in his performances over the years. Even so, it was unusual hearing the 1971 hard-rock staple delivered in such a stately and smoldering cadence graced with a violin solo. The "awh-awh-awh-awh" segment was clear as a bell, though, and Plant encouraged the audience to sing it back, which everyone did gustily. I found myself imagining that perhaps this version might be the one preferred by that old guy loaded up with the huge bundle of sticks pictured on the cover of *Led Zeppelin (4)*.

Robert Plant introduced Krauss, who took charge for three numbers while he stepped to the rear to provide backing vocals with the band. As soon as she opened her mouth, all attention on Plant vanished, for the moment. I felt what I believe everyone must have felt: a chill dance down my spine as her first heavenly and perfect notes rang vibrantly through the pavilion. Such a voice of beauty, and I had never heard it before! It took only one verse and chorus from Krauss to silence whatever doubts anyone might have harbored concerning the wisdom of such an eccentric musical liaison. Perhaps some might have resented her for obstructing the benefit of a full Robert Plant experience. Not now. Instantly, I realized that she was easily his equal: a vocal giant born with an incredible talent and one who had grown confident in being able to project her voice however she wished. She could match even the thunder of Plant's howling on the stormy "Kashmir" with her own ethereal wailing on the gentle "Trampled Rose" by Tom Waits, her voice as limpid and haunting as the eerie tones from a theremin.

Then came a switcheroo as Krauss backed off to let Plant deliver "Fortune Teller," the tongue-in-cheek R & B chestnut from 1962 covered by many including the Rolling Stones and the Who. He uncorked his solo hit "In the Mood" as well as a spirited run-through of "Black Country Woman" from *Physical Graffiti*. Further pleasures included "Who Do You Love," a tribute to blues legend Bo Diddley and then probably the best Led Zeppelin song to benefit from the stylistic junction of this collaboration: "The Battle of Evermore." Krauss pushed the emotion of Sandy Denny's original 1971 delivery with Plant into thrilling new realms: the darkness they walked through became even more ominous, the night longer still, and the risk somehow greater. The "bring it back!" chants at the end spiraled to a peak that could have ended the show, but there were still a half-dozen songs to go. After twenty-four selections and 130 minutes, including a four-song encore, the pair took their final bows and walked off. I felt utterly dazzled, exhilarated, and satiated as they disappeared, concluding that if I had to pick my top five shows of all time, this one would have to be one of them.

My wife and I loitered about for a while as most of the crowd filed out, my eyes searching about for one of my record-company friends. The possibility of going backstage had been left as undetermined; if there was a meet and greet, some passes would show up. The last time we'd met Plant was three years earlier in this same place after a spec-tacular concert with his band Strange Sensations. Carrie and I, in the company of some friends, headed backstage and blended in with the hubbub inside the catering tent, not certain whether Plant would even appear. But he did: the star was led straight through the room and over to us by folks from his record label. "Did you like the show?" he asked. "What parts?" Here he was: the questing musicologist again. Mean-while, my wife and her friend Sandra stood mutely starstruck next to us. Both held CD covers waiting for autographs, and Sandra tightly gripped a Sharpie for the request. Plant turned and smiled, "Would you like me to sign these?" The girls remained motionless and en-thralled, his godlike presence overwhelming their circuits and molding them into two beautiful statues. "Ah, I guess so," he laughed, plucking the pen from Sandra's fingers and initiating the signatures. The mo-ment was supremely amusing, and all of us, including Plant, enjoyed the humor of it. Within seconds the girls found their voices again and chatted briefly with the star before he moved on to the next group of fans. But tonight, three years later, there were no label representatives handing backstage passes to us. C'est la vie. If we had gone back, I might have been lucky enough to speak with my "buddy" Robert Plant again, but if they'd brought Alison Krauss out, I'm sure I would have been as frozen and speechless as my wife and friend had been during their own rock-star moment.

CHAPTER 49

JACK WHITE

POWER HITTER

Fenway Park "Bleacher Theater," Boston, September 17, 2014

Listen to: "I'm Shakin," "Just One Drink," "Sixteen Saltines," "Seven Nation Army"

There was no joy in Mudville. The Red Sox season had less than two weeks to go, and the team had firmly secured last place in the AL East, this after winning the World Series just a year earlier. From first to worst! With no possibility of the team making the play-offs, what was a Bostonian to do? There would, of course, be next season to start fresh, but before bidding this one good riddance I joined 7,500 others in a Fenway Park pilgrimage to celebrate a different American pastime—rock and roll. After taking a few practice swings in the batter's box, Jack White was next up in the cycle, and so far his impressive stats made a home run over the Green Monster a distinct possibility. Could he save the season? After a dazzling and meteoric rise through his farm-team years in the White Stripes and side projects like Raconteurs and Dead Weather, White's role as a solo slugger had fully taken off. The tickets appeared courtesy of my twenty-something friend

Billy, who scored a pair and urged me to go. You see, talents like this didn't come around to play too often, and when you had the chance to see one on the field, you took it. Sure, I'd been around the sun a few more times than Billy and I'd probably be older than most in the audience, but with the benefit of those years I ranked Jack White favorably among all the greats I'd been lucky enough to see and hear. He spoke principally to a generation younger than mine, but as an insightful and fearless artist, he had something to say to everyone. You just had to leave the bullpen to hear it.

Owner of his own Third Man record label, White had a new album out called *Lazaretto*, a provocative blend of screeching alt-rock bombast, traditional blues feel, and tasteful blends of every fingerboard, drumhead, or keyboard found in a well-stocked music shop. Like all his previous work, White crafted his recording meticulously, with an obsession for precision well documented in interviews and reviews. The critics loved the album, praising *Lazaretto* and his previous *Blunderbuss* as essential works of the era. "You've got to see him," Billy urged. He hadn't been the first. Nine years earlier, my assistant at work, also twenty-something at the time, began feeding me White Stripes albums. Jay extolled the virtues of the most important band to appear since the Beatles. Well, he didn't say it like that, but for all the times he brought up the subject, you would have thought that this group represented the second coming of, well, the Fab Four or, at least, U2. Every day he could get away with it, Jay consigned the office sound system to the White Stripes' *Elephant* album, cranking "Seven Nation Army" until the receptionist on the opposite side of the building buzzed us to turn it down. When the White Stripes (Jack White and Meg White) played three nights at the Boston Opera House, tickets evaporated instantly, but somehow Jay came up with a pair.

More to shut him up rather than pursuing a pure musical interest, I agreed to go, hiding my relative ambivalence carefully amid his hysterical excitement. With no expectations, no worshipful attitude or history with this band, I watched from mid-floor as Jack White displayed a seemingly boundless talent on any instrument. While Meg thumped somewhat adequately on the drums, he picked from an impressive assortment of guitars—electric to national steel acoustic plus keyboards, marimba, and percussion to adorn whatever song popped in his head. That was a big deal: the spontaneous set list. Who had the balls and the talent to do that? I'd only seen a few pull it off, and usually in an acoustic setting. Neil Young came to mind. I'd seen the same thoughtful gaze around the stage as the classic-rock veteran considered his instrumental options and what song he could play on each. With all the implements he required right there around him, Young's entire catalogue remained on the table right in front of us. With the same pondering look as the seasoned "Old Man," White pondered his choices before an idea percolated and sent the set off on a new bearing. It only took a few songs before I regarded Jack White with a profound wonder and respect. Jay smiled: not because he'd won the fight in a knockout, but because he'd shared something special. For him, the White Stripes' recently released *Get Behind Me Satan* album was his fifth White Stripes adventure, but for me, I had some catching up to do!

So I'd become a White Stripes fan, but shortly after, suffered the same disappointment of so many when the duo went on hiatus for a few years and eventually announced its dissolution in 2011. But comfort came in White's work with the Raconteurs and the cluster of sessions for other artists that he engaged in as a player or producer (often both). Billy's offer to see the solo White in action echoed strongly of the invitation nine years earlier, but this time I didn't hesitate. Like some dazzling A-list talents before him—Michael Jackson, Jim Morrison, Prince, Kurt Cobain and Jimi Hendrix—White had a prodigious talent, a booming work ethic, and an astounding focus. Critically, though, the cosmic bargain that meted out these icons their supreme artistic intellect also sprinkled in only the barest dash of the ingredients helpful in handling the onslaught of fame or even coping with the most normal of social situations. White had a reputation as a loose cannon that could easily drop a wheel and fire its shot anywhere; he'd stormed off stages and abruptly abandoned projects without notice or scarcely a reason. This opportunity to see him onstage supporting *Lazaretto* could not be squandered; now, hopefully, he'd show up for the concert.

But who would want to blow off a concert at the legendary Fenway

Park anyway? The greats had all played here, with the place preserving the rose-colored tint of baseball's classic beginnings. The right-field grandstands had been converted into a concert hall, the stage astride the bullpens looking up at the rows of bleachers and seats. We cruised past the inner concourse of hot pretzels, cotton candy, and Fenway Franks, passed through the concrete tunnel to our section, and beheld the manicured green field of dreams and stage spread out below us. Spooky blue lights illuminating the equipment and instruments hinted of Jack White's latest preferred hue, matching the indigo shades from the cover of the *Lazaretto* album cover. Unfortunately, our seats were obstructed, only permitting a half-view of the proceedings, the other part owned by a massive steel pillar slathered in Fenway Park's utilitarian green paint. "No problem," Billy insisted, "I've got a friend in security; he'll let us get down close."

When showtime arrived, White and his five-piece band took stage in truly creative fashion, darting out of the Green Monster scoreboard one by one as the soundman stated each of their names, tastefully adding the proper amount of echo you'd expect to hear from an announcer calling a game. The solo slugger got to his mic and revealed more of his reverence for Fenway Park by jesting, "What a dump I'm playing tonight. My manager promised me a bowling alley and this is what we got!" White got busy, highlighting his first few songs with wild fuzz-guitar blasts and the close accompaniment of pretty Lillie Mae Rische on fiddle. Right away, though, the sound mix emerged as a muddled mess, the problems continuing on for several songs as the crew attempted to get a handle on it. The bad sound visibly frustrated White; for a while, I worried that we'd get a five-song show and he'd walk right off the stage and back to his hotel. Fortunately, that didn't happen. The sound guy finally got the notoriously bad acoustics of the ballpark together, and White actually smiled several times, ending up playing a mammoth twenty-eight-song concert for nearly two and a half hours.

True to his word, Billy had arranged an upgrade, and we were ushered into the first row! I didn't know how and didn't care to ask — I was just happy to say goodbye to Mr. Pole. Looking around, I noted happily that I didn't look like the oldest person in the place (just the second or third) because a remarkable range in age stood singing along with just about every word. Of course, we were now hanging in front with all the fanatics, those who had waited hysterically at their computers to be right on top of the on-sale moment or pulled whatever string necessary to score seats. I wouldn't beat them on "Jack White Karaoke Night" for sure, but I loved being right in the middle of their energy. The star sported a new look, long hair long gone and replaced with a shorter, slicked-back 'do. A shift in style from song to song followed White's famously changeable muse, from a rural blues cover of "John the Revelator" to the howl of White Stripes anthems like "Ball and Biscuit" and "Seven Nation Army." It didn't stop except for one notable break in which White blasted *Rolling Stone* magazine's website: "brought to you by the Kardashian family," *US* magazine with its owner Jann Wenner, and pop music in general. The rant went viral, by the way, capturing Twitter that night and the Internet all the next day. When the band finally exited on the tail end of an exhausting eight-song mega-encore, I felt completely spent. We allowed gravity to have its wish, plopping down in the uncomfortable, but fabled, Fenway seats. We'd all done the marathon: the joyous romp from the greatest alt-rocker since . . . Cobain? Would I hang that weight around his neck? I didn't need to, as it had already been done by others before me. But White seemed to be handling the burden pretty well, even mixing in a lot of old-school history with the riveting current stuff he churned out.

I felt fortunate to have witnessed what I saw as a changing of the guard. Like T-Bone Burnett and a host of bands extending even to the pop success of Mumford and Sons, White pulled inspiration from looking back at America's vast folk heritage including blues, country, gospel — the elements that big-banged their way to form rock and roll back in the fifties. He was a new face, but fell in line on a long trail of previous travelers, from Robert Johnson to Hank Williams and Elvis Presley — musicians who regarded the music as sacred even if their lives were often chaotic and ended up wrecked and burnt along the way. Every succeeding generation covers itself with the reassuring blanket of its own era, with a father and mother's attitude regarding the "radical" trends and new heroes of their children usually draped in skepticism. A black-and-white-TV generation had gazed in horror at four mop tops on Ed Sullivan, while, in turn, their kids who gorged themselves on Beatlemania and the aftermath would later listen aghast to the scorched-earth sounds from Nirvana. But Jack White had reached back, across the generations, pulling inspiration from every era to create his own vision. The great thing was that "the kids" were digging it: accepting this charismatic and creative young star was to learn about a rich past that so often was lost as trends flew by. The hallowed surrounding of the legendary ballpark only heightened the feelings; it might have been a new team, but they were playing a very distinguished and time-honored game.

CHAPTER 50

JOE WALSH

LIFE AFTER THE FAST LANE

Orpheum Theater, Boston, October 17, 2015

Listen to: "Turn to Stone," "Rocky Mountain Way," "Life's Been Good," "Analog Man," "Wrecking Ball," "Lucky That Way"

Joe Walsh walked onstage at the Orpheum Theater, a place he'd played a couple of times in the past forty-five years, as a prodigal son returning with humility and a longing for forgiveness. The musician had wandered long and hard in the wilderness, escaping that popular and well-worn track running right off the cliff only at the very last moment. As enamored fans, we'd ignored the perils of his path, idolizing the rock-star myth, and wondering how difficult a journey could it be when you took a Lear jet to work or drove around in that Maserati that did 185. We didn't see the signs that Joe Walsh had become a walking disaster, or as he described in a new song, careening wildly from moment to moment while living his life like a "Wrecking Ball." There was no damning video clip or cellphone shot that captured the star in some grand faux pas, an extreme close-up replayed over and over again on a hundred celebrity-rumor blogs or television shows. The guitarist and singer had never supplied that spectacular prime-time gaffe or social meltdown to those professional gossipmongers whose jobs relied on tidbits of humiliation. The stories of Walsh taking a chainsaw along on the Eagles' tours to gain "emergency" access to his bandmates' or manager's room remained just that—hushed rock-star folklore. For better or for worse, Joe Walsh's fabled boozing and legendary antics remained hidden in an upper room of celebrity decadence.

As a wide-eyed teen my first concert had been the James Gang featuring a twenty-two-year-old Joe Walsh who had a lot of the same wondrous dreams for the future that I held. With his nimble fingers and an exceptionally creative mind, he'd jumped onto the national stage blasting the power chords to "Funk 49" and punching the ticket on three exceptional studio albums with that Cleveland trio. Through his following solo career and a lifelong stint in the Eagles, Walsh had remained relevant and active, even if he'd become his own worst enemy. In the wake of his monster hit "Rocky Mountain Way," I saw Walsh with his band Barnstorm play the Orpheum in 1974 and dazzle the crowd with a powerful show crackling with the creative energy he'd discovered on a pair of albums after the James Gang. The stunning performance would end up pushing the headlining Marshall Tucker Band to the wall to keep up. Then there were those amazing Eagles' concerts, Walsh lighting a flaming torch under a band of laid-back desperadoes once he joined at the end of '75. Four years later, he could look a little bleary-eyed onstage, but always managed to pick his way through the buzz. In 1988, though, came the great disillusionment.

I enthusiastically accepted the assignment from my radio station to emcee a Joe Walsh concert at Club Casino in Hampton Beach, New Hampshire, in the heat of summer '88. I hadn't seen the guitarist and singer since the Eagles retired eight years earlier. Backstage, I huddled briefly with the road manager to figure out when I'd bring the band on and was introduced to Walsh as he fiddled and diddled on his guitar moments before the show. The plan was for me to walk onstage through the narrow entrance from the dressing-room area, wind up the crowd, and introduce Walsh, then duck back through that single passageway to make way for the musicians. But, that's not how it worked out. Later, when the road manager gave me the go signal, I burst out into the bright lights and a huge shout from the sold-out house. Two spotlight beams pinioned me at the mic; I could see nothing, and as usual, I can remember none of what I said, but as a true fan my introduction would have certainly been heartfelt, ending with a shout: "Joe Walsh!" The audience responded with a roar and I whipped around to retrace my route, but the band members were already stepping through the entryway, blocking my escape. With spotlight cones targeting my back, I slid to the left to sidestep the glare. I felt like an unlucky prison inmate, exposed in front of the guard tower in a failed attempt to bust out. Joe Walsh, with one hand on a guitar strapped over his shoulder and the other clutching a blender or thermos of some happy liquid, popped into the lights as the place went nuts. But instead of doing what every other star would have done: strutting to the mic to acknowledge the mayhem, he spied me to the side trying to blend into the wall, and lurched over to enfold me in a huge embrace. The guitar slammed into my gut as the hand with the drink clamped around my back. "Thank you!" he declared with boozy breath, which was very nice, but we were, after all, hugging it up on the big stage in a supremely awkward man-dance. We rocked and tilted around for one or two rotations before the tipsy star released me to continue on his path to stage center, and I scurried desperately out of view.

That wasn't so bad, just a funny footnote, really; I was thrilled to be able to emcee for the man. What was tragic, though, was the extent to which Joe Walsh's drinking had crippled his ability to play. I almost cried as he fumbled the solo to "Life in the Fast Lane," unable to replicate or even approach the mastery of his original studio performance. While Walsh's fingers responded clumsily, as if operated by an inept puppeteer hidden in the rafters above, several extended episodes of slurry rhetoric at the microphone replaced much of the music. Afterward, with my disappointment impossible to mask, I skipped the backstage meet and greet because I couldn't face him. The rock-and-roll demon had claimed another one, I concluded, as I drove out of the parking lot and popped in a CD from one of the dozens of other artists dying for my attention. I gave it to them too: Joe Walsh slipped away and disappeared completely off my radar screen for years.

I started hearing his name again when the Eagles resumed touring in earnest in the 2000s on their never-ending "farewell" jaunt. When I went to see the band at the Boston Garden, Walsh's spirited presence and incendiary guitar work rescued the concert from its otherwise pedestrian ho-hum. Then in February 2012, he appeared on the Grammy Awards television broadcast playing marvelous acoustic guitar to back Paul McCartney on a stunning performance of the ex-Beatle's "My Valentine." Was this the fumble-fingered guitarist I'd sadly written off in 1988? Bent over his acoustic, brilliantly handling the demanding part, the veteran played effortlessly in beautiful accompaniment. Later, he'd participate in a fully-electrified finale with McCartney, Bruce Springsteen, and Dave Grohl tearing up the stage on a Beatles medley that included the legendary *Abbey Road* ax duel on "Carry That Weight"/"The End." If that wasn't a visit to the top of rock's Mount Olympus, then what was? In June 2012 Walsh released *Analog Man*, his first solo album in twenty years. Produced by Electric Light Orchestra mastermind and ex–Traveling Wilbury Jeff Lynne, the album emerged as Walsh's strongest collection of songs since the seventies. "One Day at a Time" unabashedly addressed his drinking problem and summarized the recovery plan, quoting one of its mantras. The aforementioned "Wrecking Ball" spoke of consequences realized in a life of blundering self-destructively through situations and splintering his relationships. "Family" was more a prayer than a song, thanking the almighty for rescuing Walsh and providing him with a loving and caring household. I interviewed the star on the radio in August and he talked openly of getting sober: "I'm so lucky to be alive. There's life after alcoholism and total dependency. The problem may weigh eighty pounds, but you gotta pick it up and ask for help, because there's a way out."

Walsh soaked up the delirium from the sold-out Orpheum Theater in 2015 after his first two songs, a superb blast on the James Gang "Walk Away" and the solo hit "A Life of Illusion." The versatile nine-piece band moved and rippled around him like a cloak, the bandleader completely present in directing the large and impressive ensemble. The guitar work dazzled, every bit living up to the legend of a man who had burst dynamically onto the rock-and-roll scene and cruised to its rarified heights perhaps a bit too quickly. Clearly, Walsh's lifelong madness had passed; we were left with the essence of an artist joyously celebrating his returned clarity and the ability to create unreservedly once again. From the delicate lace of his Eagles' standout "Pretty Maids All in a Row" to the metal-guitar histrionics of "The Bomber Medley" the numerous textures and moods of a life interrupted and now regained filled the theater. This was not just a greatest-hits show, but a grand celebration of Walsh's success in pushing back the darkness. The lyrics of "Life's Been Good" that had been hilarious back in '78 didn't seem so funny these days: his Maserati had crashed spectacularly and rusted for years on the freeway, but from his position now, he could at least smile about it. In encore time Walsh took his last bow at the end of an equally prophetic "Life in the Fast Lane," thanking God for allowing him to survive the hard lessons while the Boston crowd feted him and his fantastic band for minutes on end.

Worn down by hours of clapping and shouting at the triumphant return of this old soldier, I wearily gave in to the bright houselights that announced the show's finish. I sat down in my beat-up Orpheum seat, the tired springs under the worn upholstery just a hairsbreadth from giving me a vicious gouging. After the memorable performance, how could I not travel full circle in my mind back to that first James Gang show in Pennsylvania? The course of rock and roll could not be predicted then, and can't be now: and really, how boring would it be if it could? Although *Billboard* magazine steadily charted the sales success of hit albums and singles throughout the years, it's always impossible to know from whom and in what direction those songs were going to come. But that's the beauty of it, isn't it? How exciting would my life be if I could predict each coming moment? For better or for worse, my choices and mistakes had made me. So it has been with music.

Some of those moments, inflection points, that affected rock and roll were explosive: like Lynyrd Skynyrd's plane crash, Stevie's last chopper ride, Jimi's "cocktail" of drugs and alcohol, half a million showing up at a farm in upstate, Paul divorcing John, or Kurt cradling his shotgun. Most were so much more subtle; but the efforts and results of a thousand players and their millions of fans have fashioned what the music has become. Rock and roll has cruised along for more than sixty years since Carl Perkins first stepped up to the mic wearing his blue suedes. It's been my privilege to travel along with it a good part of the way. In a life of loving that moment when the lights die and the band hits the stage, I could say that I've seen it all, but I'd only be fooling myself. The next ball is always in play, and it might be the one that changes everything.

Like Walsh, many have been called and many fallen. How splendid to see one of those rise again, perhaps not as bright as in the heady days of climbing fortunes and spiraling chart numbers, but content now to be merely alive with all the fingers working and a mind restored to expertly control them. Life was good to Joe Walsh, and it was good to rock and roll too. They have both been lucky to have survived it.

ACKNOWLEDGMENTS

The main squeeze goes to my wife, Carrie, for her love, patience, and feedback — xxoo!

A special mention of my fellow travelers at WBCN: Mark Parenteau, Patrick Murray, and Wally Anacki, who all recently departed us for a better seat up front.

Kudos to Stephen Hull, Barbara Briggs, Sherri Strickland, Susan Sylvia, and all the dedicated folks at University Press of New England for their guidance and enthusiasm!

I send a big thank you to all of the following who, in some way, helped inspire the completion of this collection of rock-and-roll adventures: Tony Berardini, David Bieber, Eric Brown, Hope Denekamp, Allan Dines, Karen Durkot, Billy Finnegan, Clint Gilbert, Roger Gordy, Leo Gozbekian, Robert Guasch, Mark Hannon, Jim Harold, Lynn Jackson, Bruce Kettelle, Jill Kneerim, Thom Lane, Larry "Chachi" Loprete, John Laurenti, Sandra Laurenti, Don Law, Jay Moberg, Dave Marsden, Linda Leatherbee McKenna, Tim McKenna, John Mullaney, Steve Nelson and the Music Museum of New England (mmone.org), Oedipus, Billie Perry, Joe Perry, Sandy Pesce, Nina Ryan, Tom Sandman, Mike Thomas, Bob Walsh, Jill Weindorf, Ike Williams, and Dave Wohlman (who trained me for my first Boston radio gig — just a couple of years ago, right?).

Also, David Bowie, Glenn Frey, Paul Kantner, and Prince: for all you did, and continue to do.

SOURCES

James Gang

Crowe, Cameron. "Joe Walsh, Child of the Silent Majority: Ex-James Ganger Tends His Garden." *Rolling Stone*, February 27, 1975.

Rentlinger, Lynn. "Sly Scheduled to Perform." *Muhlenberg (College) Weekly*, February 4, 1971.

Righi, Len. "Joe Walsh Will Do More Than Fly Like an Eagle." *Allentown (PA) Morning Call*, August 10, 2007.

Smith, George. "For Joe Walsh, It's Still Jest Rock 'n' Roll." *Allentown (PA) Morning Call*, March 31, 1990.

Whitburn, Joel. *Top Pop Albums 1955–1992*. Menomonee Falls, WI: Record Research, Inc., 1993.

Neil Young

Crowe, Cameron. "So Hard to Make Arrangements for Yourself." *Rolling Stone*, August 14, 1975

Naha, Ed. *"Time Fades Away*—Neil Young's Goodbye to the Concert Scene." *Circus*, December 1973.

Ferrin, Dave. "My Least Favorite Album . . ." Radio 2 FM radio interview with Neil Young. June 5, 1987.

"Neil Young Hits the Road." *Circus*, August 1972.

Young, Neil. *Decade* album liner notes. Reprise Records, Time-Warner, 1977.

Traffic and Free

Evans, Paul. "Traffic." *Rolling Stone Album Guide*. Edited by Anthony DeCurtis and James Henke with Holly George-Warren. New York: Random House, 1992.

"Free." *The New Rolling Stone Encyclopedia of Rock and Roll*. New York: Fireside/Rolling Stone Press, 1995.

Gaines, Steve. "Behind Traffic's 'Shoot-Out'—Capaldi Flies While Winwood Hides." *Circus*, April 1973.

Hush, Michele. "How Free Fell Apart, and Why They Fell Together Again."
    Circus, December 1972.
Kirsch, Bob. "Talent in Action: Traffic/Free/John Martyn—Santa Monica
    Civic Center, Los Angeles." *Billboard*, March 10, 1973.
"Traffic." *The New Rolling Stone Encyclopedia of Rock and Roll*. New York:
    Fireside/Rolling Stone Press, 1995.
Traffic. *On the Road* album liner notes. Island Def Jam Music Group—A
    Universal Music Company, 2003 edition.
Traffic. *Shootout at the Fantasy Factory* album liner notes. Island Def Jam
    Music Group—A Universal Music Company, 2003 edition.

B. B. King

"B. B. King—1973-11-11, Berlin, Germany." Guitars 101. Accessed October
    18, 2015. http://www.guitars101.com/forums/f90/bb-king-1973–11–11
    -berlin-germany.
"B. B. King—Philharmonie, Berlin, 4 November 1983—FM." Guitars 101.
    Accessed October 18, 2015. http://guitars101.com/forumsf90/bb-king
    -philharmonie-berlin-4-november.
B. B. King. *Anthology* album liner notes. MCA Records, Universal Music &
    Video Distribution, Inc., 2000.
"B. B. King Biography." Accessed October 18, 2015. http://www.bbking.com
    /bio/.
B. B. King. *King of the Blues* box set liner notes. MCA Records, UNI Distri-
    bution Corp., 1992.
Erlewine, Michael, ed. *All Music Guide to the Blues*. San Francisco: Miller
    Freeman Books, 1999.
Milward, John. *How the Blues Shaped Rock 'n' Roll (and Rock Saved the
    Blues)*. Lebanon, NH: Northeastern University Press, 2013.
Wyman, Bill, with Richard Havers. *Bill Wyman's Blues Odyssey*. New York:
    DK Publishing, 2001.

Deep Purple

"Billboard 200" Album Sales Chart and "Hot 100" Singles Sales Charts.
    Billboard, April 15, 1972; January 20, 1973; September 29, 1973.
"Captured Decibel (Loudness) Comparison Chart." H.E.A.R.—Hearing
    Education and Awareness for Rockers. Accessed December 13, 2014.
    www.Hearnet.com.
"Dunkin' Donuts Center: Deep Purple Set List May 23, 1973." Rhode Is-
    land Rocks. www.rirocks.net.

"Hammond Hall of Fame—Jon Lord." Accessed December 8, 2014. www
.hammondorgan.co.com.

Joseph, Tim. *Deep Purple Shades 1968–1998* album box set liner notes. Warner Brothers Records and Rhino Entertainment Company, 1999.

Marks, Laurence. "Punch-Drunk Purple Power." *Circus*, April 1974.

Martinez, Arlene. "'Home of the Stars' Turns 100." *Allentown (PA) Morning Call*, September 2, 2011.

Thompson, Dave. *Smoke on the Water: The Deep Purple Story.* Toronto:
ECW Press, 2004.

Whelan, Frank. "The Allentown Fair—Its Patrons Have Seen It All."
Allentown (PA) Morning Call, August 26, 1984.

Willistein, Paul. "Valley Has Found Its Niche as a Site for Rock Concerts."
Allentown (PA) Morning Call, February 23, 1986.

Wittman, Bob. "The Great Allentown Fair, 150 Years, 1852–2002." *Allentown (PA) Morning Call*, August 25, 2002.

Ted Nugent

Buchinski, Ed. "Ice Machine Sizing." Big Screen Biz. February 14, 2005.
www.bigscreenbiz.com/forums.

"The Grand Theater History." Accessed December 28, 2014. www.thegrand
theater.org/history/.

Logan, Nick, and Bob Woffinden. "Ted Nugent." *The Illustrated Encyclopedia of Rock.* New York: Harmony Books, 1977.

Popoff, Martin. *Epic Ted Nugent.* Toronto: Power Chord Press, 2012.

Schruers, Fred. "The Ted Offensive." *Rolling Stone*, March 8, 1979.

Sharpe, Bob. "Night after Night, the Nuge Delivers." *Allentown (PA) Morning Call*, June 8, 1984.

Vickers, Tom. "Ted Nugent Unleashes His Little Ball of Fire." *Rolling
Stone*, April 8, 1976.

Yes

Fletcher, Gordon. "Psychedelic Doodles—*Tales from Topographic Oceans.*
Yes, Atlantic SD 2-008." *Rolling Stone*, March 28, 1974.

Demorest, Steve. "Yes Battles the Skeptics with *Relayer.*" *Circus*, February,
1975.

Ross, Ron. "A Rearranged Yes Says 'No' to Standing Still." *Circus*, December, 1974.

Vitale, Neal. "Yes in Concert: Rock at Brilliant Best." *Boston Globe*, February 27, 1974.

"Yes Album Reviews." Pitchfork. Accessed November 8, 2015. http://pitch
fork.com/reviews/albums/11869-the yes-album-fragile-close-to-the-edge
/tales-from-topographic-oceans/.

"Yes at Baseball Stadium, Miami, FL, USA Feb 8, 1974." Setlist.fm. Accessed November 8, 2015. www.setlist.fm/setlist/yes/1974/baseball
-stadium-miami-fl-7bdf3294.html.

Yes. *In a Word* box set liner notes. Rhino Entertainment Company, Warner
Music Group, 2002.

"Yes — *Tales From Topographic Oceans* (Atlantic)." *Circus*, April 1974.

Yes. *Tales From Topographic Oceans* album liner notes. Elektra Entertain-
ment/Warner Strategic Marketing, 2003; reissue edition.

Eric Clapton

Clapton, Eric. *461 Ocean Boulevard (Deluxe Edition)* album liner notes.
Polydor/Chronicles — A Universal Music Company, 2004 edition.

Clapton, Eric. *"Clapton: The Autobiography."* New York: Broadway Books,
2007.

"Eric Clapton — The Spectrum, Philadelphia, PA, USA. June 29, 1974."
Setlist.fm. Accessed August 3, 2015. www.setlist.fm/setlist/eric-clapton
/1974/the-spectrum-philadelphia-pa-4bd3177e.html.

Crowe, Cameron. "E. C.'s Here Again: 'There's Always Someone Faster.'"
Rolling Stone, November 20, 1975.

Turner, Steve. "Eric Clapton: The Rolling Stone Interview." *Rolling Stone*,
July 18, 1974.

"Where's Eric! 29 June 1974 — Eric Clapton & His Band." Where's Eric?
Accessed August 3, 2015. www.whereseric.com/eric-clapton-tour/29
/06/1974.

CSNY

"CSN&Y Salute Independence Eve." *Circus*, November 1974.

Fong-Torres, Ben. "The Ego Meets the Dove — The Reunion of Crosby,
Stills, Nash & Young." *Rolling Stone*, August 29, 1974.

Myers, Marc. "The First Big Stadium Tour." *The Wall Street Journal*, June
24, 2014.

Nash, Graham. *Wild Tales*. New York: Crown Archetype/Crown Publishing
Group, 2013.

Wilk, Tom. "CSN — with Y — Finally Made It to AC Race Course." *Atlantic City Weekly*, September 4, 2012. www.atlanticcityweekly.com/news
-and-views/waltz-through-time.

George Harrison

"40 Years Ago: George Harrison Begins Ill-Fated 1974 North American Tour." Ultimate Classic Rock. Accessed October 27, 2015. www.ultimate classicrock.com/george-harrison-1974-tour/.

Bailey, Andrew, and David Hamilton. "George Harrison: The Niceman Cometh." *Rolling Stone*, November 21, 1974.

Cahn, Elliot. "Rock: George Harrison Pops a Press Conference." *Real Paper*, November 13, 1974.

"Dazed and Confused: 10 Classic Drugged-Out Shows — George Harrison, 1974 Tour — Cocaine." *Rolling Stone*, June 6, 2013. http://www.rolling stone.com/music/pictures/10-classic-drugged-out-performances.

Fong-Torres, Ben. "Lumbering in the Material World." *Rolling Stone*, December 19, 1974.

"George Harrison & Ravi Shankar Setlist at Boston Garden, Boston, MA, USA." Setlist.fm. Accessed October 27, 2015. www.setlist.fm/setlist /george-harrison-and-ravi-shankar/1974/boston.

"George Harrison North American Tour 1974." Hari's On the Web. Accessed October 27, 2015. http://www.bekkoame.ne.jp/~garp/hari/live74 .htm.

Miller, Jim. "Dark Horse: Transcendental Mediocrity." *Rolling Stone*, February 13, 1975.

Santosuosso, Ernie. "George Harrison: A Strained Legend." *Boston Globe*, December 11, 1974.

———. "George Harrison Booked into Garden." *Boston Globe*, September 24, 1974.

Woffinden, Bob. "George Harrison: Dark Horse." *New Musical Express*, December 1974.

The Rolling Stones

Carr, Roy. *The Rolling Stones — An Illustrated Record*. New York: Harmony Books, 1976.

Cott, Jonathan. "Back to a Shadow in the Night." *Rolling Stone*, September 11, 1975.

McGrath, Mike. "Behind the Stones." *Philadelphia Inquirer*, August 10, 1975.

"The Rolling Stones — The Spectrum, Philadelphia, PA, USA. 30 June, 1975." Setlist.fm. Accessed February 15, 2015. www.setlist.fm/the-rolling -stones/1975.

Weitzman, Steve. "New Stones to Add Old Face." *Rolling Stone*, June 5, 1975.

Wyman, Bill. *Rolling with the Stones*. New York: DK Publishing, 2002.

The Great American Music Fair

Abbott, Deborah, and Bill Crozier. "Crowds Slog through Sea of Mud." *Syracuse Herald-Journal*, September 2, 1975.

Greenhouse, Ezra. "Rock Echoes Fade: Fans, Police Left with Memories." *Syracuse Herald-Journal*, September 3, 1975.

Miller, Gregory W. "Rock Fest a Bust." *Syracuse Post-Standard*, September 3, 1975.

———. "VIP's Miss Mass of Mud." *Syracuse Post-Standard*, September 3, 1975.

Peck, Abe. "State Fair Rock Fray: Gate Abuse in Syracuse." *Rolling Stone*, October 9, 1975.

Peters, Kenn. "Fans Jam Music Fair." *Syracuse Herald-Journal*, September 2, 1975.

Wisniewsky, John, and Laurie McGinley. "'It's a Good Fair, Not a Great One.'" *Syracuse Post-Standard*, September 3, 1975.

Whitburn, Joel. *Pop Annual 1955–1982*. Menomonee Falls, WI: Record Research, Inc., 1983.

Fleetwood Mac

Ames, Katrine, with Janet Huck. "Hey, Mac!" *Newsweek*, May 10, 1976.

Carr, Roy, and Steve Clarke. *Fleetwood Mac: Rumours 'n' Fax*. New York: Harmony Books, 1978.

Crowe, Cameron. "The Real Fleetwood Mac Stands Up." *Rolling Stone*, November 7, 1974.

———. "The True Life Confessions of Fleetwood Mac." *Rolling Stone*, March 24, 1977.

"Fleetwood Mac—Boston Garden, Boston, MA, USA 18 October, 1975." Setlist.fm. Accessed March 7, 2015. www.setlist.fm/setlist/fleetwood -mac/1975.

Fleetwood, Mick, with Stephen Davis. *Fleetwood: My Life and Adventures in Fleetwood Mac*. New York: William Morrow and Co., 1990.

Fleetwood, Mick, with text by Stephen Davis. *My Twenty-Five Years in Fleetwood Mac*. New York: Hyperion, 1992.

Forte, Dan. "Fleetwood Mac's Lindsey Buckingham." *Guitar Player*, January 1977.

Salewicz, Chris. "Fleetwood Mac Can't Go Home Again." *Trouser Press*, April 1980.

Whitburn, Joel. *Pop Annual 1955–1982*. Menomonee Falls, WI: Record Research, Inc., 1983.

Lynyrd Skynyrd

Bream, Jon. "Skynyrd Boogie Band Plays Loose, but Tough." *Minneapolis Star*, March 31, 1976.

"Cocaine Blamed in Death of Caldwell." GoUpstate.com. Accessed October 25, 2015. http://www.goupstate.com/article//19930716/NEWS/3071 60325.

Crowe, Cameron. "Lynyrd Skynyrd: Hell on Wheels Puts on the Brakes." *Los Angeles Times*, October 24, 1976.

"The Last Flight of Lynyrd Skynyrd." *Rolling Stone*, December 1, 1977.

"Lynyrd Skynyrd, April 7, 1976, Wednesday, Orpheum Theater, Boston, MA, USA." Bootleg album and liner notes.

"Lynyrd Skynyrd Set List at Orpheum Theater, Boston, MA, USA, April 7, 1976." Setlist.fm. Accessed October 23, 2015. www.setlist.fm/setlist /lynyrd-skynyrd/1976/orpheum-theater-boston-ma-4bd53bde.html.

"Orpheum Theater." Cinema Treasures. Accessed March 27, 2016. http:// www.cinematreasures.org/theaters/1789.

Perry, Joe, with David Ritz. *Rocks: My Life In and Out of Aerosmith*. New York: Simon & Schuster, 2014.

Rockwell, John. "Southern Rock Stirs up Southern Yells." *New York Times*, April 13, 1976.

Sabulis, Thomas. "Jeff Beck Tantalizes Cape Cod Audience." *Boston Globe*, August 30, 1976.

———. "Skynyrd Gives Cape Season Baptism of Fire." *Boston Globe*, June 23, 1977.

———. "Skynyrd Sparkles." *Boston Globe*, April 9, 1976.

Santosuosso, Ernie "This Should Have Been the Year." *Boston Globe*, October 22, 1977.

Van Matre, Lynn. "Southern Rock—Loud and Gutsy." *Chicago Tribune*, April 5, 1976.

Wiseman, Rich. "Lynyrd Skynyrd Turns the Tables." *Rolling Stone*, April 22, 1976.

The Eagles

Crowe, Cameron. "Eagles: Chips off the Old Buffalo." *Rolling Stone*, January 25, 1975.

"Eagles: Kingdome, Seattle, WA, USA August 9, 1976." Setlist.fm. Accessed October 4, 2015. www.setlist.fm/setlist/eagles/1976/kingdome-seattle-wa -63d8c287.html.

"Eagles: Roosevelt Stadium, Jersey City, NJ, USA July 29, 1976." Setlist.fm.

Accessed October 2, 2015. www.setlist.fm/setlist/eagles/1976/roosevelt
-stadium-jersey-city-nj-3b.

Felder, Don, with Wendy Holden. *Heaven and Hell: My Life in the Eagles
(1974–2001)*. Hoboken, NJ: John Wiley & Sons, 2008.

Sabulis, Thomas. "Three-Band Lineup for Foxboro." *Boston Globe*, July 23,
1976.

———. "Triple-Header Rock at Foxboro." *Boston Globe*, July 26, 1976.

Santosuosso, Ernie. "Elton John, Beach Boys Due." *Boston Globe*, May 21,
1976.

"Weather History Results for Foxboro, MA, (02035) July 24, 1976." Farmers'
Almanac. Accessed October 3, 2015. http://farmersalmanac.com/weather
-history/search-results.

Whitburn, Joel. *Top Pop Albums 1955–1992*. Menomonee Falls, WI: Record
Research, Inc., 1993.

———. *Top Pop Singles 1955–1990*. Menomonee Falls, WI: Record Research, Inc., 1991.

"WRKO and Don Law Presents the Eagles." Display ad, *Boston Globe*, July
4, 1976.

Talking Heads

Birch, Ian. "Sound and Vision: Talking Heads, De Montfort Hall, Leices-
ter." *Melody Maker*, December 1, 1979.

Demorest, Stephen. "Talking Heads' Stunning Debut." *Rolling Stone*, November 3, 1977.

Morse, Steve. "Ramones Headline Punk Rock Bill." *Boston Globe*, November 21, 1977.

Naprstek, Paul. "Talking Heads Get Down." *Real Paper*, November 20,
1980.

Talking Heads. *Talking Heads: 77* album liner notes. Sire Record Company,
manufactured and marketed by Rhino Entertainment Company, a Warner
Music Group Company, 2006 edition.

"The Name of This Site Is Talking Heads — Concert History: 1977 Set List
Part One." Accessed October 9, 2015. http://talkingheadsconcerthistory
.blogspot.com/2012/12/1977-setlist-part-one.

"The Name of This Site Is Talking Heads — The Early Years." Accessed
October 9, 2015. http://www.talking-heads.nl/index.php/the-early-years.

The Cars

"1977 Club Listings — Boston Punk Scene." Boston Groupie News. Accessed June 11, 2015. www.bostongroupienews.com/GigList1977.htm.

Gilmore, Mikal. "The Cars." *Rolling Stone*, October 30, 1980.

Milano, Brett. *The Cars Anthology: Just What I Needed* album liner notes. Elektra Entertainment Group, 1995.

Morse, Steve. "The Cars on Road to Success." *Boston Globe*, January 12, 1978.

———. "The Cars Spin Home." *Boston Globe*, December 7, 1978.

Pareles, Jon. "Power Steering." *Rolling Stone*, January 25, 1979.

Young, Jon. "No Puns Please, We're Cars." *Trouser Press*, November 1978.

David Bowie

Cocks, Jay. "David Bowie Rockets Onward." *Time*, July 18, 1983.

"David Bowie—Boston Garden, Boston, MA, USA, May 6, 1978." Setlist .fm. Accessed March 18, 2015. www.setlist.fm/setlist/david-bowie/1978 /boston-garden-boston-ma-13.

Carson, Tom. "Stage." *Rolling Stone*, November 30, 1978.

Connal, Kevin. "David Bowie: No More Glitz and Glitter." *CD Review*, March 1992.

Milward, John. "Low." *Rolling Stone*, April 22, 1977.

Testa, Bart. "Heroes." *Rolling Stone*, January 12, 1978.

Visconti, Tony. *Stage* album liner notes, April 2004. EMI Records Ltd. & Jones/Tintoretto Entertainment Co., 2005 edition.

Young, Charles M. "Bowie Plays Himself." *Rolling Stone*, January 12, 1978.

Ramones

"Buckley Recital Hall at Amherst College." BMOP: Boston Modern Orchestra Project. Accessed October 8, 2015. http://www.bmop.org/buckley -recital-hall-amherst-college.

Morse, Steve. "Ramones Headline Punk Rock Bill." *Boston Globe*, November 21, 1977.

Nelson, Paul. "Ramones." Record review. *Rolling Stone*, July 29, 1976.

Oedipus. *All the Stuff (and More) Volume 1* album liner notes, 1990. Sire Records Company, marketed by Warner Bros. Records, Inc.

"Ramones Biography." Rock and Roll Hall of Fame and Museum." Accessed October 7, 2015. https://rockhall.com/inductees/ramones/bio/.

Sullivan, Jim. "Ramones Rock On." *Boston Globe*, July 3, 1979.

White, Timothy. "Bang the Heads Slowly: The Importance of Being a Ramone." *Rolling Stone*, February 8, 1979.

Young, Charles. "The Ramones Are Punks and Will Beat You Up." *Rolling Stone*, August 12, 1976.

The Police

Brown, Mick. "The Case of the Bleached Blondes." *Rolling Stone*, May 3, 1979.

Henke, James. "Policing the World." *Rolling Stone*, February 19, 1981.

Nemeth, Cathy. "Police Report." *New York Rocker*, December 1978.

Pidgeon, John. "On Tour with the Police." *Guardian*, August 24, 2007.

"The Police—The Rathskeller, Boston, MA, USA, October 26, 1978." Setlist.fm. Accessed May 13, 2015. http://www.setlist.fm/setlist/the -police/1978/the-rathskeller-boston-ma-53dd.

"Roxanne." Sting.com. Accessed May 14, 2015. http://www.sting.com /discography/index/album/albumId/136/tagName/Singles.

"Tour List—The 'Outlandos' Years 1977/79." ThePolice.com. Accessed May 13, 2015. http://www.thepolice.com/tour/archive/721?page=0%2 Co%2Co%.

Young, Jon. "The Police Act Responsible." *Trouser Press*, December 1979.

The Clash

Alan, Carter. "The Clash: Audience Loyalty in a World Ruled by the Buck?" *What's New*, March 1979.

Carson, Tom. "The Clash Conquer America." *Rolling Stone*, April 5, 1979.

Christgau, Robert. "The Clash See America Second." *Village Voice*, March 5, 1979.

"The Clash—Harvard Square Theater, Cambridge, MA USA, February 16, 1979." Setlist.fm. Accessed March 16, 2015. www.setlist.fm/setlist /the-clash/1979/harvard-square-theater-cambridge.

Strummer, Joe, and Mick Jones. "The Clash." Band-written bio and discography from Epic Records, December 1979.

Sullivan, Jim. "The Clash." *Sweet Potato*, March 1979.

John Cougar & the Zone

Connelly, Christopher. "Hey, John Cougar, What's Your Problem?" *Rolling Stone*, December 9, 1982.

John Cougar, 8/18/1979 live broadcast, WBCN-FM, Boston (audiotape).

John Cougar, 8/19/1979 interview, WBCN-FM, Boston (audiotape).

"John Mellencamp, 1979–08–18—Boston, MA." Guitars 101. Accessed September 24, 2015. http://www.guitars101.com/forums/f145/john -mellencamp-1979–08–18-boston.

Rowland, Mark. "John Cougar: The Complicated Rock Brat." *Musician*, February 1983.

Shaw, Erin. "Mike Wanchic Interview/Johnny Mercer Theater Preview." *Island Packet*, June 17, 2015.

Whitburn, Joel. *Top Pop Albums 1955–1992*. Menomonee Falls, WI: Record Research, Inc., 1993.

———. *Top Pop Singles 1955–1990*. Menomonee Falls, WI: Record Research, Inc., 1991.

Tom Petty and the Heartbreakers

Gilmore, Mikal. "Tom Petty's Real-Life Nightmares." *Rolling Stone*, February 21, 1980.

Morse, Steve. "Petty Cancels at Last Minute." *Boston Globe*, November 15, 1979.

———. "Tom Petty Has Rock 'n' Roll in His Veins." *Boston Globe*, November 21, 1979.

———. "Tom Petty Is Rock 'n' Roll." *Boston Globe*, November 8, 1979.

Petty, Tom, and the Heartbreakers. *Playback — 1973–1993* box set liner notes. MCA Records, 1995.

Petty, Tom, and the Heartbreakers. *Runnin' Down a Dream*. Edited by Warren Zanes. San Francisco: Chronicle Books, 2007.

Rayl, Sally. "Tom Petty Files for Bankruptcy." *Rolling Stone*, August 9, 1979.

"Tom Petty and the Heartbreakers — Orpheum Theater, Boston, MA, USA November 19, 1979." Setlist.fm. Accessed August 18, 2015. www.setlist .fm/setlist/tom-petty-and-the-heartbreakers/1979/orpheum-theater -boston.

Whitburn, Joel. *Top Pop Singles 1955–1990*. Menomonee Falls, WI: Record Research, Inc., 1991.

Prince

"Billboard's Top Album Picks — *Dirty Mind* Warner Brothers BSK 3478." *Billboard*, November 8, 1980.

Morse, Steve. "Prince a Complete Showman at 20." *Boston Globe*, March 19, 1981.

Partridge, Kenneth. "Prince's 'Dirty Mind' at 35: Classic Track-by-Track Album Review." *Billboard*, October 8, 2015.

"Prince Setlist at the Ritz, New York, NY, USA, March 22, 1981." Setlist .fm. Accessed November 4, 2015. http://www.setlist.fm/setlist/prince /1981/the-ritz-new-york-ny-73d85ab1/.

"Prince Setlist at Uncle Sams, Minneapolis, MN, USA, March 9, 1981." Setlist.fm. Accessed November 4, 2015. http://www.setlist.fm/setlist /prince/1981/uncle-sams-minneapolis-mn-23ddf.

R.I.A.A. Gold and Platinum Searchable Database—"Prince." Accessed November 6, 2015. https://www.riaa.com/goldandplatinumdata.php.

Whitburn, Joel. *Top Pop Singles 1955–1990*. Menomonee Falls, WI: Record Research, Inc., 1991.

AC/DC

"AC/DC—Providence, RI USA, Civic Center." AC/DC: The Official Site. Accessed May 31, 2015. www.acdc.com/us/event/1981/12/04/providence -ri-usa-civic-center.

Dome, Malcolm. *AC/DC*. New York: Proteus Publishing Co., 1982.

Fink, Jesse. *The Youngs: The Brothers Who Built AC/DC*. New York: St. Martin's Press, 2013.

Fricke, David. "AC/DC Shrugs Off a Death and Rocks On." *Rolling Stone*, October 30, 1980.

Morse, Steve. "AC/DC Sits Atop the Rock Pile." *Boston Globe*, December 18, 1981.

———. "Another Jolt of Power from AC/DC." *Boston Globe*, December 15, 1981.

"Previous AC/DC Tour Dates & AC/DC Concerts" AC/DC: The Official Site. Accessed June 8, 2015. www.acdc.com/us/tour.

U2

Alan, Carter. "The Unsinkable U2." *Boston Rock*, March 1982.

———. *Outside Is America*. Boston: Faber and Faber, 1992.

Bono, The Edge, Adam Clayton, Larry Mullen Jr., with Neil McCormick. *U2 by U2*. London: Harper Collins, 2006.

Green, Jim. "Pluck of the Irish." *Trouser Press*, March 1982.

McCormick, Neil. *October* album liner notes. Universal-Island Records Ltd., 2008 edition.

"U2 Concert: February 11, 1982, at New Orleans, LA." @U2. Accessed August 7, 2015. http://tours.atu2.com/concert/ss-president-riverboat-new -orleans-feb-11-1982.

"U2 Tour: *October*—4th Leg (North America) 1982." @U2. Accessed August 7, 2015. http://tours.atu2.com/tour/october-4th-leg-north-america.

J. Geils Band

"The J. Geils Band: Boston Garden, Boston, MA, USA, February 23, 1982." Setlist.fm. Accessed September 18, 2015. www.setlist.fm/ setlistthe-j-geils-band/1982/boston-garden-boston-ma.

"J. Geils Band Kicks Out Peter Wolf." *Rolling Stone*, November 24, 1983.

"The J. Geils Band: Tour Dates 1970–1983." The J. Geils Band.net. Accessed September 17, 2015. http://jgeilsband.net/the-j-geils-band-tour -dates-1970–1983/.

Loder, Kurt. "Starting Over on Top." *Rolling Stone*, March 4, 1982.

Mehler, Mark. "Keeping the Feeling and the Faith." *Record*, March 1985.

Morse, Steve. "Hothouse Rock . . . and More." *Boston Globe*, February 23, 1982.

———. "On Top at Last: After 14 Years, J. Geils Has a No. 1 Album and No. 1 Single." *The Boston Globe*, February 18, 1982.

Whitburn, Joel. *Top Pop Albums 1955–1992*. Menomonee Falls, WI: Record Research, Inc., 1993.

———. *Top Pop Singles 1955–1990*. Menomonee Falls, WI: Record Research, Inc., 1991.

"Wolf Quits J. Geils Band." *Boston Globe*, October 15, 1983.

Black Sabbath and Ozzy Osbourne

Alan, Carter. "Black Sabbath: Life After Ozzy." *Boston Rock*, April/May 1982.

"Black Sabbath Online: 1981–1982 Mob Rules Tour." Black Sabbath Online. Accessed April 20 2015. www.black-sabbath.com/tourdates/1981tour/.

Frame, Pete. "Ozzy Osbourne: Twenty Years of Mayhem." Family tree chart included with Epic Records promo kit, 1988.

Osbourne, Ozzy. *I Am Ozzy*. New York: Grand Central Publishing/ Hachette Book Group, 2009.

"Ozzy Osbourne—Boston Garden, Boston, MA, USA, April 2, 1982" Setlist.fm. Accessed April 13, 2015. www.setlist.fm/setlist/ozzy-osbourne /1982/boston-garden-boston-ma.

"Ozzy Osbourne Tour Dates." Ozzyhead. Accessed April 19, 2015. www .ozzyhead.com/olddates/olddates.htm.

Sullivan, Jim. "Osbourne's Garden Concert Canceled." *Boston Globe*, April 1, 1982.

Welch, Chris. *Black Sabbath*. New York: Proteus Publishing, 1982.

The Who

Alan, Carter. "The Who Tour Diary." Unpublished, 1982.

———. "Who's Last." *Boston Rock*, October 1982.

Cocks, Jay. "Rock's Outer Limits." *Time*, December 17, 1982.

Evans, Paul. "The Who." *Rolling Stone Album Guide*. New York: Random House, 1992.

Harrington, Richard. "Townshend, Before He Grows Old." *Washington Post*, September 23, 1982.

Henke, James. "Who to Rake in Millions on Tour." *Rolling Stone*, October 14, 1982.

Loder, Kurt. "Who in Top Form as Tour Opens." *Rolling Stone*, October 28, 1982.

Pareles, Jon. "Whose Who?" *Real Paper*, April 9, 1981.

White, Adam. "Members of Who Assert They Intend to Continue." *Billboard*, September 23, 1978.

"The Who Tour Archive: 1982." The Who Concert Guide. Accessed April 5, 2015. www.thewholive.net/tour-list/index.php?GroupID=1&Year=1982.

Aerosmith

"Aerosmith — The Centrum, Worcester, MA, USA, November 11, 1982." Setlist.fm. Accessed May 21, 2015. http://www.setlist.fm/setlist/aerosmith/1982/the-centrum-worcester-ma-23bd.

"Aerosmith — The Centrum, Worcester, MA, USA, November 16, 1982." Setlist.fm. Accessed May 21, 2015. http://www.setlist.fm/setlist/aerosmith/1982/the-centrum-worcester-ma-23d.

"82–84 Rock in a Hard Place Tour." Aerosmith Temple. Accessed May 21 2015. http://www.aerosmithtemple.com/rock-in-a-hard-place-tour-dates-1982–1984.

Aerosmith, with Stephen Davis. *Walk This Way: The Autobiography of Aerosmith*. New York: Avon Books, 1997.

"Aerosmith Worcester, MA (November 16, 1982)." Audio tracks for entire concert. YouTube. Accessed May 30, 2015. https://www.youtube.com/playlist?list=PL8037AB7708C217C0.

"Interview with Jimmy Part 1." Riff & Roll — The Jimmy Crespo Website. Accessed May 21, 2015. http://www.jimmycrespo.com/jcint1.html.

Morse, Steve. "Aerosmith Is Back with a Vengeance." *Boston Globe*, November 13, 1982

Perry, Joe, with David Ritz. *Rocks: My Life In and Out of Aerosmith*. New York: Simon & Schuster, 2014.

Sullivan, Jim. "Tyler Collapses on Stage." *Boston Globe*, November 18, 1982.

Tyler, Steven, with David Dalton. *Does the Noise in My Head Bother You?* New York: HarperCollins 2011.

Wild, David. "Aerosmith: The Band That Wouldn't Die." *Rolling Stone*, April 5, 1990.

Joan Jett

Doyle, Patrick, Caryn Ganz, Andy Greene, Brian Hiatt, Christian Hoard, Nick Murray, and Simon Vozick-Levinson. "20 Best Moments at the Rock and Roll Hall of Fame Induction," *Rolling Stone*, April 11, 2014.

Fricke, David. "Joan Jett: Built to Rock." *Rolling Stone*, April 24, 2015.

"Glorious Results of a Misspent Youth" (press kit). Blackheart Records/ MCA Records, September 1984. Accessed April 28, 2016. http://joan jettbadrep.com/PressKits/pkgr.shtml.

"Joan Jett & the Blackhearts Biography." The Rock and Roll Hall of Fame and Museum. Accessed April 28, 2016. https://rockhall.com/inductees /joan-jett-and-the-blackhearts/bio/.

Joan Jett and Kenny Laguna, 9/22/1983 interview, WBCN-FM, Boston (audiotape).

Johnson, Dean. "Schemers Top Rock Rumble Heap." *Boston Herald*, June 30, 1984.

Morse, Steve. "Schemers Triumph in Rock 'n' Roll Rumble." *Boston Globe*, June 30, 1984.

Robinson, Lisa. "Banned Song Makes Joan Jett 'Album' Cassette a Rarity." *Newark (NJ) Star-Ledger*, August 24, 1983.

Whitburn, Joel. *Top Pop Albums 1955–1992*. Menomonee Falls, WI: Record Research, Inc., 1993.

———. *Top Pop Singles 1955–1990*. Menomonee Falls, WI: Record Research, Inc., 1991.

Bruce Springsteen and the E Street Band

Barol, Bill, with Mark D. Uehling, Nikki Finke Greenberg, and Shawn Doherty. "He's On Fire." *Newsweek*, August 5, 1985.

Hinckley, David. "30 Years after 'Born in the U.S.A,' Bruce Springsteen Went from Star to Supernova." *New York Daily News*, June 1, 2014.

Knobler, Peter. "Running on the Backstreets with Bruce Springsteen." *Crawdaddy*, October 1975.

Landau, Jon. "Growing Young with Rock and Roll." *Real Paper*, May 22, 1974.

"Bruce Springsteen—Providence Civic Center, Providence, RI, USA, December 11, 1980." Setlist.fm. Accessed April 26, 2015. www.setlist.fm /setlist/bruce-springsteen/1980/providence-civic-center.

"Bruce Springsteen—06-Aug-1984 E. Rutherford, NJ, Meadowlands Arena, USA [set list]." Bruce Springsteen Database. Accessed April 22, 2015. www.brucespringsteen.it/DB/mn.aspx?yr=1984&mt=08.

Bruce Springsteen & the E Street Band. *Live/1975–85* album liner notes. Bruce Springsteen/Columbia Records/CBS Inc., 1986.

Whitburn, Joel. *Top Pop Albums 1955–1992.* Menomonee Falls, WI: Record Research, Inc., 1993.

———. *Top Pop Singles 1955–1990.* Menomonee Falls, WI: Record Research, Inc., 1991.

Live Aid

Alan, Carter. "Bob Geldof Interview." *Boston Rock* no. 13, April 1981.

Coleman, Mark. "The Revival of Conscience." *Rolling Stone*, November 15, 1990.

Geldof, Bob. *Is That It?* New York: Penguin Books, 1986.

"July 13, 1985, this was Live Aid . . ." (Detailed set list). Live-Aid.info. Accessed November 26, 2015. http://liveaid.free.fr/pages/liveaidtimes detaileduk.html.

Live Aid Concert Program. London: Concert Publishing Co. and Concessions Ltd. for Xylopark Ltd., 1985.

Tannenbaum, Rob. "Bob Geldof." *Rolling Stone*, November 15, 1990.

Mötley Crüe

"Accept — Manning Bowl, Lynn, MA, USA Aug 3, 1985." Setlist.fm. Accessed July 5, 2015. www.setlist.fm/setlist/accept/1985/manning-bowl -lynn-ma-63d92a13.

Bryson, Donna. "15,000 Attend Mötley Crüe Concert in Lynn." *Boston Globe*, August 4, 1985.

"City of Lynn Attractions — Manning Field." City of Lynn website. Accessed July 5, 2015. www.ci.lynn.ma.us/attractions_manningfield.shtml.

Grein, Paul. "August Yields Bumper Crop of Gold, Platinum Albums." *Billboard*, September 14, 1985.

"Inside Track — Vince Neil." *Billboard*, October 5, 1985.

Morse, Steve. "A Mellow Tribute to Metal Mania." *Boston Globe*, August 5, 1985.

"Mötley Crüe — Manning Bowl, Lynn, MA, USA Aug 3, 1985." Setlist.fm. Accessed July 5, 2015. www.setlist.fm/setlist/motley-crue/1985/manning -bowl-lynn-ma-53db7.

Ribadeneira, Diego. "Rock 'n' Roll Concert that N.H. Town Didn't Want Is Rescheduled for Lynn." *Boston Globe*, July 31, 1985.

Vare, Ethlie Ann. "Talent in Action — Motley Crue — The Forum, Los Angeles." *Billboard*, September 14, 1985.

Waters, Tim. "Rock 'n' Roller's Song Sobered by Fatal Crash." *L.A. Times*, July, 21, 1985.

Whitburn, Joel. *Top Pop Singles 1955–1990*. Menomonee Falls, Wisconsin: Record Research, Inc., 1991.

"Y & T—Manning Bowl, Lynn, MA, USA Aug 3, 1985." setlist.fm. Accessed July 5, 2015. www.setlist.fm/setlist/y-and-t/1985/manning-bowl-lynn-ma-7bd92a18.

Stevie Ray Vaughan

Alan, Carter, and Stevie Ray Vaughan. WBCN audio file, February 24, 1987.

Erlewine, Michael, ed. *All Music Guide to the Blues*. San Francisco: Miller Freeman Books, 1999.

Govenar, Alan. *Meeting the Blues*. Dallas: Taylor Publishing Company, 1988.

Patoski, Joe Nick, and Bill Crawford. *Stevie Ray Vaughan: Caught in the Crossfire*. Boston: Little, Brown and Company, 1993.

Swenson, Jon. "Stevie Ray Vaughan [1954–1990]." *Rolling Stone*, October 4, 1990.

Pink Floyd and Roger Waters

"A Momentary Lapse of Reason—Pink Floyd, 1987." The Pink Floyd Archives. Accessed May 5, 2015. http://pinkfloydarchives.com/tourdate.htm.

Cohen, Scott. "Treading Waters." *Spin*, September 1988.

Fricke, David. "Pink Floyd Hits the Road." *Rolling Stone*, October 22, 1987.

———. "Roger Waters—Madison Square Garden." *Rolling Stone*, October 22, 1987.

———. "Pink Floyd: The Inside Story." *Rolling Stone*, November 19, 1987.

"Live Press Conference with Roger Waters" Abbey Road Studios, London. Script from radio program, August 4, 1987.

"Roger Waters On Tour Presents Radio Kaos Tour 1987." Pink Floyd—A Fleeting Glimpse. Accessed May 5, 2015. http://www.pinkfloydz.com/jollyrogerwaters/radiokaos.htm.

Sharp, Keith, and Dimo Safari. "Equal Time." *Rock Express*, October/November 1987.

Wild, David. "Pink Floyd Plays the Name Game." *Rolling Stone*, January 15, 1987.

Guns N' Roses

Davis, Stephen. *Watch You Bleed: The Saga of Guns N' Roses*. New York: Gotham Books, 2008

"Guns N' Roses Setlist at Paradise Rock Club, Boston, MA, USA, October 27, 1987." Setlist.fm. Accessed December 2, 2015. http://www.setlist.fm /setlist/guns-n-roses/1987/paradise-rocck-club-boston-ma-2bd6dc3a .html.

Holdship, Bill. "Days of Guns N' Roses." *Spin*, May 1988.

Sullivan, Jim. "New Band That's Special." *Boston Globe*, October 28, 1987.

Tannenbaum, Rob. "The Hard Truth About Guns N' Roses." *Rolling Stone*, November 17, 1988.

Whitburn, Joel. *Top Pop Albums 1955–1992*. Menomonee Falls, WI: Record Research, Inc., 1993.

———. *Top Pop Singles 1955–1990*. Menomonee Falls, WI: Record Research, Inc., 1991.

Roger Waters (Berlin)

Rogers, Sheila. "Random Notes." *Rolling Stone*, September 6, 1990.

Schaffner, Nicholas. *A Saucerful of Secrets*. New York: Harmony Books, 1991.

"The Wall Live in Berlin." REG: The International Roger Waters Fan Club. Accessed November 21, 2014. http://www.rogerwaters.org/about_berlin .html.

Waters, Roger. *The Wall Live in Berlin*. Universal Music DVD, 2003.

———. "The Wall Berlin '90" (official press kit). Mercury Records, 1990.

Paul McCartney

Fricke, David. "One for the Road." *Rolling Stone*, February 8, 1990.

Henke, James. "Can Paul McCartney Get Back?" *Rolling Stone*, June 15, 1989.

"July 26, 1990, Boston" set list. Paul McCartney: The Official Site. Accessed May 9, 2015. http://www.paulmccartney.com/live/boston-7.

"McCartney's Best Box Scores — Top Concerts from Tokyo to Tacoma." *Billboard*, September 3, 2005.

McCartney, Paul. *Tripping the Live Fantastic* album liner notes. Capitol Records Inc., a subsidiary of Capitol-EMI Music, 1990.

The Paul McCartney World Tour official program. London: Emap Metro, 1989.

"The Paul McCartney World Tour [1990]." Paul McCartney: The Official Site. Accessed May 9, 2015. http://www.paulmccartney.com/live/tour -archives/the-paul-mccartney-world-tour.

Stadiums of Pro Football, "Foxboro Stadium." Accessed May 9, 2015. http:// www.stadiumsofprofootball.com/past/FoxboroStadium.htm.

Whitburn, Joel. *Top Pop Albums 1955–1992*. Menomonee Falls, WI: Record Research, Inc., 1993.

The Black Crowes

Alan, Carter, and Chris Robinson. Transcript of Atlanta Interview, May 2, 1992.

"The Black Crowes Album Release Party May 2 1992," Def American Recordings information kit.

Bloom, Steve. "Flyin' High with the Black Crowes." *High Times*, July 1992.

Curtis, Gregory. "Solid as the Crowes Rock." *Rolling Stone*, June 25, 1992.

Holdship, Bill. "It's Only Rock 'n' Roll." *Spin*, May 1991.

Neely, Kim. "As the Crowes Fly." *Rolling Stone*, January 24, 1991.

Whithall, Susan. "Black & Blues." *Boston Herald*, August 28, 1992.

The Allman Brothers Band

"Boston Tea Party, the (1967–1970)." The American Revolution. Accessed November 6, 2009. http://www.theamericanrevolution.fm.

Morse, Steve. "Allman Brothers Forge Some Raging Rock Out of Chaos." *Boston Globe*, August 2, 1993.

Paul, Alan. *One Way Out: The Inside History of the Allman Brothers Band*. New York: St. Martin's Press, 2014.

"Show Setlists for August 1, 1993." Hittin' the Web With the Allman Brothers Band. Accessed July 13, 2015. http://allmanbrothersband.com/modules.php.

"Show Setlists for July 1993." Hittin' the Web With the Allman Brothers Band. Accessed July 13, 2015. http://allmanbrothersband.com/modules.php.

"Show Setlists for Mansfield, MA." Hittin' the Web With the Allman Brothers Band. Accessed July 26, 2015. http://allmanbrothersband.com/modules.php.

Walker, Michael. "When the Starship Ruled the Skies." *Billboard*, May 23, 2015.

Nirvana

Azerrad, Michael. "Live Through This." *Rolling Stone*, June 2, 1994.

DeCurtis, Anthony. "Kurt Cobain 1967–1994." *Rolling Stone*, June 2, 1994.

Fricke, David. "Kurt Cobain: The Rolling Stone Interview." *Rolling Stone*, January 27, 1994.

"Nirvana Setlist at Wallace Civic Center, Fitchburg, MA, USA, November 12, 1993." Setlist.fm Accessed November 20, 2015. http://www.setlist

.fm/setlist/nirvana/1993/wallace-civic-center-fitchburg-ma-63d67e8b .html.

Strauss, Neil. "The Downward Spiral." *Rolling Stone*, June 2, 1994.

Sullivan, Jim. "Nirvana Down but Defiant, the Seattle Sensation Rages On with New Album." *Boston Globe*, September 17, 1993.

———. "Pop-Grunge Grind Intact, Nirvana Still Smells Like Teen Angst." *Boston Globe*, November 12, 1993.

Pearl Jam

Burke, Bill. "Nirvana Singer's Death Haunts Pearl Jam Fans." *Boston Globe*, April 11, 1994.

Crowe, Cameron. "5 Against the World." *Rolling Stone*, October 28, 1993.

Lozaw, Tristram. "A Heavy Concert for Pearl Jam." *Boston Globe*, April 11, 1994.

Neely, Kim. "Where Angels Fear to Tread." *Rolling Stone*, May 5, 1994.

"Pearl Jam and Neil Young—'Rockin' in the Free World' (1993)." Rolling Stone.com. Accessed June 29, 2015. http://www.rollingstone.com/music /lists/readers-poll-the-10-best-mtv-vmas.

"Pearl Jam—Boston Garden, Boston, Massachusetts. Sun. 10 April, 1994." Pearl Jam: The Official Site. Accessed June 26, 2015. http://pearljam.com /setlists/1009/1994/20065/boston_garden.

"Pearl Jam—Boston Garden, Boston, Massachusetts. Mon. 11 April, 1994." Pearl Jam: The Official Site. Accessed June 26, 2015. http://pearljam.com /setlists/1009/1994/20066/boston_garden.

Pearl Jam. *Twenty*. New York: Simon & Schuster, 2011.

Bush, Goo Goo Dolls, and No Doubt

Bernstein, Jonathan. "Get Happy." *Spin*, November 1996.

"Bush, Goo Goo Dolls, Providence Civic Center, April 10, 1995." Whatever Magazine. Accessed May 19, 2015. http://whateverhq.tmok.com/issues /3/bush.html.

"Bush *Sixteen Stone*." RIAA—Gold and Platinum Searchable Database. Accessed May 19, 2015. https://www.riaa.com/goldandplatinumdata.php ?content.

Daley, Steven. "Bush: Nirvanawannabes." *Rolling Stone*, April 18, 1996.

"Goo Goo Dolls, *A Boy Named Goo*." RIAA—Gold and Platinum Searchable Database. Accessed May 19, 2015. https://www.riaa.com/goldand platinumdata.php?content.

"Goo Goo Dolls Biography." Goo Goo Fans website. Accessed May 18, 2015. http://googoofans.com/index.php?page=biography.

"No Doubt *Tragic Kingdom*." RIAA—Golden and Platinum Searchable Database. Accessed May 19, 2015. https://riaa.com/goldandplatinum dataphp?content.

Toure. "No Doubt: Music from the Big Pink." *Rolling Stone*, July 6, 2000.

Phish

"137,000 Turn Out for Phish Fest." *Music News of the World*, August 20, 1996.

"Boxscore: Top 10 Concert Grosses." *Billboard*, August 31, 1996.

"Cliff's Notes." The Clifford Ball official festival booklet, August 1996.

"Friday, 08/16/1996 Plattsburgh Air Force Base, Plattsburgh, NY." Phish .net. Accessed August 25, 2015. http://phish.net/setlists/?d=1996–08 –16.

"Phish Building City for Weekend Festival." Great Northeast Productions press release, August 7, 1996.

Puterbaugh, Parke. "Phresh Phish." *Rolling Stone*, February 20, 1997.

Richmond, Peter. "Phishstock." *GQ*, January 1997.

"Saturday, 08/17/1996 Plattsburgh Air Force Base, Plattsburgh, NY." Phish .net. Accessed August 25, 2015. http://phish.net/setlists/?d=1996–08–17.

"Small Adirondack Town Is Host of a Giant Concert." Associated Press, *New York Times*, August 18, 1996.

"What Was the Clifford Ball?" Phish.net. Accessed August 25, 2015. http:// phish.net/faq/clifford.html.

Joe Perry and Cheap Trick

Bell, Mach. "About Joe Perry's Birthday Party." Aerosmith News. Accessed September 12, 2015. http://www.angelfire.com/rock2/aerorockcom/sept 00news.htm.

Bergeron, Jennifer. "How Slash Reunited Joe Perry with a Prized '59 Les Paul." *Guitar Player*, July 23, 2014.

Drozdowski, Ted. "Joe Perry on the New "Joe Perry 1959 Les Paul." Gibson .com. Accessed September 8, 2015. http://www.gibson.com/New-Life style/Features/en-us/Joe-Perry.

Gisborne, Kim. "Unofficial Cheap Trick UK/Europe Newsletter," no. 24, November 2000. Accessed September 9, 2015. http://www.ctnewseurope .co.uk/nov00.htm.

"Locals Schmooze at Aerosmith Celebrity Restaurant Opening." *Duxbury (MA) Clipper*, August 13, 1997.

Perry, Joe, with David Ritz. *Rocks: My Life In and Out of Aerosmith*. New York: Simon & Schuster, 2014.

U2

DeCurtis, Anthony. "Raw Power." *Revolver*, Winter 2000.

Heath, Chris. "U2: Band of the Year." *Rolling Stone*, January 18, 2001.

Hunter, James. "'All That You Can't Leave Behind.'" *Rolling Stone*, November 9, 2000.

Katz, Larry. "It's a B-U2-ful Day." *Boston Herald*, June 6, 2001.

———. "Return of U2 is a 'Beautiful' Thing." *Boston Herald*, October 30, 2000.

Light, Alan. "Rock's Unbreakable Heart." *Spin*, January 2002.

Morse, Steve. "U2 Kicks Off 'Elevation' Tour with a Blast." *Boston Globe*, March 26, 2001.

Nesch, Elliot. "U2 Frontman Bono: Christian or Antichrist?" Holy Bible Prophecy, August 12, 2012. Accessed August 14, 2015. http://www.holy bibleprophecy.org/2012/08/12/u2-frontman-bono-christian-or-anti christ-by-elliot-nesch.

Sullivan, Jim. "U2 Leaves Many Memories Behind at the Fleet Center." *Boston Globe*, June 11, 2001.

"U2 Concert: June 5, 2001 at Boston, MA." @U2. Accessed August 13, 2015. http://tours.atu2.com/concert/fleet-center-boston-jun-05-2001.

"U2 Concert: Jun 06, 2001 at Boston, MA." @U2. Accessed August 13, 2015. http://tours.atu2.com/concert/fleet-center-boston-jun-06-2001.

U2. *Elevation 2001/Live from Boston* album liner notes. U2 Limited, licensed in the USA to Interscope Records, 2001.

"U2 Tour" Elevation— 1st Leg (North America)." @U2. Accessed August 13, 2015. http://tours.atu2.com/tour/elevation=1st-leg-north-america.

Robert Plant and Alison Krauss

Anderman, Joan. "Two Voices—Krauss and Plant—In Perfect Harmony." *Boston Globe*, June 7, 2008.

"Alison Krauss." *The New Rolling Stone Encyclopedia of Rock and Roll*. New York: Fireside/Rolling Stone Press, 1995.

"Robert Plant & Alison Krauss Setlist at Bank of America Pavilion, Boston, MA, USA, June 5, 2008." Setlist.fm. Accessed December 5, 2015. http://www.setlist.fm/setlist/robert-plant-and-alison-krauss/2008/bank-of-america-pavilion-boston-ma-23d0f0cb.html.

Pareles, Jon. "When It Takes Three People to Make a Duet." *New York Times*, October 21, 2007.

Remz, Jeffrey B. "Alison Krauss, Robert Plant Make Magic—Bank of

America Pavilion, Boston, June 5, 2008." Country Standard Time. Accessed December 5, 2015. http://www.countrystandardtime.com/d/concertreview.asp?xid=289.

Spencer, Neil. "Robert Plant and Alison Krauss, Raising Sand." *Guardian*, October 14, 2007. http://www.theguardian.com/music/2007/oct/14/folk.shopping.

Whitburn, Joel. *Top Pop Albums 1955–1992*. Menomonee Falls, WI: Record Research, Inc., 1993.

Jack White

Farr, Heather. "Jack White, the Chicago Theater, Chicago, IL, July 23." *Relix*, September 2014.

Fricke, David. "*Lazaretto*-Jack White-Third Man/Columbia." *Rolling Stone*, June 10, 2014.

Gottlieb, Jeff. "Last Best Show: Jack White at Fenway Park." *Boston Herald*, September 17, 2014.

"Jack White Setlist at Bleacher Theater at Fenway Park, Boston, MA, USA, September 17, 2014." Accessed December 9, 2015. Setlist.fm. http://www.setlist.fm/setlist/jack-white/2014/bleacher-theater-at-fenway-park-boston-ma-13cfc31.html.

Lynch, Joe. "Jack White Mocks Foo Fighters, Rolling Stone in 'Kanye-esque Rant.'" *Billboard*, September 18, 2014. http://www.Billboard.com/articles/6258707/jac-white-mocks-foo-fighters-rolling-stone-kayne-rant.

NESN Staff, "Jack White to Play at Fenway Park's 'Bleacher Theater' on Sept. 17." NESN. Accessed December 9, 2015. http://nesn.com/2014/06/jack-white-to-play-at-fenway-parks-bleacher-theater-on-sept-17/.

Rodman, Sarah. "Jack White Outstanding in the Field at Fenway." *Boston Globe*, September 18, 2014.

Joe Walsh

Alan, Carter, and Joe Walsh. Live Interview on WZLX-FM, Boston, August 2, 2012.

"Joe Walsh Setlist at Orpheum Theater, Boston, MA, USA, Oct 17, 2015." Setlist.fm. December 14, 2015. http://www.setlist.fm/setlist/joe-walsh/2015/orpheum-theatre-boston-ma-bf4515e.html.

Lacatell, Marc. "Joe Walsh Digs Deep into Catalog & Shares Comical Stories in Boston." *Glide*, October 19, 2015. http://www.glidemagazine

.com/150351/joe-walsh-digs-deep-catalog-shares-comical-stories-boston
-show-reviewphotos/.

Obrecht, Jas. "Joe Walsh Carries On." *Guitar Player*, April 1988.

Rodman, Sarah. "Life's Still Good for a Solo Joe Walsh." *Boston Globe*,
October 10, 2015.